I Never Saw Colour Again

Pro libertate!

Rick Oliver

I Never Saw Colour Again

Sergeant James Philip Keenan
ROYAL CANADIAN AIR FORCE

AND

RICHARD W. OLIVER

Interactive MultiMedia Associates
885 Curtiswood Lane, Nashville, TN 37204

For more information or to order additional copies,
please visit www.Lancaster850.com

Interactive MultiMedia Associates
885 Curtiswood Lane
Nashville, TN 37204

Interactive MultiMedia Associates produces and publishes works of non-fiction and fiction in a variety of media.

ISBN 978-0-9961046-0-9

Photos and letters provided to the co-author by Elaine Walsh
George Collins photos and notes courtesy of Ann Collins
Cover by GKS Creative, Nashville, TN (gkscreative.com)
Photo restorations by Len Buckland Design (lbdesign@bmts.com)

Dedicated to the Memory
of
Sergeant James Philip Keenan
Royal Canadian Air Force
3 February 1921 – 27 April 1944

May his soul always live in the hearts
Of those who knew and loved him in life and
Those who came to know and love him in death.

And to his fiancé
Elizabeth Elaine Ellis
3 August 1921 – 14 April 2013

And to the people of Chauffourt, France
Who since April 1944 have cared for the graves
& honoured the memories of
Jim Keenan, John Moffat & Henry Peebles

Elizabeth Elaine Ellis   Sergeant James Philip Keenan

Contents

Preface

Sergeant James (Jim) Philip Keenan, Royal Canadian Air Force (RCAF), was the Tail Gunner on Lancaster ND. 850 No. 106 Squadron, Royal Air Force (RAF) Metheringham, England. Attached to the RAF during WWII, Sergeant Keenan wrote to his fiancé Elaine Ellis in Hamilton, Ontario, from the time he shipped out to England in 1943 until days before his untimely death on 27 April 1944. He was shot down over France on the way to a bombing raid on Schweinfurt, Germany.

I first learned about Jim Keenan from my wife's aunt, Elaine Walsh (nee Ellis). This book is the result of several years of research into Jim and Elaine's romance and the events that led to his death. Through my research I also came to know about the heroic crew of Lancaster No. 850, the plane in which Jim lost his life.

Part I briefly describes the search for Jim Keenan's grave and story, as well as finding his sister and one of the (then) surviving crew members of the Lancaster. A short section called the "The Ring" in many ways brings the story full circle and makes perhaps as satisfying an end to this sad story as is possible.

Part II of book contains Jim's letters to Elaine. For those wishing a little more historical context, Part I contains several brief accounts about Bomber Command, No. 106 Squadron, the raid that took Jim's life, what was learned about the others in the crew and their training, the German Luftwaffe pilot who shot down the Lancaster, the Messerschmitt Bf 110, and finally, short descriptions of the four locations important to this story: Metheringham, England; Schweinfurt, Germany; the small village of Chauffourt, France, where Jim and his two companions found their eternal rest; and Laon-Athies air field that was the base for the German Luftwaffe's Nachtjagdgeschwader 1 Night Fighters.

The first edition of this book was produced specifically for a 70th anniversary ceremony, held on 27 April, 2014, honouring the three RCAF airmen buried at Chauffourt. The second edition of this book includes a Part III to tell "the rest of the story." It includes a number of documents, memorabilia and information that came into my possession from Elaine's estate after the publication of first edition, and excerpts from an unpublished document by Navigator George Collins that describe his escape and return to England. This second edition includes some brief information about the memorials held at Chauffourt, a particularly costly American raid on Schweinfurt, and some final reflections on the events and people in this book.

The heart of this story, however, belongs to Jim Keenan through his letters home to his fiancé, Elaine Ellis. The reader should not expect grand observations about war and peace, but simply an expression of the heartfelt desire of a single airman wanting to do his duty, return home, and marry his sweetheart.

Readers should note that I use British/Canadian spellings and the time designations appropriate to their era. There are occasional corrections or explanations added where needed.

Finally, I hope readers will forgive me for attributing words to Jim Keenan in the Foreword. I never met him, but having read his letters and talked extensively to those who did know him, I feel reasonably certain he would have approved.

Richard W. Oliver
Nashville, Tennessee
2017

Foreword

View from Chauffourt Cemetery

There is a beautiful view of the rolling hills of the French countryside from the cemetery behind the old church in the tiny village of Chauffourt where I have rested peacefully for the past 70 years. I came here in the dark night of 27 April 1944, when the British Lancaster in which I was the Rear Gunner was shot down by a German Mersserschmitt. Beside me are two young Canadians, John Moffat from Toronto and Hank Peebles from Heart Valley, Alberta. Both were just 20 years-old and on their first combat missions. I was on what turned out to be my unlucky third mission. We were young men who never had a chance to experience life in the many ways that you, the readers of this book, enjoy.

My eternal companions and I are here, in a strange country, an ocean away from our families, for reasons beyond our control and because of a war that none of us wanted. We did our jobs because that was expected of us. Our deepest dreams were to do our job and get back to Canada. For the three of us, as for many thousands of others, that was not to be. The war took our most precious possesion, our lives.

Throughout this book, you'll read more about the war, my views and experiences and even about the German pilot, Martin Drewes, who took my life. I bear him no ill will. He was doing his job; I was doing mine. Today, I prefer to focus not on war and destruction, but on peace.

From the cemetery, the vistas are magnificent and the people of Chauffourt treat me and my companions, forever young, with dignity and respect. They even consider us heroes who came to save them. We, however, don't think of ourselves as heroes, but as young men who volunteered to do a job that few others wanted. We believe we did those jobs well, but in the process, paid a very steep price.

Were it different, I hope the three of us, who had experienced the worst of life, our war, would have rejoiced in the many precious gifts of life – love, children, grandchildren, careers, and beautiful spring days.

Those things were not to be. Yet we rest here peacefully, without remorse, because we achieved what we came to do: liberate a continent from oppression and make the world safe for those we loved, but left behind.

Had I lived, there are many other things I'm sure I'd tell you. As that was not to be, I'll select a select a few of my final words from letters to my fiancé, Elaine:

The sooner I am in action the sooner I go home, so it has its advantages...
—Friday August 20, 1943

Gosh the last few nights have been lovely due to the moon; I guess you have noticed it too. Tomorrow I shall go to Mass at the church of St. Anslem and St. Cecelia, which is but a few blocks from here, and I will remember you, and "us" in my prayers...
—Saturday, February 5, 1944

The first day I am home I'm going to sleep at your place if I must stay on the chesterfield [couch, ed.], and I might even stay for a week!!!!! You're going to have your hands full getting rid of me but you could always have your father toss me out, and then I'd sleep on the steps!!
Tomorrow's letter shall be the last from here until I return a month hence.
—Tuesday, February 22, 1944

This as you know is my last day here, and I have come through all of my examinations today with flying colours... The lads have all made their way into Nottingham tonight, as usual, and yours truly is behaving himself and remaining on the station as per custom; I have no desire to go on a spree...
—Wednesday, February 23, 1944

Love,
Jim.

Sergeant James Keenan
No. 106, Royal Air Force,
Chauffourt, France

Part I
"I Never Saw Colour Again."

One of my strongest memories as a youngster growing up in Canada was the annual Remembrance Day poppies. I proudly wore a plastic red poppy on my shirt, meant to symbolize the many people killed in WWI and II.

In school, I learned some of the history of the wars, but I had only a sketchy understanding of its impact on millions of individuals. My rather limited understanding about the wars had as much to do with not paying attention in class as to infrequent references by my father, Pilot Officer Harry Thomas Oliver, Royal Canadian Air Force (RCAF), who told me almost nothing of his wartime experiences. All I remember is he was "in Belgium, Holland and Germany." In our entire house, there was not one memento or indication that my father had served from 1939-45 in the RCAF.

In later years, I became interested in Winston Churchill's role in the war, and in frequent travel to Japan on business, intrigued about the war in the Pacific. I read extensively about both, but my understanding was about the "grand strategies" of the various combatants, and little about the war's impact on individual lives.

All of that changed in late 2002. My wife, Susan (Elaine), and I were visiting her Aunt Elaine, her namesake, at her home in Dundas, Ontario. Aunt Elaine was preparing for the next phase of her life. At 80, she was quietly and privately mourning the loss of her youngest son, and wanting to clear many of the memories of her past. Elaine married about five years after the war and her life not always happy. She bore three sons, all of whom preceded her in death.

She asked me to move a piece of furniture, and while doing so, I found a trove of artwork. "Aunt Elaine," I said, "who painted these?" I was struck by the colour and composition that bore a striking resemblance to the compelling style of impressionist landscape painting made famous by the Canadian "Group of Seven."

A brief discussion uncovered that Elaine was the artist. I didn't known that she painted, although we had several pieces in our home painted by Elaine's mother and sister. I said, "I didn't know you painted?"

"I never painted after the Second World War," she replied.

Somewhat confused, I asked: "Why not?" Although not an expert, the paintings exuded passion, talent and potential to me.

"After the war, I never saw colour again."

"Why?" I said. Her answer started the rest of this story.

She told me that she had been engaged to an RCAF tail gunner who had been shot down over France. She knew nothing more about what happened.

Later, I asked my wife why she never told about Elaine's art and the war. As it turned out, Susan knew nothing about it. No one in her family had ever talked about it.

It was up to Susan and me to discover what actually happened.

In short, the love of Elaine's life, her soul mate, fiancé and fellow artist, James (Jim) Philip Keenan, was a Tail Gunner on a British Lancaster who was shot down and killed on April 27, 1944 by a German Messerschmitt Bf 110 over Chauffourt, France. It was just Jim's third operational flight. His Lancaster was one of several planes downed by the Luftwaffe that evening.

When our visit to Aunt Elaine was at an end, we returned to our home in Nashville, Tennessee, with the barest of outlines of the story. I set about trying to fill in the blanks. I had repeatedly asked Aunt Elaine over the previous few days to tell me more, but she was reticent to bring up an obviously painful memory, and truthfully, as I was to learn, "They didn't tell the fiancé much."

What we did learn is that two letters had informed her; one that Jim was missing; and then, some months later another confirming him dead. Neither letter had much information. Her memory was sketchy about the details but she confessed she had long wished to know what had happened.

What she did tell me was that Jim had written to her every several days. Since Elaine was known as Susan's family "pack rat," I eagerly asked to see the letters. "Sorry," she said, "I burned them after the war." I thought that was the end of the story!

More than a year later, Susan was once again in Canada to visit Elaine and called me and said: "You remember that Aunt Elaine burned all those letters from her fiancé? Well, she transcribed them all before she burned them and wants to know if you want the transcriptions?"

Needless to say the answer was yes, and what happened next turned into a search that would take us to Europe three times, several trips back to Canada, and countless days of research.

Finding Sergeant Keenan

Our search to find the story of Sergeant Keenan began in earnest in May 2004, when Susan and I travelled to the UK to check service records. Unsure where to start, for most of a week we canvassed several military museums in England and asked lots of questions. On our last day before leaving for home empty-handed, we travelled to the RAF Museum that houses the Bomber Command Museum in London. They have a Lancaster on display and it was our first look at that magnificent airplane. The museum also houses the RAF records from the war, but it was closed the day we were there. As luck would have it, a staffer was in the office on his day off and helped us to get the basic information about the raid, the crew names and some other basic information we needed, and information about the Lancaster No. 850 that was shot down. Officially, as noted on overleaf, the plane was Lancaster ND. 850 Mark III Merlin 38 PO247377 P 1247025 S1244238 SO248504. For simplicity in this text, I will simply use ND. 850.

We returned home and began an Internet search in earnest. We knew Jim was buried in Chauffourt, France, and with the help of the great resources of the Internet, were able to locate his grave – at least on the

NW/n.   TELEGRAM EN CLAIR.   145/27.

TO:- AIR MINISTRY KINGSWAY, AIR GROUP OXFORD,
HQ.B.C., 5 GROUP, 54 BASE, RECORDS GLOS.,
INFO METHERINGHAM.
FROM:- 106 SQUADRON.

RECEIVED A.M.C.S.2220 HRS.27TH APR.44.

IMMEDIATE. SECRET NOT. T.

A.25 27TH APRIL. (ATTENTION
AT AIR MINISTRY OF ACCIDENTS CI AND P.4.CAS.) F.B.
(A) LANCASTER ND.850 MARK III MERLIN 38 P0247377
P1247015 51244238 S0248504.
(B) 106 SQUADRON.
(C) RESUMED OVER ENEMY TERRITORY. NOTHING HEARD FROM
AIRCRAFT AFTER LEAVING BASE AT 2130 HOURS ON 26TH
APRIL 1944.
(D) P/O W.G. FRASER, CAPTAIN. SGT. D.A.
SIMPSON, FLT.ENGINEER. R160042. W/O G.A. COLLINS
(CAN.) NAVIGATOR. R171606 SGT. H.T. PEEBLES (CAN.)
AIR BOMBER. SGT. A. MCKENZIE, W/OPERATOR.
R199304 SGT. J.A. MOFFAT (C) GUNNER. R173638 SGT.
J.P. KEENAN (CAN.) GUNNER. ALL MISSING.
(E) NOT KNOWN.
(F) 1800 x 4 LB INC SAA FISHPOND. H2S FULL OPERATIONAL
EQUIPMENT.
(G) PRESUMED ENEMY ACTION. AIRCRAFT FAILED TO RETURN
FROM BOMBING RAID ON SCHWEINFURT.
(H) NOT KNOWN.
(J) NIL. informed
(K) P/O FRASER, NEXT OF KIN, MOTHER, MRS.A. FRASER,
SGT. SIMPSON,
NEXT OF KIN, FATHER, MR. A.A. SIMPSON,
KINFORMED. W/O
COLLINS, NEXT OF KIN, FATHER, MR. E.C. COLLINS, 84
SPRINGHURST AVENUE, TORONTO, CANADA, KINNOT. SGT.
PEEBLES, NEXT OF KIN, MOTHER, MRS. E.V. PEEBLES,
KINNOT. SGT. MCKENZIE,
NEXT OF KIN, FATHER, MR. A. MCKENZIE,
KINFORMED. SGT. MOFFAT,
NEXT OF KIN, FATHER, MR. J.R. MOFFAT,
KINNOT. SGT. KEENAN, NEXT
OF KIN, MOTHER, MRS. E.M. KEENAN,
KINNOT.

TIME OF ORIGIN. 271103B HRS.

"CRASH" CIRCULATION. (P.4.CAS.10 COPIES).
P.4.CAS.(CAN) (6 COPIES).
ADVANCE COPY TO: P.4.CAS.

RAF telegram notification of the shooting down of ND. 850

screen. We also began developing information about Bomber Command and the air war.

The following summer we were back in Europe, this time in France for the three-hour car drive from Paris to Chauffourt. The drive took us a lot longer than expected as Google maps unfortunately led us in the wrong direction several times. We did however get to see a lot of the French countryside. By late afternoon we had about given up when we received some good advice from a friendly farmer and found our way to Chauffourt.

Finding Chauffourt and the Graves

It was with a great degree of trepidation that we parked in front of what looked like a no longer used church. It was closed, but luck was with us again as a woman who apparently had been doing some work inside the church came out as we were about to leave. My French is marginal after not using it for more than 30 years, but I was able to communicate that we were looking for the graves of the three airmen. Waving us to follow, she took us behind the church and pointed at three extremely well attended plots in the small cemetery.

We didn't know what we would find, so we were very pleased we found them so well taken care of. It was an emotional moment. Perhaps it was the long trip, the uncertainty of many wrong turns in our research and on the road to Chauffourt, but mostly it was the enormity of seeing the graves, and knowing the story of Jim and Elaine through his letters that impacted us so. The woman left us, stepping quietly back into the church to give us some time alone with the graves. We had prepared pictures of Jim and Elaine and put them in a waterproof metal frame and placed them on Jim's grave.

I sought out the woman again to ask about where we could find more information. She pointed across the fields to a town (Montigny Le Roi) in the distance. It was nearing the dinner hour by that time and we decided to see if there was anyone around. We drove the short distance to the town and had a quick look around for any building that might look official enough to house war documents. Nothing was readily apparent, but Susan suggested we try the library. I asked the lone librarian if they had any books on the war. She took me to the shelves that had a few standard books on the war, but nothing that looked like it would give us local information about the downed Lancaster.

After several failed attempts, I finally got the message across that we were there looking for information about the Lancaster that had crashed in nearby Chauffourt. Her face lit up, her arms went up and she asked me to stay in the library while she went up stairs. She returned very quickly with a woman who identified herself as Mary-Christine Pinot, Directeur Général des Services, Mairie de Val de Meuse. Ms. Pinot invited us to come to her second floor offices where she provided us with coffee and some basic information about the plane and graves. She told us there were people she would like us to meet if we could return the next day. We had been planning on returning to Paris, but agreed to return the next morning.

We found a hotel in the center of Langres (about 30 miles away) and spent the evening walking around the ancient walled city. The following morning we returned to Ms. Pinot's office, stopping off to look once again at the graves. Overnight Canadian flags had been added to the graves and, again, we were very touched by the reverence and care the graves received.

At Ms. Pinot's office we were greeted with a huge binder with photocopies of newspaper stories and pictures about the crash. I thought that whoever put it together, must have worked late into the night. Also in her office were two gentlemen introduced as local citizens with an interest in the Lancaster as they had seen the wreckage. One was there to help with translation. The other had been a young boy at the time of the crash and showed us pieces of the plane that he had gathered from the site. We spent about an hour discussing the story and they presented us with three parts of the plane.

They suggested we follow them back toward Chauffourt and detoured down a small lane near the village. There we visited a memorial that had been erected by the people of the village. We then travelled to the cemetery and were joined by the mayor of Chauffourt, along with a woman reporter from a local paper. After some discussions with the mayor, we were taken to a farmhouse on the edge of the village. For the next hour or so, we sat in the kitchen of the farmhouse with a farmer and his wife while he described, in an animated manner, the aftermath of the crash, and the attempts of the villagers to retrieve the bodies.

Monument erected by the people of Chauffourt

Interestingly the farmer showed us some of the pieces of the wreckage he had collected as a young boy and proudly kept all these years. He had a propeller from the Lancaster on a wall in the barn attached to the house. What was truly shocking however, is that he pulled out a large well-maintained poster describing the Lancaster in a significant amount of detail. But the poster was in English and had been procured for him from outside France. He then pulled out an obviously much-reviewed set of papers that translated the poster text into French. We could clearly tell that this Lancaster loomed large, not just in the history of the village, but was very much alive in the minds of the townspeople.

We learned the Germans had kept local people away from the site and left the bodies in the field for two days. The people from the village had tried to visit the crash site, but German soldiers with machineguns prevented it. Eventually, they were allowed to visit the site and many of them collected parts of the plane. As usual, the Germans took the Rolls-Royce engines and shipped them back to Germany.

While the Germans wanted to have the bodies buried without any fanfare, in defiance, the villagers held a proper church service and burial for them.

Funeral at the church in Chauffourt held by the villagers against German orders

The people of the village also told us about the escape of the four crewmen who had parachuted to safety. They were picked up by the French underground who, at great peril themselves, hid the airmen and took them to Switzerland. From there, some months later, they were able to return to England. Susan and I visited the nearby village where they had been hidden.

Just before leaving the village for Paris, the farmer hugged me and with tears in his eyes (and mine too) he said: "Your people came twice to save us and we will never forget it."

Some months later, we received an article in the mail, clipped from the local newspaper. It was the story of our visit to Chauffourt and finding the graves. With a picture of Susan and me at the memorial, the article was titled "Finding Sergeant Keenan." We made copies of the article and made plans to visit Aunt Elaine in her new home in an assisted-living facility. We used the article and other information, pictures and the like to tell her the story of what happened to her fiancé. Elaine had the article translated and took it around to show her surviving wartime friends about our search for Jim. I asked Elaine if she wanted the entire story, but she demurred, saying she was satisfied to know that his grave was being cared for so well.

The Ring

Back home in Nashville, I continued my Internet search and Susan began looking for Jim's relatives. Using a Hamilton, Ontario phone book, she started making calls. After about four such calls, she found the daughter of Jim's sister Bernice. We called Bernice and introduced ourselves and ask to

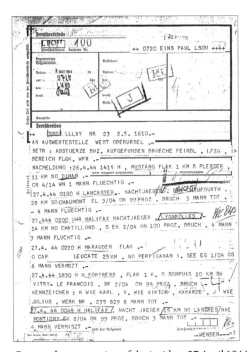

German documentation of the incident 27 April 1944

meet. We went to Canada and met her and her husband told us they had visited Jim's grave several years earlier. Bernice told us she had not really known Jim's fiancé, Elaine, as she had only been eleven years old when Jim went off to war. We had the good fortune to visit with Bernice and her husband Jim Galea over the next few years and learned more about Jim's family.

Susan arranged for Bernice and Jim Galea to meet Elaine and they had a great reunion. Unbeknownst to us, Jim Keenan had given Elaine an engagement ring that had been his grandmother's. In the trauma following the news of Jim's death, the ring had never been returned. At their meeting, Elaine returned the ring to Jim's family over 60 years after she had accepted his proposal.

Susan continued her diligent research and found the navigator from the Lancaster, George Collins. He had returned to Canada after the war and was living, and retired in Lynden, a rural area near Hamilton about 20 minutes from Elaine's home. Again, we returned to Canada and arranged to meet George and his wife, Ann. We had a pleasant visit with them; unfortunately George was suffering from memory loss and was only able to give us the barest outlines of the story. Importantly, he did explain why the plane was near Chauffourt, as they had been told to take the "southern route to Schweinfurt."

George also told us that the pilot of Jim's plane, Gordon Fraser, now lived in Calgary, Alberta, Canada. I made plans to visit him and called his home, only to learn he had passed away a few months previous. More information about Gordon Fraser, George Collins, and the two other airman killed in this brief battle, is included below.

Meeting Martin Drewes

In the meantime, I was honing my Internet research skills and was digging deeply into a number of promising looking websites that contained information about the Luftwaffe and the RAF. There was a lot of general information, but nothing about this one plane that had been shot down. I wasn't surprised as nearly half (3249) of the 7377 Lancasters built for the war were lost. I did, however, begin to query websites that had contact information, but frankly didn't expect much additional information. In fact, I didn't receive answers to any of my queries and had given up hope. So, I was surprised one day when I received an email from a person in Belgium, who I later discovered was one of the foremost living authorities on the Luftwaffe. He sent me the German documentation of the incident (originally it was not known if the plane had been shot down by a German night fighter or ground fire) and told me the pilot of the Messerschmitt was named Martin Drewes, and that he was alive and living in Brazil.

I started making plans to go to Brazil and talked with Drewes by phone. He was most understanding and pleasant and welcomed my visit. Because of my busy work schedule, I found it difficult to find time for the trip. The only time I could arrange to go to Brazil, he was away in what he said was "likely my final trip back to Germany to see friends." We subsequently spoke several times on the phone, and I was pleased to acquire signed photos of him, as well as a copy of his wartime remembrances. Replicas of his Messerschmitt BF 110G-4 (from 1944) are available, and, of course, I acquired several of them, hoping for autographs when we finally met. I was truly disappointed to learn that he too had passed away (late in 2013) before I could meet him face to face. I have included more information on Martin Drewes below.

Over the last dozen years I have had the opportunity to read extensively about the air war, and, in particular, the role the British Lancaster and the German Messerschmitt played in it. It is truly an amazing story. I offer here only the briefest information on Bomber Command, No. 106 Squadron, and the two aircraft so central to the story. I highly recommend further reading of some of the numerous books available on the RAF, Bomber Command and the Luftwaffe.

Bomber Command

Bomber Command was the name given to the unit of the RAF concerned with bombing the enemy during WWII. Other major command units included Coastal Command and Fighter Command, the later being the RAF unit responsible for its fighter aircraft. It was Fighter Command that fought so valiantly, outnumbered and outgunned, against such great odds during

Bomber Command Crest   Royal Canadian Air Force crest

the Battle of Britain. The battle inspired British Prime Minister Winston Churchill to famously say, "Never in the field of human conflict has so much been owed by so many to so few."

For the greater part of the war, however, it was Bomber Command that carried the lion share of the battle to Germany. Although there were significant battles occurring in North Africa and in the Pacific, until the invasion on June 6, 1944, the only real British effort against the German homeland was the almost nightly work of Bomber Command. So extensive were Bomber Commands (and later the US Eight Army Air Force) raids that they eventually destroyed almost all of Germany's war supply and manufacturing facilities and, in the process, most major German cities.

As a relatively new invention, the airplane was used in WWI largely for reconnaissance, although there were some famous air battles and "aces," the most notable being the German Manfred von Richtofen (the notorious Red Baron), Canadian ace, Billy Bishop, the French ace, Rene Fonck (with 80, 75 and 72 victories respectively). The Americans who joined later in the war were led by Eddie Rickenbaker with 26 victories.

German bombers are generally cited as introducing the concept of bombing cities, with major strikes against Spanish dissidents prior to WWII, on Poland, the Low countries and then London (the "Blitz"), and other British cities, most notably Coventry. Many revisionists now feel that British bombing of Germany was largely for revenge, and the extent of the raids was far beyond what was necessary. Some were truly devastating to German cities such as Hamburg, Dresden and Cologne. Most contemporary accounts suggest, however, that British war planners used the bombing raids as the only effective means to carry the war to Hitler.

Bomber Command's unique place in war history is now unquestioned. For much of the war, Bomber Command was headed by Sir Arthur Harris, Marshall of the Air Force. In his book, Bomber Offensive, he reminds readers that: "It is worth noting that no other country in the world had at that time conceived of the possibility of using an air force in this way, to fight a war by itself and within certain limits, win a war outright." Bomber Command was organized into Squadrons, designated by a number, of which there were hundreds by the end of the war.

At the outbreak of the war, the RAF was grossly undermanned. With few planes, Bomber Command was initially used to provide tactical support to the Army and Navy. Later, as more bombers became available, particularly the Lancaster, capable of carrying heavier payloads over longer distances, Bomber Command came into its own as a fighting force. Early results of targeted bombing on discrete military and manufacturing sites proved largely ineffective. Technical limitations in navigation and communications also hindered its effectiveness. Later, as various technologies improved almost every part of the bomber, Bomber Command began to use a "strategic bombing" approach. This approach included large area bombing and significant numbers of civilian areas. Bomber Command used a number of different bombers in the early part of the war, but it was the introduction of the Lancaster in 1942 that proved most effective in carrying the war to the Germans.

As John R. Bruning describes in Bombs Away!, "The 'Lanc,' as the RAF's crews called it, came into service gradually through 1942. By the following year, it formed the Bomber Command's backbone. Eventually over several years, thousands were built at a cost of fifty thousands pounds each. For Great Britain, the Lancaster program marked a prodigious event of treasure and effort. Once in service, the aircraft exceeded all expectations. Over the course of the final three years of the war, Lancasters flew over 158,000 sorties and dropped 608,612 tons of bombs."

On 16 April 1943, Jim Keenan was assigned to the No. 106 Squadron and began his training as an Air Gunner on a Lancaster.

No. 106 Squadron

Based at Metheringham, the No. 106 Squadron was one of the most renowned Bomber Command squadrons of WWII. The 106 was formed in 1917, disbanded in 1919, and then re-formed in 1938 as the No. 106 (Bomber) Squadron. It was disbanded after the war, re-formed sometime later and then disbanded again, presumably forever, on May 24, 1963.

Its motto was "Pro libertate" ("For freedom"), while its badge was a lion, rampant, with a banner and crown. The badge was based on the crest of Doncaster near where the Squadron was formed. Flying the Hampton, then Manchester airplanes, the 106 served as a training squadron until 1941, when it took on operational duties in the bombing of Europe. It also started flying Lancasters in 1942.

No. 106 Squadron Crest

In total, the Squadron operated on 496 nights and 46 days, flying 5,834 operational sorties, losing 187 aircraft, but shooting down 20 enemy aircraft (with 3 more probable) and 29 damaged others. A total of 267 decorations were won by the Squadron. On the 26/27 April 1944 raid on Schweinfurt that claimed Lancaster ND. 850, Sergeant N.C. Jackson of the 106 won the Victoria Cross for conspicuous bravery during the attack.

The No. 106 Squadron participated in the 1,000-bomber raids on Cologne, Essen and Bremen. The raid on Le Creusot was lead by Wing Commander Guy Gibson, who later became famous for the Dam Busters raid with the No. 167. No. 106 Squadron also took part in the raids on Montchanin, Friedrichshafen and Spezia, and the important attack on Peenemunde. In 1944, the 106 bombed a coastal gun battery at St. Pierre du Mont and the

V1 (rockets) storage sites at St. Leu d'Esserent. In 1944, it made a nearly 2,000 mile round trip to bomb the German Baltic Fleet at Gdynia, while in 1945, it was among the bombers force that attacked Wesel just before the Rhine crossing, saving many Allied lives. In early 1945, its last bombing attacks were on an oil refinery in Norway, and a mine-laying raid in the Oslo fjord.

The Lancaster ("the Lanc")

Today, there are only two flight-worthy Lancasters left: one in the UK and the other, ironically enough, in Hamilton, Ontario. During the war, however, more than 7,300 Lancaster's saw service in most of the theatres of war.

Designed by Roy Chadwick for the Avro Company, the Lancaster went into service in February 1942 and established itself by 1945 as the war's most successful night bomber. The Lancaster could carry varying payloads with the heaviest bomb at 12,000 lbs. A number of Lancasters were modified and became famous for a daring raid on German dams (the "Dam Buster raid") with a special "bouncing bomb" of 22,000 pounds. With four engines, usually Rolls Royce, it is a metal-bodied plane with wings (with a span of 32 meters) about midway on the fuselage. It was built for fighting and not for comfort, as the crew needed heavy clothing and masks to protect them from the cold and thin air.

The "Lanc"

Two crew positions in the plane were particularly vulnerable. The Bomb Aimers main position was in the exposed front of the plane, where he laid flat on his stomach, looking out of a large transparent nose cupola made of perspex (thermoplastic). When finished bombing, he could sit up and man the front guns.

At the other end of the plane was the Rear Turret, also with a transparent cupola. It was manned by the Rear or Tail Gunner, often referred to as "Tail End Charlie." It was a very small, cramped space and tall Tail Gunners like Jim Keenan had no room to wear a parachute, which was hung behind or to the side. When needing to bail out, the Tail Gunner had a few seconds to release his seat and get his parachute. The Tail Gunner, flying backwards in the exposed, unheated copula, had to wear electrically heated suits to prevent hypothermia during flights that could last from 8 to 12 hours. With two guns, the Tail Gunner could fire 2500 rounds-per-gun. Despite its critical role in defense of the airplane, the Rear Turret was never as functional as needed and was re-designed several times throughout the war. Many Tail Gunners had the centerpiece of perplex removed to improve night vision. Because this rear position was so exposed, and so critical to the Lancaster's defenses, German night fighters would typically sneak up on the side or from below and try to take out the Tail Gunner first. Tail Gunners experienced the highest death rate of any position in the RAF, with generally a 50-50 chance of returning home after a raid. For the Tail Gunner, an operational sortie must have often been eight hours of boredom punctuated by eight minutes of sheer terror.

Messerschmitt Bf 110

Adolph Hitler spared no expense in building his war machine, and as part of his ambitious plans, he rescued a near bankrupt airplane manufacturer, Messerschmitt AG, and turned it to making the most important fighter of the Luftwaffe. Although it manufactured a number of different planes, the company eventually designed and built the workhorse of the German Air Force, the Messerschmitt Bf 109 and 110. The company introduced the world's first jet powered fighter before the war was over, but it was too late to have a major impact.

Messerschmitt Bf 110

Pilots on both sides of the conflict considered the Messerschmitt one of the best fighters of the war. With Daimler-Benz engines it could soar more that 30,000 feet at speeds of nearly 400 miles per hour. It was armored with both machine guns and rockets. Weighing in at just over 5,900 lbs. and a wingspan of 32 ½ feet, it was a highly maneuverable aircraft that eventually carried technologies that made it an excellent night fighter. Until the end of the war, it was the main aircraft used in the defense of Germany.

The Crew of Lancaster ND. 850

Captain	Pilot Officer W.G. Fraser	173136
Flight Engineer	Sergeant D.A. Simpson	1860709
Navigator	Warrant Officer G. Collins	R160042
Wireless Operator	Sergeant A. MacKenzie	15363940
Air Bomber	Sergeant H.T. Peebles	R171606
Mid-Upper Gunner	Sergeant J.A. Moffat	R199304
Rear Gunner	Sergeant J.P. Keenan	R173638

A typical Lancaster crew was comprised of seven airmen: a Pilot, Flight Engineer, Navigator, Wireless Operator, Bomb Aimer, Mid-Upper Gunner, and a Tail Gunner. (often called the Rear Gunner). Officially, the Tail Gunner was classified as an Air Gunner but the Tail or Rear Gunner term is often used to identify that particular position.

As was the case through much of the war, the crew was a mixture of British and Commonwealth airmen. The RAF just used numbers to identify the individual airman, while the RCAF designations began with the letter R (as shown above). In Lancaster ND. 850, three were English/Scots (Fraser, Simpson and MacKenzie) while the others were Canadians.

Except for exceptional raids, such as the famous Dam Busters raid, where the planes and crew were handpicked by senior officers, the RAF crews were able to self-select, usually led by the Captain. As Group Captain Tom Sawyer DFC (Distinguished Flying Cross) describes in his book Only Owls and Bloody Fools Fly At Night, "When pilots were sufficiently [trained] … they [picked a crew and] flew together from then on… And it was at this stage that the really tremendous crew spirit was created. Once a crew had decided to fly together ... then that was it. Forever after they only wanted to fly with each other, and when circumstances forced them to fly with other crews ... they really did not like it." As the reader will find in the letters of Jim Keenan, the crew of Lancaster No. 850 were, in the main, quite close.

Lancaster ND. 850 was just one of many Lancasters to lift into the air over the RAF Station in Metheringham, England on the night 27 April, 1944, at 2130 hours. The tension among the crew must have been palpable. The Captain was on his third operational flight and many of the others were similarly lacking in operations experience. With orders to bomb the ball bearing factories at Schweinfurt, the Captain signed off on takeoff and headed into the dark English sky. It was not a welcome assignment as Schweinfurt was deep in Germany and they would have to y over long stretches of well-defended German territory. The Navigator, Collins, plotted their route and the rest of the crew checked and re-checked their gear. After the Captain's sign-off, nothing was heard from the plane again.

On orders, George Collins, the Navigator, took the four-engine Lancaster on a "southern route" across France, to avoid as much of Germany as possible. Near Chauffourt, France, flying at 15,000 feet, at around 23:59 BST (British Summer Time)., they encountered Gruppenkommandeur Martin Drewes, a German ace, flying a Messerschmitt Bf 110, and in a short duel, the Lancaster was hit twice, caught fire and crashed.

Before it did so, four members of the crew (Fraser, Simpson, Collins and MacKenzie) were able to bail out, and three others, John Moffat, Henry Peebles and Jim Keenan died in the crash.

Reports vary as to the actual exit from the plane, but it seems Collins was the first to bail out, followed by MacKenzie, Fraser and then Simpson. All four were hidden by the French Underground in a nearby village and secreted out of France to Switzerland. Collins was initially reported among the dead but, despite a very rough landing (as he told us, he apparently landed from the jump without his boots), he later turned up alive and joined his fellow crewmembers.

The bodies of three dead Canadian airmen (Peebles, Moffat and Keenan) were left untouched by a German Army unit, stationed nearby. For two

Villagers search the wreckage of Lancaster ND. 850

days, they lay where the fell in a farm field until the villagers were allowed to bury them. Despite protests from the German military, the villagers of Chauffourt gave the Canadians a proper burial behind their tiny stone church, where they rest today, well-tended by the town's people. A plaque of remembrance from the French military and occasionally a small, pristine

Canadian flag sit atop the graves. They are interred, left to right: Moffat, Peebles and Keenan.

Except that they successfully returned to England, at this writing, little could be found about two of the crew who escaped: Gordon Fraser returned on 5 September 1944, and George Collins, the first to exit the plane, returned the day after. Simpson arrived in England via Switzerland on 8 November 1944; while MacKenzie returned the same way a couple of days earlier, on 6 November 1944.

Three of the survivors out of their RAF uniforms ready for the escape

From the available Canadian war records, it was possible to put together some brief information, and it is presented here, along with selected documents from the Canadian military archives. Some of the correspondence from the official records regarding the ill-fated flight were essentially duplicates and sent to several locations and families. For simplicity, they are only presented once. The information on Pilot Officer Fraser is from his obituary (with slight corrections derived from the official records).

Pilot Officer W. George Gordon Fraser, 173136
Captain, Lancaster, ND. 805
No. 106 Squadron,
Royal Air Force,
Metheringham, Lincoln

The following is from the Calgary Herald, December, 9, 2005:
"Gordon Fraser died (in Calgary, Alberta, Canada) on Wednesday December 7, 2005 following a four month struggle with cancer. As he had wished, he died at home, surrounded by his family and with his best friend beside him.

Born in Liverpool, England, on June 16, 1922, Gordon was seventeen when, in 1939, he and thousands like him volunteered to serve with the Allied Forces during World War II. He earned his wings on February 1, 1941 and was immediately posted to the Royal Air Force College at Cranwell where he trained as a flight instructor.

He arrived in Canada in September 1941 to train Canadian and Commonwealth pilots in Penhold and Medicine Hat, Alberta and Moose Jaw, Saskatchewan until the spring of 1943. Posted back to Britain, he completed heavy conversion training to fly the Lancaster and joined 106 Bomber Squadron flying out of Metheringham, Lincoln.

On his third raid, April 27, 1944, he was shot down near Langres, France. With the help of the French Resistance, he made his way back to Britain four months later. He completed his wartime service flying Yorks for Transport Command to India, the Middle East and North Africa.

Demobilized from the RAF, he returned to Moose Jaw, Sask. in 1946 and married Dorothy Mary Pritchard, the beautiful girl he had fallen for three years earlier. He worked for several years as a private pilot, and then joined the RCAF in November 1950.

His career spanned fifteen years and took the family from Claresholm, Alberta where he was Squadron Commander and instructor, to London, Ont. where he was an instructor at RCAF Staff College, then to Trier and Ramstein, Germany where he served as Aide-de-Camp to the Canadian Chief of Staff RCAF for NATO.

Back to Canada in 1960, he worked as project pilot and test pilot at CEPE in Uplands, Ottawa, then with 111 Communication Unit (Search and Rescue) out of Winnipeg. Gordon retired from the RCAF in 1965 and the family moved to Calgary where he began a successful career as a human resources specialist and management consultant in the oil and gas industry until his final retirement in 1987.

His last few years, spent with his friend and partner, May Froud, were full of adventures and good times with friends and family. He was predeceased by his parents, Jessie Maggie Leah and Captain Robert Yule Kennedy Fraser; and his beloved wife of fifty-two years, Dorothy Mary Fraser (nee Pritchard).

He leaves two daughters, Janice Lee Robertson, Lorna Dianne Fraser; one grandson, Matthew Fraser Robertson; his brother Robert Graham Kennedy Fraser; and nephew Graham Ian Fraser in Yorkshire, England; and three nieces, Bonnie Pritchard, Barbara Pritchard and Penny Davies."

One of Captain Fraser's first crew choices was Tail Gunner Jim Keenan. During their training they became fast friends.

Gordon Fraser in later life

Warrant Officer George Collins, R160042
Navigator, Lancaster, ND. 805
No. 106 Squadron,
Royal Air Force,
Metheringham, Lincoln

My wife and I met George Collins and his wife in their home outside Hamilton, Ontario, shortly before George's death in 2007. Susan had tracked him down using the Internet and phone directories. Unfortunately George was having memory issues and was unable to provide much detail about the ill-fated flight. He was, however, able to provide some confirmation of details about the flight ("We took the southern route through France."), the shooting down of the plane, his escape and the whereabouts of Gordon Fraser.

Born in Toronto, George, like many of his generation enlisted as soon as he could and chose the Air Force because he was more technically inclined. He underwent the service training typical of the times (described below) and was ultimately assigned as a Navigator to the 106 Squadron.

Following the war, George translated his technical skills into a series of jobs that saw him travel extensively. He married and had one son who now lives in Vancouver, Canada. He married a second time and he and his wife, Ann (from South Africa) eventually settled in a rural home in Lynden, Ontario.

George was convinced that the Allies had made a major mistake in not using more technical warfare (electrical interference and the like) to defeat the Germans, and spent much of his leisure time in the pursuit of the theory, eventually publishing a small pamphlet to describe his ideas. The war was long over of course, and his work met little interest from those weary of the war years and perhaps defensive about its conduct.

After his death, George's widow sold their home and moved to a seniors' facility not far away in Dundas, Ontario. My wife and I began a correspondence with her and even found occasion to visit her in her new home.

Perhaps in one of this story's most interesting coincidences, the windows of Ann's new home looked directly across the street at the seniors' home that Elaine (Ellis) Walsh had by this time occupied. Although they met once after we had made the connection, they were both at points in their lives where there seemed little to sustain a friendship. Their first meeting was to be the only one.

At the time he was shot down, he was making only his second operational flight. While growing up in Toronto, he lived near and knew John Moffat.

Sergeant John Agnew Moffat R196304
Mid-Upper Gunner, Lancaster, ND. 805
No. 106 Squadron,
Royal Air Force,
Metheringham, Lincoln

"Willing worker"

Sergeant John Moffat, of Toronto, Ontario, was just two months shy of his 21st birthday when he died in the crash a little after midnight in Lancaster ND. 805 over Chauffourt, France. It was his first operation flight.

Months before, H.P. Crabb, Officer Commanding, Number 9 Bombing and Gunnery School, RCAF Halifax, where John trained for four months, described him as a "willing worker."

Born in Toronto, June 22, 1923, to John Kitching and Gertrude Eileen Moffat, he grew up at 95 Marion Street, Toronto, with a brother, Stanley P.D. Moffat, and a sister Doris E. K. Moffat.

An athletic young man, John Moffat particularly enjoyed ice-skating and baseball. Handy with his hands, his hobby was woodworking. After his schooling in a Toronto high school and at Western Technical-Commercial, he worked a variety of jobs in a hardware store (Lyall-Lyall), a machine shop (Sedgwick Electric) and in the tool shop, Cribbs Small Arms Ltd.

Enlisting on 29 October 1942, he trained in Halifax and Montreal at the McGill University Pre-Aircrew Education Detachment in May 1943, before sailing out to England from New York on 8 October 1943, arriving eight days later on 16 October. His training continued in England and he was posted to the 106 on 16 April 1944, just 11 days before he died. In his Will, he left $35 in savings and a $1,000 life insurance policy.

During his training and service, he was promoted as follows:

Air Crew 2	29 October 1942
Leading Aircraftman Corporal (LAC)	24 July 1943
Technical Sergeant	3 September 1943
Pilot Officer	25 April 1944

Moffat was awarded his Air Gunner Badge on 3 March 1943, and posthumously, the following medals:

39-45 Star

Air Crew Europe

Defense medal

General Service Medal

Canadian Volunteer Service Medal and clasp

On 5 December 1946, his family received his Operational Wings.

Sergeant John Agnew Moffat

COMPLETED BY
1563940 SGT A. MacKenzie

QUESTIONNAIRE for completion by returned evaders and escapers.

NOTE   Please read the whole questionnaire before starting to
              write your answers.

QUESTION 1.   Approximately where did the aircraft crash?

              In the vicinity of Langres, France

QUESTION 2.   Did you bale out? If so state (a) the number and, if
              possible, the identity of any other occupants of the aircraft
              whom you know to have baled out before you. Have you any
              evidence direct or hearsay of what happened to them subsequently?
              (B) the number and, if possible, identity of any other occupants
              whom you know to have still been in the aircraft when you left it.
              Give any details which may have a bearing on the probable fate
              of these men.

              F/Eng. & Navigator baled out before me.
              Pilot baled out after. The M.U.G. Sgt. Moffatt
              R/G Sgt. Keenan, B/Aimer Sgt. Peebles were
              left in aircraft. All were killed, according to
              French People who saw identity tags.

QUESTION 3.   Have you any other information touching on what happened or
              what probably happened to the other occupants?

              The three men were buried at Chaumont near Langres.

QUESTION 4.   Have you information of any Royal Air Force personnel other
              than members of your own crew?

              No.

NOTE   Information given in this report will be passed on to the
              next-of-kin only at the Air Ministry's discretion. Neverthe
              less details of a very secret nature such as identity or exact
              location of aiders are not required, but only such general
              remarks which may enable the Air Ministry Casualty Branch to
              assess the probable fate of the other occupants.

              In every case be careful, if the facts stated have been learnt,
              not by your own observation, but through any other person, e.g.
              the enemy or inhabitants, to say so.

                                    Signature A. MacKenzie
                                    Rank   Sgt.
                                    Squadron or Unit 106 Sqdn
                                    Date   7.10.44

Attestation of the downing of ND. 850 by Sergeant A. MacKenzie

21

MINUTE 1.

D.P.S.

1. No.106 Squadron reported that Lancaster aircraft, ND.860, with a crew of 7, failed to return from an operational attack on Schweinfurt. It left base at 21.30 hours on the 26th. April, 1944, after which no further news was received. P/O. J.A. Moffat, F/Sgt. J.P. Keenan and P/O. H.T. Peebles were members of this crew.

2. Information received from Air Intelligence states that on the night of the 26/27th. April, 1944, at 00.45 hours , a Lancaster aircraft No.ZHG-JC 680 (not certain) crashed at Chauffourt near Montigny-le-Roi (Haute Marne) at a distance of 400 yards from a German Radar Station. Four members of the crew baled out and are either on their way to Switzerland or already there, but F/Sgt. Peebles, F/Sgt. Keenan and Sgt. Moffat were killed and buried at Chauffourt. The report further states 'the aircraft caught fire after having been attacked by a fighter. For a period of two days the bodies were left unattended by the Germans. In view of this information, F/Sgt. Keenan, F/Sgt. Peebles and F/Sgt. Moffat were reclassified "Missing Believed Killed in Action".

3. It is accordingly submitted that the death of CAN/R193304 SGT. J.A. MOFFAT, CAN/R173838 F/SGT. J.P. KEENAN, and, CAN/J90560 P/O. H.T. PEEBLES, be presumed, for official purposes, to have occurred on the 27th. April, 1944.

4. The one remaining R.C.A.F. member of this crew, W.O.2. G. Collins is now safe in the United Kingdom and the three remaining members of this crew were not R.C.A.F. personnel.

13/1/45.   *M. M. Goldberg* AC

13/1/45.   *M. Cameron* S/L
                                                 for R.C.A.F. Casualties Officer.

MINUTE 2.

                                        of Minute 1. approved.

ORIGINAL ON P4/CAS/CAN.
"RETURNS" 4-17. VOL: 2. FOLIO 159

R. O. D. let to Ottawa 57A. 15/1/45

C. 1 2 N.C.O. 1/C *M. M. Goldberg* (A)   **J. S. HARRIS.**

13/1/45.   Wing Commander,
                                                 for Director of Personal Services.

RCAF Minute of the crash

S.14 (Cas.)C.5   POST PRESUMPTION MEMORANDUM NO. 3270/48

                    FILE NUMBER P.416464/44   DATE 23.6.48

              Relating to LANCASTER ND.850   Missing on 26-27.4.44

                        Crashed near MONTIGNY, FRANCE

NUMBER	RANK	NAME	BURIAL DETAILS	INFORMATION
			CHAUFFORD PARISH CEMETERY	FRANCE
J.92010	Plt.Off.	MOFFAT J.A.	Grave 1	F.3372 shows burial
J.90569	Plt.Off.	PEEBLES H.T.	" 2	details of these 3
R.173638	Flt.Sgt.	KEENAN J.P.	" 3	members.
				Remaining 4 members
173136	Flt.Off.	FRASER W.G.)		safe.
1860709	Sgt.	SIMPSON D.A.)	Safe	
1563940	Flt.Sgt.	MACKENZIE A.)		Case closed.
R.160042	W.O.2.	COLLINS G.A.)		
Circulation:	S.14. (Cas.C.4)			
P.File	S.14. (Cas.C.5)			
B.1(Alpha)	Cas. Can.4			
B.1(Chron.Cards)				G.203146(e)/JBD/6/48
B.1(MSM)				

"Case closed"

CONFIDENTIAL

100 6/A.I.1(a)F/W

P.4 Cas(Miss Baker)

The following report has been received and may be of interest to you:

"On the night of 26/27 April, at 0045 hrs. a Lancaster No. ___ - JU 650 (not certain) crashed at Chauffourt near Montigay-le-Roi (Haute Marne) at a distance of 400 yards from a German radar Station:

Crew:

Pilot: Lieutenant Gordon FRASER: baled out, was
        rescued by French people, is on his way to)
        Switzerland.

Radio Operator: Alex Mackenzie: Baled out, was
        rescued by French people, is on his way to)
        Switzerland.

Navigator: George Collins: -do-

Co Pilot: Sergeant Dennie SIMPSON: Has reached
        Switzerland with the help of French civilian.)

Bombardier: Harry PEEBLES: Killed and buried at
                             CHAUFFORT - RCAF -

1st Gunner: James KIERAN: - do -   RCAF

2nd Gunner: Don MOFFAT: - do -   RCAF

Aircraft caught on fire after being attacked by a fighter - was based at Metheringham - target was Schweinfurt.

For a period of two days, bodies were left unattended by the Germans. When asked by the Major of the town what action was to be taken as regards the disposal of the bodies, the Germans' answer was that he could do as he wished and that they took no interest in the matter."

                              Signed
                              A.S. Thomson F/Lt Officer

A.I.1(a) F/W
1.7.44

Inquiry about the crew graves. Note Fraser was originally reported killed

J92010   (RC)

REGISTERED   OTTAWA, Canada, 5th December, 1946.

Mr. John K. Moffat,
95 Marion Street,
Toronto 3, Ont.

Dear Mr. Moffat:

It is a privilege to have the opportunity of sending you the Operational Wings and Certificate in recognition of the gallant services rendered by your son, Pilot Officer J.A. Moffat.

I realize there is little which may be said or done to lessen your sorrow, but it is my hope that these "Wings", indicative of operations against the enemy, will be a treasured memento of a young life offered on the altar of freedom in defence of his Home and Country.

Yours very sincerely,

(W.A. Dicks)
Wing Commander
for Chief of the Air Staff.

/BRO

Awarding Sergeant Moffat his operational wings

J92010   R 3-2-1

Ottawa, Ontario,   June 21th, 1945.

Mr. J.K. Moffat
95 Marion St.
Toronto, Ont.

Dear Mr. Moffat:

I have the honour to forward, herewith,
the Royal Canadian Air Force Officer's Commission Script
for your son Pilot Officer John Agnew Moffat.
This Script, which is being forwarded to you for safekeeping,
represents the authority vested in   Pilot Officer Moffat,
as well as the trust placed in him by His Majesty, The King.

Would you be good enough to sign and return
the enclosed receipt as evidence that the script has been
received by you in good condition.

Yours very truly,

(F.K. McDougall)
Group Captain
for Chief of the Air Staff.

Encl. - 3
F/L C.T. ALLAN/GB

Awarding Sergeant Moffat his script. Obviously not a personalized letter, suggesting the tremendous volume of such correspondence

Sergeant Henry Thomas Peebles R171606
Bomb Aimer, Lancaster, ND. 850
No. 106 Squadron,
Royal Air Force,
Metheringham, Lincoln

"Above average in air work."

"Very keen" "This Air Bomber should progress satisfactorily"

At 5'8 1/4" and 130 lbs., Henry (Hank) Peebles was eager to do his part in the war. And, he was perfect for the tight confines of a Lancaster on a long flight. He had trained rigorously for the job in Canada and England, ranking "above average in airwork," but ironically only "average in ground work." Ironic because when he applied to the RCAF in 1941, he wrote on his application that "I would like to be called soon after January 21st, 1942 and would be willing to join for general ground work if not accepted for a mechanic." He got his wish and was inducted in the RCAF on 3 March 1942, just a couple of months after his 18th birthday. His examination report from the RCAF Recruiting Center in the Provincial Building, Edmonton, Alberta, noted he was "healthy and fit."

As well he should have been from working on his parent's farm in Heart River, Alberta, following his high school years. He was born to Harold George Henry (originally from Ontario, Canada) and Emmie Beatrice Peebles (nee David, born in Cleobury, Mortimer, England). Henry Peebles' father travelled to England to marry Emmie at Christ's Church in Birmingham on 4 March 1920. After their marriage, they moved to Alberta and raised a family. In addition to Henry, the Peebles raised three children: George, Ruth and Allen, who were respectively 24, 16 and 14 when Henry went off to war. Henry joined the family on 21 January 1924.

Henry completed school in Grande Prairie and then Wanham high schools, essential credentials to be in NCO program in the RCAF. Henry did some part-time woodworking and garage work while in school, and following his schooling, worked with his father on their farm.

Hank, as he was called by his friends, was good looking young man with brown hair, blue eyes, and a fair complexion. When he arrived on station at

Metheringham for his training as a Bomb Aimer, he was 20 years old. Like his crewmates on ND. 850, he was athletic having played softball and done track as a jumper and runner while growing up.

Henry followed the same path through training and promotions as John Moffat and Jim Keenan were undergoing in other parts of Canada. By that time, Canada had become critical in training RCAF crews for the RAF. One of Henry's instructors (Chief Instructor A. F. McKillop, in Rivere, Manitoba) noted he was "a good map reader," "usually capable in the air," "a conscientious, reliable student," and "young but very keen." His promotions followed the traditional path for the time, and he received his Sergeant stripes on 11 March 1944. In England, he attended Battle School at Scampton, and was sent to join the 106 on the 16 April, just 11 days before the raid on Schweinfurt. He never got the chance to use the training in which he had excelled.

Three graves correctly identified after the war

Sergeant Henry Peebles

Mr. Harold George H. PEEBLES

Heart Valley,

ALBERTA

Any further communication on this subject should
be addressed to:—

THE DIRECTOR OF ESTATES,
DEPARTMENT OF NATIONAL DEFENCE,
OTTAWA, ONTARIO.

and the following number quoted:—

H.Q. J90560 FD 19

DEPARTMENT OF NATIONAL DEFENCE
ESTATES BRANCH
OTTAWA, ONT.

12th February 1945

For the purpose of record and in the event of there being any Service estate available for distribution (according to law) on account of the late

PEEBLES, Henry Thomas   P/O

J90560   R.C.A.F.

ESTATES
BRANCH
MAR 12 1945
H.Q.
NAL DEFENCE

it is necessary that certain information regarding the deceased and his relatives should be furnished the Estates Branch. You are asked therefore to read the enclosed memorandum before completing pages 2 and 3 of this form. The particulars required are to be carefully filled in and the Declaration on page 4 should then be signed in the presence of a Clergyman, Priest, Local Magistrate, Commissioner for Oaths, Notary Public or a Commissioned Officer of any of His Majesty's Forces who should be asked to complete and sign the Certificate. This form should then be returned to the above address.

If there is insufficient space for complete particulars to be given opposite any question on pages 2 and 3 of this form, the space under "additional remarks" on page 4 should be used.

Director of Estates.

DOG/MJ

M.F.W. 77
103M-10-44 (5854)
H.Q. 1772-39-072

Clearing up the estate

4.

DECLARATION

*Insert degree of relationship for example. "Widow". "Father". "Brother". etc.

I hereby declare that all the particulars shown on this form are correct, and a true and complete statement of all the relatives that the deceased ever had in the degrees specified; and that I am the *_Father_____of the deceased.

N.B.—To be signed in full in the presence of a Clergyman, Priest, Local Magistrate, Commissioner or Notary Public or Commissioned Officer of any of His Majesty's Forces.

Harold Peebles.

JM.   Heart Valley Grande Prairie Alta

Signature of Informant   HEART VALLEY
Address   ALTA

CERTIFICATE

I hereby certify that to the best of my knowledge and belief........................

See above.   Harold Peebles { Name of Informant } is the* *lawful father*..........of the Deceased above described. The above Declaration was made by the Informant and signed in my presence.

Dated at *Grande Prairie Alta* this *7th* day of *March* 19 *48*

Signature of Clergyman, Priest, Magistrate, Commissioner or Notary Public or Commissioned Officer of any of His Majesty's Forces.

JW Lawlor.   Qualification *Barrister.*

Address........*Grande Prairie Alta.*

NOTE.—Before granting the above Certificate, care should be taken to see that the Informant gives particulars concerning the death of any Relative stated by him or her to have died, and that the full name and address and age of each surviving Relative specified is stated in its proper place in the Statement opposite.

(If the deceased has no living relatives of the degrees shown on page 2, the names and addresses and relationship of other relatives should be set out below.)

USE SPACE BELOW FOR ANY ADDITIONAL REMARKS YOU MAY WISH TO MAKE

I have not received any of my Son's personal belongings as yet with the exception of his bicycle which was sent to his Uncle in Birmingham Eng.

My Son mentioned in one of his letters from Eng. that he had a Post Office Saving account in both Canada & England now.

HP.

Clearing up the estate

RAF Record Sheet. Note disposition of effects at bottom

C O P Y

4th December, 1945

F.416464/44/MR1/B.

Officer i/c No.1 Section(France),
Missing Research and Enquiry Service,
Royal Air Force,
c/o British Army Staff,
Paris,   France.

Casualty Enquiry No. F.254

With reference to your 1 MRES/S.201/11/
CEP254S/CTH of 23rd November, particulars of the three
deceased airmen are:-

pa/CR

R.199304	Sgt.	J.A. Moffat	Mid-Upper Gunner
R.171606	"	H.J. Peebles	Air Bomber
R.173638	"	J.P. Keenan	Rear Gunner

reported missing 26th/27th April, 1944, in Lancaster MD.850.

It is confirmed that the remaining four members
of the crew returned to the U.K., and the case may now be
regarded as closed.

Signed   W. TOYNTON

for Director of Personal Services.

Casualty Enquiry

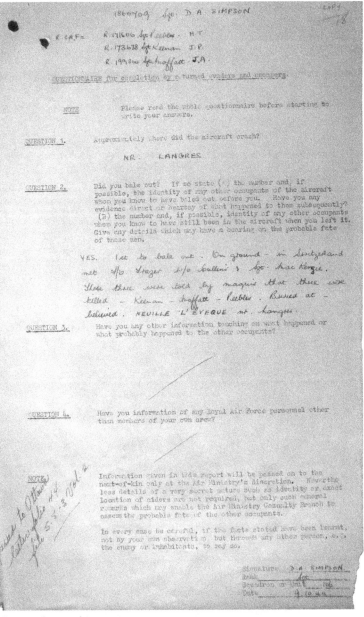

Sergeant Simpson's report

Peebles H.T.

P.416464

6

No. 106 Squadron,
Royal Air Force,
Metheringham, Lincoln.

106S/S10/162.   30th April, 1944.

Sir,

I have the honour to submit the following report of
the loss on operations of Lancaster aircraft ND.850 as reported
to you in my signal A.25 dated 27th April 1944. The aircraft,
which left here at 2130 hours on 26.4.44, was one of sixteen
detailed to bomb Schweinfurt. Nothing was heard after take off
and I regret the aircraft did not return. The crew was as
follows:-

Captain	P/O.	W.G.Fraser	173136
F/Engineer	Sgt.	Simpson D.A.	1860709
Nav.	W/O.	Collins C.	R.160042
A/Bomber	Sgt.	Peebles H.T.	R.171606
W/Operator	Sgt.	Mackenzie A.	1563540
M.U.Gunner	Sgt.	Moffat J.A.	R.199304
Rear Gunner	Sgt.	Keenan J.F.	R.173638

2.   P/O Fraser, the Captain, was making his third operational
sortie, and Warrant Officer Collins, the Navigator, his second.

                         I have the honour to be,
                              Sir,
                         Your obedient Servant,

                         Wing Commander, Commanding,
                         No.106 Squadron,   R.A.F.

Wing Commander's Report

5

No. 106 Squadron,
Royal Air Force,
Metheringham, Lincoln.

EWP/DO.   30th. April 1944.

Dear Mr. Peebles

      I am writing to express my sympathy in the anxiety which must be yours upon receipt of the news that your Son is missing from an operational flight.
      He was the Air Bomber of an aircraft which left here on the night of 24th. April 1944 to carry out a bombing raid on Karlsruhe. Nothing was heard after take-off, and I regret the aircraft did not return. There is absolutely no knowledge of what happened, and it can only be assumed that the aircraft was a victim of enemy fighters or ground defences. In either case, however, there is a possibility that the crew were able to bale-out and that, although prisoners-of-war, they are all quite safe. We all hope that this is indeed the case.
      Your Son had been with my Squadron for but a few days and this was in fact only his second operational sortie. He was, however, already showing excellent promise as an operational Air Bomber, and I am sure that, given the opportunity, he would have served the Squadron well.
      We are most appreciative of the motives which brought him from Canada to help us in our great fight, and I can assure you he will not soon be forgotten.
      Once again, both personally and on behalf of the whole Squadron, I offer you my deep sympathy.

Yours sincerely

Wing Commander Commanding.
No. 106 Squadron, R.A.F.

Mrs.E.B.Peebles,
Heart Valley,
Alberta,
CANADA.

5 MAY 1944

Wing Commander's letter to Mrs. Peebles

ADDRESS REPLY TO:
The Secretary,
Department of National Defence for Air,
OTTAWA, Canada.

X171606 (R.O.4)

A I R M A I L   8th May   4

Mr. G.H.H. Peebles,
Heart Valley,
Alberta.

Dear Mr Peebles:

It is with deep regret that I must confirm the telegram
recently received by you which informed you that your son, Sergeant
Henry Thomas Peebles, is reported missing on Active Service.

Advice has been received from the Royal Canadian Air
Force Casualties Officer, Overseas, that your son was a member of the
crew of an aircraft which failed to return to its base after a bombing
raid over Schweinfurt, Germany, on the night of April 26th and the early
morning of April 27th, 1944. There were three other members of the
Royal Canadian Air Force in the crew and they also have been reported
missing. Since you may wish to know their names and next-of-kin, we
are listing them below:

Warrant Officer Second Class G.A. Collins,
Next-of-kin, Mr. H.C. Collins, (father)
84 Springhurst Avenue, Toronto, Ontario.

Sergeant J.A. Moffat,
Next-of-kin, Mr. J.K. Moffat (father)
95 Marion Street, Toronto, Ontario.

Sergeant J.P. Keenan,
Next-of-kin, Mrs. J.G. Keenan, (mother)
657½ Barton Street, East Hamilton, Ontario.

This does not necessarily mean that your son has been
killed or wounded. He may have landed in enemy territory and might be
a Prisoner of War. Enquiries have been made through the International
Red Cross Society and all other appropriate sources and you may be
assured that any further information received will be communicated to
you immediately.

Your son's name will not appear on the official casualty list for five weeks. You may, however, release to the Press or
Radio the fact that he is reported missing but not disclosing the date,
place or his unit.

May I join with you and the members of your family in
the hope that better news will be forthcoming in the near future.

Yours sincerely,

R.C.A.F. Casualty Officer,
for Chief of the Air Staff.

Canadian Department of Defense notification to family 8 May 1944

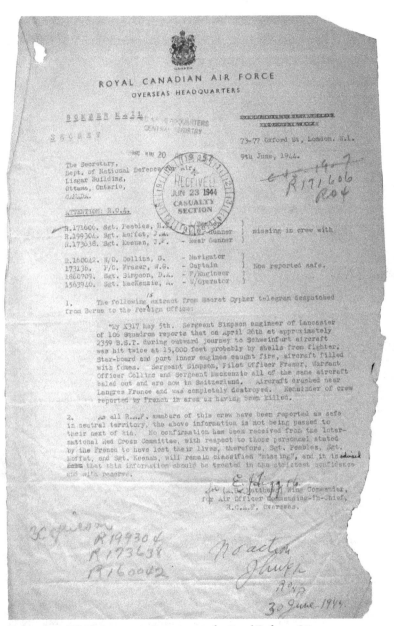

Report from RCAF Overseas to Department of national Defense, Ottawa

Training an Air Gunner

The war-time booklet, Pilots, Observers and Air Gunners for the Royal Canadian Air Force, the training of aircrew outlines the training schedule for Air Gunners who were also partly trained as Wireless Operators:

Chart of Aircrew Training (actual text)

WIRELESS OPERATORS (AIR GUNNERS)

Manning Depot – Training period from two to four weeks. Designated at enlistment as Wireless Operators (Air gunners). Preliminary training is carried out. Transition carried out from Civil to Service life.

Wireless School – Training period twenty weeks. Enters as Aircraftman Class 2. At the end of one month becomes Leading Air Craftman. Receives Wireless badge on completion of course.

Bombing and Gunnery School – Training period four weeks. Graduates as Wireless Operator (Air Gunner) with the rank of Sergeant. Receives Air Gunner wing.

Overseas Pool – Here trained efficient teams are assembled. The special training each man has received equips him to play his particular part in the science of modern sky fighting.

Scales of Pay for R.C.A.F. Aircrew

The following are the scales of pay for R.C.A.F. aircrew at various stages in their training:

AC2. (upon enlistment)............................$1.30 per day.
LAC. Airman Pilot, Air Observer or Wireless Operator (Air Gunner) (Received soon after training is commenced).............................$1.50 per day.

If you are selected for training as pilot or air observer, after completing training at an Initial Training School, you will be entitled to a special allowance of 75 cents per day, in addition to pay and allowances to which you are entitled at the time selected. This special allowance is paid continuously for the whole period during which you are undergoing flying training.

Over and above the daily rates of pay you receive, in addition, your meals and living quarters. You are also clothed, completely at the government's expense.

When you are mustered as sergeants at the conclusion of your training under the British Commonwealth Air Training Plan, your daily rates of pay, including flying pay, are as follows:

Airman Pilots	$3.70
Air Observers	$3.70
Wireless Operators (Air Gunners)	$3.20
Air Gunners	$2.95

In addition to the above rates you are also still provided with meals, quarters and complete clothing.

Upon embarking for overseas with, or in conjunction with the Royal Air Force, your pay will be in accordance with the scale of pay and allowances of the Royal Air Force. The deficiency, if any, in this rate from that of the Royal Canadian Air Force will be issued to you by the government of Canada as deferred pay, either on termination of service or otherwise in special circumstances.

For those selected as officers, the daily rates of pay, including flying pay are as follows:

Pilot Officer	$6.25
Flying Officer	$7.00
Flight Lieutenant	$8.50
Squadron Leader	$9.75

Officers are allowed $150.00 towards the purchase of their uniforms and receive, in addition free quarters and meals.

The three airmen (Moffat, Peebles & Keenan) earned C$6.25 to $7.00 per day

Major Martin Drewes, Gruppenkommandeur
Nachtjagdgeschwader III/1 (NJG 1—1st Night Fighter Wing)
Laon-Athies, France
Messerschmitt Bf 110G-4 G9-WD

Martin Drewes died on October 13, 2013 in Blumenau, Brazil, where he had made his home following the war. In his published memoirs, Sombras da Noite (roughly translated as Shadows of the Night, or Dark Shadows) in 2002, he recounted his war experiences, which included some 252 operational sorties, including those in North Africa, shooting down 52 Allied planes. Of those, 43 were at night, and 33 were Lancasters. His adjutant in the group at the time was Oberleutnant Walter Scheel, who later became the President of Germany (July 1974 to June 1979).

Martin Drewes' book

As was the custom on both sides of the war, Drewes' Bf 110 had his victories painted on the tail. He added a personal touch with a rendering of the Knights Cross above the tail's scoreboard.

After a short tour in North Africa, Drewes returned to Germany and fought the Allies in the skies over his own country. He took command of Nachtjagdgeschwader (NJG) 111/1 in 1944 and was basically a night fighter defending against British raids by attacking the British bombers over France. By the end of the war, NJG 1 was part of the Luftwaffe's most successful night fighter unit, claiming more than 2,300 victories and 676 Allied crewmen killed. NJG 1 was based in Laon-Athies, France.

Martin Drewes with Iron Cross

Drewes was awarded many of the most prestigious German military honours, including:

Iron Cross (1939)

2nd Class (26 May 1941)

1st Class (9 April 1943)

German Cross in Gold on 24 February 1944 as Oberleutnant
    in the 11./NJG 1

Ehrenpokal der Luftwaffe (31 March 1944)

Knight's Cross on as Hauptmann and Gruppenkommandeur III./NJG 1
    (27 July 1944)

Knight's Cross of the Iron Cross with Oak Leaves (17 Aprile 1945)

The Ehrenpokal der Luftwaffe (Honor Goblet of the Luftwaffe)

The Ehrenpokal der Luftwaffe (Honor Goblet of the Luftwaffe) was an award established by Reichsmarschall Hermann Göring, "For Special Achievement in the Air War," given only to pilots and aircrew. The actual goblet was either in fine silver or nickel silver.

Originally created in 1813, the Knight's Cross of the Iron Cross was re-issued beginning in 1939, essentially the highest award made by Nazi Germany to recognize extreme battlefield bravery or outstanding military leadership. The only higher award was the Grand Cross of the Iron Cross given only once, by Hitler to his second-in-command, Hermann Göring. The Iron Cross eventually had several additional levels, the second level being with Oak Leaves. Drewes Iron Cross with Oak Leaves as Major was the 839th of only 890 awarded at this level.

The son of a pharmacist, Drewes was born on 20 October 1918 in Lobmachtersen-bei-Braunschweig, a small village near Hannover in northwestern Germany. In the late 1930s, before the outbreak of war, Drewes was accepted into the German Army's officer's school, but transferred to the Luftwaffe in 1939. At the end of the war, he was captured by the British Army and eventually released. He emigrated to Brazil and married his wife Dolce; they had one son, Klaus. After a brief career as a commercial pilot, he established his own business, and by all accounts, was very successful.

Drewes signing his book

Metheringham, England

The small village of Metheringham, located about 10 miles south east of Lincoln, was established in Saxon times, ironically enough by the German Alamanni people from the Black Forest area around the upper Rhine

River. Once an independent country, the region was also known as Germani. Thus, the Alamanni gave their name to Germany and the German language. (allemand) The Alamanni were tribal warriors known best for their defense against the Romans. Like Schweinfurt, Germany, it was nearly destroyed by fire in the 1500s.

Perhaps it is fitting then that the RAF chose it for one of their Bomber Command bases in WWII. England was often referred to during WWII as an "aircraft carrier" because of its many airfields, and Metheringham, one of several hundred RAF stations, was home to the 106 Squadron.

Today as a housing community for nearby RAF personnel and serving local farming needs, the village has about 4,500 inhabitants.

Schweinfurt, Germany

Established around 740 AD, the city was almost destroyed by fire in the 1544. On the banks of the Main River, the city was rebuilt as the centerpiece of a beautiful German countryside filled with historic castles.

During the war, it was the target of a massive bombing raid in 1942, with the objective of wiping out the important German ball bearing factories. The raid, in the end, was a failure and in 1944 it was still on the list of important German targets for the Allies. The raid on 27 April 1944 had the same objective.

An industrial city today, making ball bearings among other industrial goods, the city has about fifty thousand residents, and is home to the US Army base for the First Infantry Division.

Chauffourt, France

The smallest of the three towns central to this story is located in the northeast corner of France, in a region known as Champagne-Ardenne. It is in the Department of Haute-Marne, in the township of Val-de-Meuse, in the district of Langres. With about 100 houses and buildings, it is home to about 200 people, and of course, the graves of the three airman killed in Lancaster ND. 805.

There are two war memorials in Chauffourt: one to the villagers' war dead from the WWI, and the other built for the three Canadian airmen by the grateful people of the village.

Laon-Athies

Built as a French civilian airfield in the northeast corner of France, Laon-Athiens was used by the Germans as a bomber base to attack England. It was then converted to a night fighter base for the NJG 1 to intercept RAF bombers. It was decommissioned after the war, then opened again as a NATO base in the 1950s. It was closed in 1967. In April 1944, it was home to Gruppenkommandeur, Major Martin Drewes.

Sergeant James Philip Keenan
Rear Gunner, Lancaster, ND. 850
No. 106 Squadron,
Royal Air Force,
Metheringham, Lincoln

"Very willing worker, takes a keen interest in all he undertakes, has a sound basic knowledge of his trade."

Jim Keenan relaxing in the English
countryside.

At six feet tall (with his great wavy hair seeming to add another couple of inches), and a 32 1/2 inch waist and ramrod straight back, Jim Keenan was every inch a trim and athletic young man. In fact, as an athlete, he played baseball, football, hockey, golf and, as he freely admitted, was moderate at tennis. More important than his athleticism, however, as he added in answer to a question about any useful skills for the RCAF, was his "sketching ability." Neither the RCAF nor RAF took him up on it.

Jim saw commercial art as a potential career after the war and had attended a local technical to study the field for four years. Although we don't know how often he drew pictures in his letters to Elaine, a surviving letter to Elaine's mother has a funny sketch of him with a bulging stomach, full of the goodies she had sent him in England.

Strikingly handsome, with a ready smile and always well dressed, Jim constantly looked for the bright side of everything. His letters to Elaine are full of hope and happiness, and seldom a complaint. In his pictures, he always has a broad, playful grin, even in his "serious" photos in uniform.

Pictures of Jim and Elaine before he shipped out to the war reveal a sense of artistic awareness and shy and playful sensuousness. Although they lived not far apart, in the middle-sized city of Hamilton, Ontario, they met at a small summer retreat, Cedar Springs, near Hamilton, where both parents had cottages. Apparently the attraction was immediate and strongly felt. Elaine was truly smitten and very protective of their relationship. When asked about Jim, one of Elaine's cousins demurred, saying they didn't know him all that well because "the two of them were always off doing something together." Both artistic and athletic, the photos of the time suggest they particularly enjoyed being in the outdoors while skiing, swimming, picnicking and hiking. Of the hundreds of photos Elaine kept in her albums, not one of the couple together was taken inside.

Jim was born on 3 February 1921 and raised in Hamilton, although he lived in Cleveland, Ohio, for several years as a youngster. He was born James Prowse, but his mother remarried and Jim changed his name to Keenan in 1940. Hamilton is known best as Canada's steel city, and Jim's adopted father, James Gardiner Keenan, worked at the National Steel Car Company. His mother, Evangeline (nee Dyer, and born in England), was a hairdresser. The family lived at 657 ½ Barton Street in Hamilton, not far from Elaine's family, who owned a steel trucking company.

Jim's sister Bernice was only 11 when Jim left for the war. She has remained highly interested in Jim's service and she and her husband visited his grave in Chauffourt. Jim's brother, George Bernard Prowse, was 28 at the time Jim enlisted. Another brother, John Joseph Keenan, 21, was with the U.S. Army Air Force stationed in Sioux Falls, South Dakota.

Jim attended St. Bright's School through the primary grades and then Hamilton Technical High School where he studied Commercial Art. His school records show he was ranked above average in his academic "accuracy, judgment, deportment and, reliability," and significantly above average in his art related subjects of "lettering, design and colour." His highest rank was in Physical Education.

Jim's tests for the RCAF noted that he was a "bright, active applicant, and should prove readily adaptable to training." His application included Elaine's father, George Ellis, as a personal reference. After being accepted, he trained in RCAF facilities in Toronto, Guelph, Belleville and Trenton, in Ontario. After arriving in England, he trained at Scampton Battle School and was posted to No. 106 on 16 April 1944 to train as an Air Gunner.

Jim shipped out to England on 3 August 1943 and arrived in the England on 11 August 1943.

As to the true character of the man, his letters speak louder than anything I could write.

Elaine and Jim outside Hamilton

Elaine and Jim on a hike

Elaine on one of their hikes

Elaine striking a pensive pose

Beside the lake at Cedar Springs

Jim hiking in the winter

Skiing

Jim, always smiling and immaculately dressed

Elaine striking a shy pose for the camera

Jim with his mother Evangeline and sister Bernice (11) before leaving for the war

Both Jim and Elaine were artistic. While Elaine primarily painted landscapes, she also made hand illustrated cards like this one for her father. Unfortunately none she sent to Jim, nor any art by Jim, except one card, remain.

Sharing a quiet moment before Jim leaves for training and then on to England

Jim (middle) in training in Canada enjoying a bit of free time

\ee REPLY TO:
Secretary,
rtment of National Defence for Air,
OTTAWA, Canada.

R173635 (R.C.b)

8th May   b

Mrs. J.Q. Keenan,
657½ Barton Street East,
Hamilton, Ontario.

Dear Mrs. Keenan:

It is with deep regret that I must confirm the telegram recently received by you which informed you that your son, Sergeant James Philip Keenan, is reported missing on Active Service.

Advice has been received from the Royal Canadian Air Force Casualties Officer, Overseas, that your son was a member of the crew of an aircraft which failed to return to its base after a bombing raid over Schweinfurt, Germany, on the night of April 26th and the early morning of April 27th, 1944. There were three other members of the Royal Canadian Air Force in the crew and they also have been reported missing. Since you may wish to know their names and next-of-kin, we are listing them below:

Warrant Officer Second Class G.A. Collins,
Next-of-kin, Mr. E.G. Collins, (father)
54 Springhurst Avenue, Toronto, Ontario.

Sergeant H.T. Peebles,
Next-of-kin, Mr. C.H.E. Peebles (father)
Heart Valley, Alberta.

Sergeant J.A. Moffat,
Next-of-kin, Mr. J.K. Moffat (father)
95 Marion Street, Toronto, Ontario.

This does not necessarily mean that your son has been killed or wounded. He may have landed in enemy territory and might be a Prisoner of War. Enquiries have been made through the International Red Cross Society and all other appropriate sources and you may be assured that any further information received will be communicated to you immediately.

Your son's name will not appear on the official casualty list for five weeks. You may, however, release to the Press or Radio the fact that he is reported missing but not disclosing the date, place, or his unit.

May I join with you and the members of your family in the hope that better news will be forthcoming in the near future.

Yours sincerely,

R.C.A.F. Casualty Officer,
for Chief of the Air Staff.

R173638 (R.O.4)

OTTAWA, Canada, November 15th, 1944.

Mrs. J.G. Keenan,
657½ Barton Street, East,
Hamilton, Ontario.

Dear Mrs. Keenan:

Further to my letter dated September 12th concerning
your son, Sergeant James Philip Keenan, a report has been received
from one of the members of your son's crew who has been reported safe
and it states as follows:

"At approximately 11:59 p.m. on April 26th during
the outward journey to Schweinfurt the aircraft was hit at approximately 15,000 feet, probably by shells from an enemy fighter.
The starboard and port inner engines caught fire and the aircraft
filled with fumes. Sergeant Simpson, Pilot Officer Fraser, Warrant
Officer Collins and Sergeant Mackenzie baled out and are known to
be safe. The aircraft crashed near Langres, France, and was completely
destroyed. The remainder of the crew were reported by French people
in the area to have been killed."

A subsequent report received states that information
obtained from the Air Intelligence Branch confirms the above details
and states that your son, Sergeant Moffatt and Sergeant Peebles were
buried at Chauffort, France.

Please be assured that if any further information
is received concerning your son I will again communicate with you.

May I again express to you and the members of your
family my most sincere sympathy in your great loss.

Yours sincerely,

R.C.A.F. Casualty Officer,
for Chief of the Air Staff.

DEJ

ROYAL CANADIAN AIR FORCE
OVERSEAS HEADQUARTERS

20, LINCOLN'S INN FIELDS,
LONDON. W.C.2.
18 Aug., 1944.

Dear Mr. Ellis:

Re: Parcel containing assorted articles addressed to Sgt. J.P. Keenan.

The above noted parcel unfortunately arrived in the United Kingdom too late to be delivered to the addressee and therefore the Canadian Overseas Postal Depot has forwarded it to this Headquarters for disposal.

This procedure was followed because the parcel did not have an alternative address, and it fell within the category of a parcel having a declared value of less than $3. In view of the great demand for ocean shipping space needed for the transportation of essential war materials, the Postal Authorities did not think it advisable to return the parcel to you. We have therefore supervised the distribution of the contents to other airmen of the R.C.A.F.

It is disappointing that the parcel could not be delivered as you originally intended but it may be a consolation to you to know that your kindness has brought pleasure to other Canadians of the R.C.A.F. serving overseas. I trust that you will approve of the action taken.

Yours sincerely,

(L.S. Breadner) Air Marshal,
Air Officer Commanding-in-Chief.

Part II
Letters from Home: "Life-Breath"

Today's soldier deployed to a war zone communicates home by email and social media like Facebook. Public media provide up-to-the-minute information about conditions at the front, and often provide opportunities to send video sound bites to those at home. The soldier in WW II, however, faced numerous obstacles in sending and receiving information in the form of letters, parcels, or even public media. Jim Keenan was no exception. While his letters describe the many problems he and Elaine faced in maintaining contact through an erratic postal system, his letter of July 4, 1943, shortly after arriving in England, clearly shows that he understands how vital this correspondence is. This perhaps accounts for the steady stream of correspondence between the two and the reluctance Elaine had in destroying Jim's letters some 60 years after his death.

While I have maintained the text as transcribed by Elaine, I have added editorial notes where needed and on a couple of occasions, eliminated direct reference to individuals. The reasons will be obvious by the context. Readers should be aware that correspondence from Elaine and others to Jim was destroyed by the RAF after his death, a normal procedure at the time.

Jim wrote to Elaine almost every other day. He seemed to know that his writing inspired others to write to him. The letters he received he called, "life-breath," and "the high spot of my life these days." Letters sometimes came in batches and often crossed in the mail. As such, they used a numbering system to try to keep the messages coherent. I have exerpted one letter that references how important these letters were to the men overseas.

July 4 , 1943
   After church parade I made my morning pilgrimage to the unit post office.
You have no idea how everyone here rushed to that place whenever there is a
spare moment, and anxiously cross examines the harried postal clerks. The mail
comes in here 2 batches of many hundreds so that it may take a whole day for
the understaffed post office to sort the lot. Mail is our very life-breath over here.

Love,
Jim.

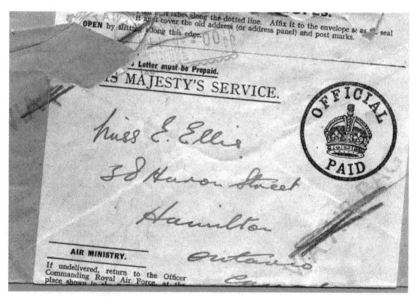

Jim's mail to Elaine arrived in many forms but mostly as letters written on the very poor
quality of paper available to him

At Sea (date unknown)

Our stay at Transit camp was not very comfortable due to the camp being not yet finished and very overcrowded.

This morning we came to the embarkation port, we got up at 4 a.m. Can you imagine me doing that? We left port amidst a drizzly rain, although we had had fine weather previously. While in port I felt I was so close to you and yet so far away, because we were not allowed to contact any one ashore either by telephone or any other means.

As you probably already know we were somewhat disappointed when we boarded a ship other than the one we hoped for. However, she seems to ride nicely, and day bunk is quite comfortable. So far I don't think anyone has been sea sick, but the sea is relatively calm. Some of the boys saw a school of porpoises after supper, but I was not on deck-at the time.

We have had several life boat drills already, and we are beginning to know our way around the ship. Well, it is rather late, and the boys (eleven) want to get to sleep with the lights out, so I shall close for now.

Love,

Jim.

At Sea (date unknown)

Mist and rain, and it is blowing--and how. The ship is rocking worse evey hour. I have won my first round with "mal de mer," although it cheated me out of breakfast this morning. I got as far as the dining-room, but only ate a few bites before I decided to return to my bunk. Dinner and supper went down fine. Another twenty-four hours should see me feeling 100% again. I am just beginning to get the knack of rolling with the boat. Even placid Cecil Green commenced to feel woozy this morning. Out of twelve in this cabin, three feel definitely sick. Only about two seem to be perfectly normal.

Love,

Jim.

At Sea (date unknown)

We have been through a very choppy storm which really made the boat roll and heave, and added many more to the sick list. I am still fighting a victorious battle to keep all my meals down. Breakfast seems to be the worst one to force down. I imagine I feel much like you did when we went to Halifax on the train. I am now in a position to fully sympathize with the way you felt. Certainly hope it wears off so I can enjoy the voyage.

The wind has died down and the sea now has a gentle roll so that the boat only turns half on end now as it plunges down-down-down and then rolls-rolls-rolls, and jerks! The fog is quite close, which we all feel is an advantage as far as safety is concerned.

I overslept all three divine services this morning. I understand that the R.C. Padre (McGivern) has been quite sea-sick. I have not seen and do not know who the Protestant padre is.

The turkey dinner this evening was very excellent, although I had no appetite beforehand. We have a very excellent diningroom and lovely meals, but it is really fun to to see the boys get up suddenly after merely looking at the meal and bolting for the door. However, most of them feel slightly better this evening.

Love,
Jim.

1

At Sea

Our stay at Transit Camp was not very comfortable due to the camp being not yet finished and very overcrowded.

The morning we came to the embarkation port, we got up at 4 a.m. Can you imagine me doing that? We left port amidst a drizzly rain, although we had had fine weather previously. While in port I felt I was so close to you and yet so far away, because we were not allowed to contact any one ashore either by telephone or any other means.

As you probably already know we were somewhat disappointed when we boarded a ship other than the one we hoped for. However, she seems to ride nicely, and my bunk is quite comfortable. So far I don't think anyone has been sea sick, but the sea is relatively calm. Some of the boys saw a school of porpoises after supper, but I was not on deck at the time.

We have had several life boat drills already, and we are beginning to know our way around the ship. Well, it is rather late, and the boys (eleven) want to get to sleep with the lights out, so I shall close for now.

XX

Mist and rain, and it is blowing--and how! The ship is rocking worse evey hour. I have won my first round with "mal de mer", although it cheated me out of breakfast this morning. I got as far as the dining-room, but only ate a few bites before I decided to return to my bunk. Dinner and supper went down fine. Another twenty-four hours should see me feeling 100% again. I am just beginning to get the knack of rolling with the boat. Even placid Cecil Green commenced to feel woozy this morning. Out of twelve in this cabin, three feel definitely sick. Only about two seem to be perfectly normal.

XX

We have been through a very choppy storm which really made the boat roll and heave, and added many more to the sick list. I am still fighting a victorious battle to keep all my meals down. Breakfast seems to be the worst one to force down. I imagine I feel much like you did when we went to Halifax on the train. I am now in a position to fully sympathize with the way you felt. Certainly hope it wears off so I can enjoy the voyage.

The wind has died down and the sea now has a gentle roll so that the boat only turns half on end now as it plunges down-down-down and then rolls-rolls-rolls, and jerks! The fog is quite close, which we all feel is an advantage as far as safety is concerned.

I overslept all three divine services this morning. I understand that the R.C. Padre (McGivern) has been quite sea-sick. I have not seen and do not know who the Protestant padre is.

The turkey dinner this evening was very excellent, although I had no appetite beforehand. We have a very excellent diningroom and lovey meals, but it is really funnto to see the boys get up suddenly after merely looking at the meal and bolting for the door. However, most of them feel slightly better this evening.

I had a

First page of typed versions of letters provided to the co-author

At Sea (date unknown)

Having had a good sleep and having seen a funny movie I am in much better spirits - thank goodness. If I were you I suppose I would tear up the first part of this letter and send a fresh one, which would not sound so depressing. However, I am going to brave the effect it might have and send it along so that you may know that I too can feel low.

I had a hot salt water bath after dinner. All it did for me was make me warm, because in spite of using special salt water soap, there was absolutely no lather, and so no dirt was removed.

This business of sleeping fully clothed every night is convenient, as far as going to bed is concerned, but I am beginning to feel quite filthy. My long underwear went on at the beginning of the voyage not because of the cold on board, but because of the possibility of being in an open life boat for days.

All sea-sickness aboard has disappeared, because the sea has become very calm. We have not seen the sun since we left port, and are ploughing through a dense fog most of the time.

As you will notice I blotted out the date at the top of the letter. Dates and places must not be mentioned. Also we cannot tell about those aboard, nor any other ships or planes that we might see, nor about any escort that we might have.

We are all feeling much better now, both pysically and mentally. Every hour brings us closer to land, and won't we be glad to get off this confined space!

We have changed our time twice so far, which is another indication of distance covered, however, our miles are rather long, as true to navy fashion: we are zigzagging continuously every sharp turn usually upsets something. Today the piano in the recreation room almost fell over.

I bought a two volume booklet biography of Winston Churchill. That is helping me fill in the many idle hours.

What a gala day! This afternoon we sighted land and ships. We feel like we are part of the world once more and that there are other people living on it. The sun shone yesterday and today for the first time, and the sea is like a mill pond. The coast line is very interesting. We do not know what port we are headed for, but we hope to be there sometime during the night. That will mean that with luck (and leave) I should be able to see Weatherhead three days from now.

So far, to my knowledge, war has not come near us. Possibly we have been very lucky.

Love,
Jim.

Sunday, June 20, 1943

I might quite appropriately give a title to this letter such as "So this is England". Due to a rapidity of changing events during the past forty-eight hours I have been unable to keep up my more or less daily diary to you.

Probably first impressions should come first, so I shall try to remember them in order, and present them to you. The first thing of course, are the quaint little light trains. They look like the little toy trains that take people around amusement parks. I assure you they are quite comfortable and fast. The second thing that struck us was the extreme cleanliness of all public as well as private property. If any debris had to be present it was carefully swept into a neat pile. Then the houses attracted us. In the first place the very numerous chimneys are very striking. The houses are mostly red brick and nearly all are exactly the same. This latter fact applies equally well to the middle class homes, with the only difference that these houses are separated from each other instead of being joined as in the slums. Every middle class house has a beautiful flower garden. In many cases this place is surrounded by a high board-fence, so that no one can see in except by invitation.

After having lunch we did a little walking to see the sights walking along The Mall to Buckingham Palace, passing on the way St. James Palace. After looking the palace over we sat in St.James Park - this is a bird park. Then we viewed the Parliament Buildings and listened to Big Ben strike. Crossing the Thames on the Westminster Bridge, we saw the London County Hall and the St.Thomas Hospital. We then recrossed the Thames on the Lambeth Bridge and walked back to the Parliament Buildings, and went into Westminster Abbey, which proved to be a most interesting place. Among other important people that have been buried there, I noticed that Henricus Puroell (1645) had had this honour.

We then proceeded along the Thames to Waterloo Bridge (the new bridge). We passed Cleopatra's Needle on the way. Crossing the Waterloo Bridge we went to the Waterloo Station where we had supper, and then got on the train and came back here to write this letter.

I should say a word about their subway system. It is quite stupendous and cheap, costing 1 ½ d. to travel from Waterloo Station to Trafalgar Square. The stairs down to them are very steep and long, and fitted with escalators after the style of Simpson & Co.

love,

Jim.

Photo Jim took in London

(date unknown)

I made my pilgrimage to the post office this morning and delivered happiness to many, and in so doing derived some myself. (This Q [queue or line, ed] enough to make me continue writing as often as I possibly can so you will have mail often.)

The war news seems bitter now that we are definitely on the offensive and in Europe too. The waste of life will probably be terrific, but for the sake of the present generation it is worth it if our leaders and ourselves make proper use of the peace which will follow our victory.

Love,
Jim.

Saturday, June 26

I did some rifle practice today and felt quite proud of my efforts considering my amateur status and poor eyesight.

The meals here are just so so, and we do not get enough to fill us. There is lots of hot water here but we are warned to use it sparingly. The tubs are very narrow and long.

Love,
Jim.

Monday, June 28

Well, well it has happened. Just as I was finishing above sentence someone brought your Air Mail #2 in to me. I notice that it is postmarked June 22 - 8 days isn't too bad. I feel quite content now. I had given up for the day after trotting down to the post office twice already. I am glad my friends have enquired after me. I feel content enough to write to some of them whenever I get a chance. I do not think I am telling too much if I say I am on a course here preparatory to going into the field. I am out in the open a great deal and have become sunburned, because we must keep our shirt sleeves rolled up to one inch above the elbow.

Love,
Jim.

Saturday, July 3

I put money in the local bank (Lloyd's Bank) here the other day. They didn't seem very fussy about taking my money but I persuaded them to do so. They do not issue bank books, but do give a receipt for your deposit. Every so often they mail you a statement regarding the status of the account.

We have had a rather busy week. We were at the 30 yd. range twice. The first time we fired our 303 Lee Enfield rifle. I do not like firing this weapon because it has quite a kick to it. Also the noise is quite painful to my ears. The second time we fired the Bren gun. Although it makes just as much noise, there is absolutely no kick to it, so that it is easy to fire.

Yesterday we went more than six miles out to the grenade ranges. We spent the afternoon tossing hand grenades. There is a considerable blast with these which makes you feel as though someone had shoved you, but the actual noise was easier to take than the 303 bullets.

The meals continue to be of a low grade. Possibly this is just part of our training as we cannot expect more than sustenence when we get in the active field.

Love,
Jim.

Sunday, July 4

After church parade I made my morning pilgrimage to the unit post office. You have no idea how everyone here rushed to that place whenever there is a spare moment, and anxiously cross examines the harried postal clerks. The mail comes in here 2 batches of many hundreds so that it may take a whole day for the understaffed post office to sort the lot. Mail is our very life-breath over here.

Love,
Jim.

Monday, July 5

Notice I say above that I am awaiting supper time. To tell you the truth, the meals here are not worth waiting for. The boys are quite disgusted with them. The reason is not because we are in England, because other messes nearby got much better fare than we do, and we are paying top mess dues.

Have I told you about the type of beds we sleep on? They are low iron folding army cots. There are no sheets, nor pillows. The blankets are very rough and wiry. The first night here I woke up many times to scratch all over where the blacket was pricking me.

Love,
Jim.

Tuesday, July 6

I didn't go to London this Sunday, but attended my first church parade instead. I felt that it was altogether too formal and had too much of the compulsory atmosphere to it. I hope they do some good, but I came away with the feeling that a padre certainly has the hardest job in the army, as is also in civil life. They usually receive little or none, or else merely token support from the officers. Of course we have already seen great indifference to the church in civil life, and the only difference in the army is that they can be compelled to attend church, but remember the old saying "You can lead a horse to water...".

Love,
Jim.

Jim happy to get an air mail letter from Elaine

Monday, July 12

Well I an climbing back up on top of the world again quite rapidly due to a dose of the right medicine I received this afternoon. Of course it was an Air Letter from you. Not receiving anything from you in this mornings mail, I proceeded to send you another cable at noon. I am sending an Air Letter scurrying out after it to explain that I now know that you have heard from me.

Love,
Jim.

Tuesday, July 13

The course we are on here has become quite dull and stupid. (Sounds like you honey child) We are all bored stiff most of the time except when we are on motorcycles or out on the ranges. When they are going to show us how the Medical aspect of warfare is conducted remains a deep dark mystery. So far it looks like we will be made into primary infantry privates—very poor ones at that.

I feel much improved since knowing that you have heard from me, and that you are apparently getting mail quickly and regularly.

Love,
Jim.

Wednesday, July 14

This evening Giberson and I went down to a burlesque show. I haven't been to one since long before I was married [humerous reference to his status as engaged, ed]. The joking over here is of a much higher grade, but the jokes are just about as crude.

Love,
Jim.

Jim relaxing between training sessions

Thursday, July 15

I received the grandest surprise this morning when they handed me Air Letter #9, which is one of the loveliest letters I have ever received from you. Your catalogue of letters sent to me makes me ashamed of my weak effort. To date I have received letters #2, 7, 9, only which would indicate that we have once more become entangled with the Mail service. Your letter has made me feel quite happy, like my old self. Such letters seem so necessary to me now.

Love,
Jim.

Sunday, July 18

Today must be my lucky day. Imagine getting two letters from you and one from Max at one mail time. The one from Max came over in four days—the speediest yet.

My bed is very hard. In fact almost every morning I awaken suddenly almost crying out with pain and feel as though I couldn't move the shoulder on which I have been lying.

I haven't said anything about the sex morals existing in this country. It would appear as though they were rather loose and low. Dr. Temple, Archbishop of Canterbury, had a piece about it in the paper the other day. The sex indulgence is carried on, literally, right in the open. The divorces after the war are going to be very numerous due to unfaithful wives and husbands. Some sections of London now have the unenviable reputation as being the greatest red light district in the world. During blackouts soldiers cannot make their way peacably through Piccadilly Circus. (You have already mentioned about that in one of your letters).

Love,
Jim.

Thursday, July 22

None of us have had any mail since last Sat. I understand there is plenty of mail for us but it is being held back. The significance of this keeps us all guessing. Is our mail being held up?

Love,
Jim.

Wednesday, July 28

We are learning a little about chemical warfare, and I am receiving confirmation of the feeling which I often expressed in Canada, that gas warfare is quite a humane form of warfare in comparison with present forms in use. The thought I was crazy to argue like that but now I know I was right.

The weather has been real warm during past two days, and the evenings are grand. Wish you were here so we could go out walking and really enjoy this beautiful countryside.

Love,
Jim.

Saturday, July 31

I am being swamped with mail—goody. I am very happy now.

Love,
Jim.

Friday, August 6

A most ridiculous episode occurred this morning. As I told you in a previous letter, a number of us did not turn out on parade yesterday morning. This was so noticeable that disciplinary actions was decided upon. In true army fashion, innocent and guilty were treated alike in that we all had to report at 0800 hours and were drilled for fifteen minutes by a Sgt. on the empty parade square. Whilst we were marching up and down, with the innocent cursing in their anger (being guilty I felt quite cheerful), three black mongrels, possibly sensing the pent up emotions, started to yelp and bark at our heels in a very excited manner. I wish I had had a recording made so you might also hear the sounds made in our battle training. I have yet to figure out whether the punishment was good
or bad.

Love,
Jim.

Saturdy, August 7

Giberson and I bought tickets for the R.A.M.C. symphony concert of tomorrow evening. We both looked in at the post office on the way back but there was no mail this afternoon. Gib. hasn't had a letter for a week— poor fellow. We will both be hanging about the P.O. in the morning.

Love,
Jim.

Sunday, August 8

I was very lazy this morning and didn't drag myself out of bed until 10:30, thereby missing breakfast and also missing going down for the mail. Luckily, Gib. went down and got all the mail and your Air Mail #21 was thrown into me before I had gotten around to shaving. The Air Letters are taking much longer to come over now. Probably because the Can. Gov't is now operating a "New and Better Service" (Sarcasm).

Dinner was good today. There was a grand steak, french fried potatoes and cauliflower. The meals have improved a great deal. Probably there is a new cook.

Love,
Jim.

Jim after receiving his Sergeant stripes

Friday, Aug. 13

I am experimenting with this system for my first letter so be sure and let me know how satisfactory it is. (Airgraph).

I had an uneventful voyage, and a most uncomfortable one, although the ocean was for the most part as calm as a mill pond.

I hope you received all of my letters and cards which I scribbled off through the U.S.A.

This country is very pretty, but give me Ontario any day! I can have films developed here, so I shall be able to send some prints along shortly.

Don't worry about me, especially in regard to the feminine species here; I shall enlarge upon that later! I should be here for a while before I do any flying at all.

The summer seems like fall here, minus the fall foliage. I met Danny Begin on this station, a lad that attended C.H.S. with me. If I receive a leave I shall probably find other lads too.

I cabled you and Mother last night.

The food on this station is remarkably good, in fact much better than at the "Y" Depot; England is not starving, let me assure you.

I was not seasick at any time, no doubt because of the size of our transport and because we had good weather. The meals on board were terrible and until we were half way here it was almost impossible to sleep due to the heat of our quarters; we had much better cabins than the majority, especially those who were bunked in the hold. After we dropped anchor we spent the afternoon and night on an English train (no berths) and it was torture because we had to sleep sitting up and the seats were so hard it even hurt to sit!

You should have seen us when we left Halifax camp; we were marched about four miles with our full kit on our backs at an hour when we should have been in bed and then we had to lug our kit bags about another mile and believe me, mine was heavy!

I met Jack Porter at dinner today and if you see Dot tell her that he is in perfect condition. He had just returned from a short course at an R.A.F. station somewhere. Some chap in civilian clothes was looking for me in my barracks last noon so the fellows tell me; I am very curious to find out who it was; he left his name but my friend forgot it!

This is a pretty city, and the buildings are very modern, especially our mess hall. I had my first ride on an omnibus last night, most of them are electrically operated as in the U.S. The women here are not a bit like our Canadian girls, they are, as a rule, large hipped, fat faced and about as symetrical at the ankle as they are at the hip!! The W.A.A.F. girls are the worst, very sloppy looking uniforms and silly hats but they are doing a grand job despite what we think of their appearance. They seem to have sufficient cosmetics if you can judge by the lipstick they wear. It all sounds very catty, but that is my opinion.

I will be issued with an R.A.F. uniform here, if you please:I shall wear it on all parades and use mine for leaves, if I get any.

[text intrupted, ed]…the town a little more since I wrote last and I sure wish I had a colour film. I saw some Russian Officers for the first time today; they look quite efficient. I see Yanks and I have even met a Canadian Sailor. I have not seen anyone else that we know.

Love,
Jim.

Wednesday, August 18, 1943

I had this morning off and this afternoon I was supposed to go swimming in the ocean but I have a very bad cold so I went out to an athletic field instead. The Air Force had chartered busses so it was alright. We have free Tennis, Golf, and other games here but these hills have taken so much out of me that I have not gotten round to anything like that yet.

If you receive the card you will know where I was when I sent it, but I will be moved by that time. [Elaine's added a note: "The card was from Bournemouth", ed.]

Love,
Jim.

Friday, August 20, 1943

This is the first Air Mail letter that I have been able to lay my hands on as they are quite rare. I hope you don't mind my crowding words in everywhere. It is a very discouraging business this writing and never receiving an answer; it would be a God-send if the mail were as prompt here as at home. You must be having the same difficulty.

I am fine, and went to a theatre last night but it was the usual propaganda, but for a Henry Aldrich picture called "Henry Swings It".

Harry Venn has left. I will not receive a leave till I finish O.T.W. and perhaps not then. The sooner I am in action the sooner I go home, so it has its advantages.

I lead a life of wasted time here, which seems to be taken up with meals mostly; that will change now as we may have some classes for one or two days.

I visited an Air Force Exhibition which was interesting this morning; there was captured German equipment and large displays of our own. I sat in a nice park that we have and listened to
a good band concert this morning too.

If Bob [Elaine's brother, ed] ever mentions the Navy again tell him that they work under the Royal Navy here and that they are treated very poorly

in every way; a Canadian sailor told me about it. All English Servicemen
are treated poorly in relation to us. A soldier gets about .44 per day.

Jack Porter is still here, but, I don't know for how long. By the way,
how is Earl doing on his course? It won't be long till he leaves too. But they
have oodles of his trade here so he should have almost a year before he sees
action. (Earl is training for a pilot and doing very well at present). Mine are
the only ones who do not stay on this station long enough for a leave, and
it is not due to casualties, it is the low number that have been trained for
the job in comparison with the number of aircraft to be supplied. Most of
what is rumoured in Canada is false, believe me.

Love,
Jim.

Sunday, August 22, 1943

I am afraid that I won't hear from you perhaps till after I leave my next
station which I expect to be on for about two weeks. It is rumoured that
Canadian mail is due tomorrow, so I am keeping my fingers crossed.

I have been retiring very early in the evenings this week in an attempt
to break up a heavy cold I have had from the voyage.

It is very boring wandering about all day trying to find something
interesting to do, hoping that perhaps we will have some excitement somehow, a raid, or a building falling in, anything at all.

I expect to be near David's hometown on Wednesday and I may stay
for a while; too bad he is not with me, but in any case I shall have my hands
full without him.

I believe I am to be attached to the R.A.F. and am not sure whether
that is good or bad yet. I have heard that promotions there are non-exis-
tent. I have also heard that all graduated A.G.'s are to be W.O.2 and W.O.1's
[Warrant Officer, ed] now instead of Sergeants; I always was lucky!

By the time I was dismissed from parade this morning, I had to go to
11 o'clock, Mass; we were really hungry when that was over!

You should know where I have been for the past eleven days, or do
you? Some fellows knew before we left Canada.

I have just noticed that the wall calendars are from the Royal Bank of Canada, no less. They sure get around.

Love,
Jim.

Monday, August 23, 1943

There is little chance of me hearing from you now until next week, Canadians can smile at home, and be smug about how hard they work and grumble about taxes and buying bonds; I should like to have a few of them here! I was the same, so I am no different. I guess so much idle time here and the characters of a lot of the population have made me excessively bitter. Perhaps when I am moved I will meet nicer people and that always helps a lot.

Love,
Jim.

Wednesday August 25, 1943

The above will be my address for the next eleven weeks at least, and twill [I will, ed] notify you of any change in my "attachments". I hope to eventually be on an all Canadian Squadron, as they sure have rotten meals here, and no canteen, in fact at dinner we drink water and no tea; it may sound funny to you but when you are in England tea assumes quite an importance because there are no other beverages other than beer, and it turns my stomach. In Bournemouth it was possible to buy a snack between meals, and in the evenings but we are, so isolated that it cannot be done here.

I have seen much of London (from the rear of an army lorry;) and it appears quite interesting. I shall have no leave till I finish here and I don't know about then, or I would be sure to look London over more thoroughly. The war can end tomorrow and I will be very happy, as I don't like it here.

I saw "H.M. Pulham Esq." tonight in the station theatre; it was a good picture too, a trifle sad here and there, but good. The theatre is the only good thing they have here.

My cold sticks with me, but some Cough Syrup that I bought is getting the best of the situation now.

David lived but fifteen miles from here, and I may visit the place one of these evenings.

Love,
Jim.

Saturday, August 28, 1943

At present I am on an indefinite leave in London and I am with three Canadian colleagues of mine. We have been having a quiet time of it so far; I have been to see Buckingham Palace and I took a snap of it, and Trafalgar Square. If the days were nice I would have gotten a snap of Big Ben and Cleopatra's Needle.

It requires a fortnight to have a film developed so I shall wait till I am more settled before I leave it in to be done. I met a fellow from Cathedral here in the Beaver Club, Harry Close, you don't know him, and also the brother of another chap that I went there with. I am a member of the Beaver Club now, and also the Chevrons Club, where I sleep and have breakfast. London is very large, and quaint. There are inumerable old-fashioned taxis with bulb horns (squeeze for sound). We travel exclusively by Tube (Subway) as it is cheap and fast and direct. I do not intend to pass all of my time in London as it would become boring and if I can I shall visit some of these addresses that I have. I don't know how far Wales is but I may even get there. I more or less stick with the fellows as after all they are Canadian and that is something. There are hundreds from Canada at this club naturally but I do not know them.

News is very good over here and perhaps this will not go on much longer. I heard the bombers flying over the city toward Europe in steady streams for hours last night, and according to this morning's paper, the

Axis got it in the neck in a big way. I hope to have a few letters waiting for me when I return to camp, so when I think of that I don't mind returning to the R.A.F. The R.A.F. chaps seem much easier to get along with over here than they were in Canada.

By the by, not that I am bragging, but we were each questioned by two English Officers on our trade knowledge and they tell me that I am the only one who knows my business. The others must be stupid.

Love,
Jim.

Tuesday, August 31, 1943

I am still in London and I expect to stay here until Sept. 7th when I shall report back to my station. If I get additional leave, which I expect, and also some money I will go to Ireland or Wales, I don't know which. I have not been doing anything exciting so far; I have seen St. Pauls, 10 Downing Street, Westminster Abbey, Big Ben & the Houses of Parliament, Buckingham Palace, and I have walked down The Mall. (Just an ordinary boulevard leading to Buckingham Palace!) None of these places are particularly impressive, in fact none of London is. Trafalgar Square which you hear of so often is quite insignificant, perhaps it is different in peace-time but it does not amount to a hill of beans now. I have been to several movies, "Mr. Lucky" "Battle of The North Atlantic", "Strip Tease Lady", which is no good!, "Above Suspicion", "Five Graves To Cairo", other than that I have done little as London closes down at black-out time, unless you drink a lot, and I have been retiring early each night. The patterns in the sky caused by search lights at night over London is quite fascinating and also the myriad barrage balloons hovering over the city day and night. There is still much evidence throughout London of the terrible raids that she has experienced, but most of it is cleared away.

I met Jerry Lynam yesterday in the Beaver Club and he is very well. He is an L.A.C. Radio Meehanic.

I have changed my residence from the Chevrons Club to The Canadian Legion Club as there are only two to a room there and there is a separate wash room for each two rooms, and also it is much cheaper. Chevrons Club 4 shillings per night, Legion only 2 shillings, sixpence, a key to your room, a nice canteen that remains open till midnight & which also has Coca Cola which is darned rare.

Eddie Lehman, a fellow from Cargill Ont. and myself, visited R.C.A.F. Headquarters today and got 100 cigarettes free and two handkerchiefs. We can do that every time we get a leave, so I won't forget.

Neither of us has any interest in the women of England. I hope that there are oodles of letters waiting for me on the station because I haven't had a letter now for a month; how about you? I am still carrying that letter that you gave me, and I almost know it by heart.

I was at mass in St. Mary's Church in Cadegan Gardens last Sunday; it was bombed during the blitz and is considerably damaged. A Bishop said Mass.

Jim in training

Thursday, September 2, 1943

I am staying here at the Canadian Legion Club and it is where I shall stay if I ever spend a night in London again as it is as close to perfect as any place I have yet found. It was a modern hotel at one time and we sleep two to a room and there is a separate bath and washroom for every two rooms. The rooms are especially nice, there is a secretary in one corner with shelves, pidgeon holes, and drawers, and on one side of the room stands a large wardrobe with double doors and a full length mirror on one door and half the wardrobe is filled with shelves. There is an easy chair, a small table and a straight backed chair to use at the secretary, a rug on the floor. There are two self-operated elevators, a nice canteen downstairs, a lounge, and billiard room, table tennis, All of this only costs 2 shillings six pence per night, about 60¢ a day and that included breakfast! Of course that is per person.

This afternoon I went on a tour of a Brewery and now I know how they make the junk. I could have had all the free beer I could drink but fortunately, or unfortunately, I don't care for for the stuff! This evening I went to an entertainment given by an old woman in the West End of London for Canadian Servicemen. Beer was free, coffee and sandwiches, and there were hostesses too, but I have already described the English women to you. There was an R.C.A.F photographer present and he took a picture of us all, which was definitely posed and should appear in the Canadian papers; propaganda you know. It was a tiny apartment and there was only standing room and about six men to each "female". All naval officers, Majors, Captains, Wing Commanders, etc. We left early—sneaked out as it were and beat it back to our rooms and here I am writing to you about it.

Travelling about London in the blackout is definitely hazardous, cars and bicycles whiz by, you stub your toes on curbs, walk into lamp-posts, postal boxes, and of course people! We have an unpredictable time of it trying to travel by tube, underground and ending up where we are headed for.

By the by, The British Empire Club arranged all of today's doings for us and we may go on a tour of Windsor Castle or the Tower of London some day this week.

Love,
Jim.

Saturday, September 4, 1943

Yesterday afternoon I went to the "Cinema" to see Dot Lamour and Bing Crosby in "Dixie" which was not a bad picture considering that it had a rather abrupt ending. On the way home we met a rather tipsy Yank soldier and we had to get him a taxi to his club. After that we returned to our own Club and had sandwiches and a Coke before retiring.

If my leave is prolonged and I get some cash I think I shall go to Ireland; they say the food is good there and rationing is not so strict. I'll let you know anyway. I am going out now as it is a fine day and it is 2 P.M. and we haven't been out today yet.

Love,
Jim.

Monday, September 6, 1943

It is another nice day today but it rained most of yesterday. I have traced Lawrence and he is on leave somewhere over here, I gave my address to his corporal and told him to tell Lawrence to write.

This will be my last night in London for three months at least because my pass ends tomorrow so back to the old grind, and the R.A.F. I was thinking yesterday that I have done no P.T. since June! I am the worse for it too! I bumped into John Nelligan last night in the Underground as I was going "home". He is an officer in a Canadian Transport Unit. He is the same as ever and looks very out of place in his uniform; I guess it is because he looks so young in the face. I hear that Alex Sturroc is at Bournemouth and was there when I was, but I didn't see him.

Love,
Jim.

Wednesday, September 8, 1943

I received 9 letters from you last night when I returned to my unit, one written Aug. l to Halifax, and numbers 4, 5 ,6 ,9, 10, 13, 14, 15. I am now back in London with six more days leave; apparently they sent me a telegram telling me to stay here but I left London before it arrived. I am back at the Canadian Legion Club and I shall remain there for the six days because it is quiet and more home-like than any place I have yet found. We did not get any more money so if I am very careful I should be able to stretch what I have.

This is the first Air Mail letter that I have been issued with or I would have been using them sooner; we are only allowed 4 of them per month, but I hope to be able to chisel more.

Tonight at 6 I heard the good news of Italy's surrender so with God's further help, the war should not last much longer. I can imagine Bob breezing about town in his car; I think he will be hard to keep track of now!

None of your letters have been censored; how have mine made out? I cabled to you on the 12th or 13th, so it seems the Spectator got the news ahead of you. Well, I am dead tired, why I don't know, so I am going to bed, and shall finish this tomorrow.

Love,
Jim.

Thursday, September 9, 1943

Here I am again, much better for getting a good night's rest. I have a little clipping that was in the R.C.A.F. paper, Wings Abroad, about me— something for the scrap-book which I shall enclose in another letter.

I checked at R.C.A.F. Headquarters about Jim Melrose, and he is still listed as missing. Don't spend all of your time knitting socks for me as I have scads of them at the present. Give my best to June and Mary.

I like England well enough, but there is something about my station that is awfully depressing. I feel it whenever I near it, but then I have only been on it three days and it rained each of those. The people in London are amusing to us and we see many queer things. I would not like to live here after the war, but as a novelty it is fun. The sights one sees here are unbelievable at times.

This afternoon I am going to Confession and then Communion on Sunday as it will be the last time that I see a Catholic Church for about 10 weeks as there is none on my station.

What you have mentioned about the box your mother is sending is very interesting! Gum and choc. bars are the scarcest things here, and even more so on an R.A.F. station. I got the R.A.F. uniform in addition to my own. Thanks for the snaps of Harry & the boys! You will look quite sophisticated and charming with your Kolinsky's so I hope someone doesn't grab you before I get home. Remember me to your Aunt Elizabeth and tell her I am very well, when you see her. Do I like fried chicken! What a question. I wish I could get some! Thanks heaps for writing so often. As soon as I am settled I hope to keep you better informed on what goes on over here every day.

Love,
Jim.

Sunday, September 12, 1943

I have been to Mass this morning with Eddie at the Church of Saints Anslem and Cecilia, a tiny church on Kingsway. We could not get to confession so we are going tomorrow morning and then to 8 o'clock Mass on Tuesday morning before we return to Upper. Heyford.

Every morning different groups of men stop in front of our Club and play instruments for the pennies that the fellows throw. Sometimes one man dances while another plays an ancient piano on wheels, as well as sings. This goes on till they figure they have enough money to spend in the nearest Pub I believe. Sometimes they are comical and sometimes pitiful. There are a lot of queer people on the streets, perhaps I should say eccentric! Yesterday I saw an aged man walking along with a mass of medals and badges completely covering the front of his suitcoat; he sounded like a milk wagon on a cobble-stone road. I saw another old geezer sauntering along with a basket of vegetables on his head, both hands in his pockets and a butt drooping from his lips.

Fountain pens are so scarce over here a man offered a chum of mine two pounds for his! I am hanging on to mine, needless to say.

Yesterday Eddie and I hung around the club except to get our uniforms pressed in the afternoon because we had been caught in the rain on Friday. The other day we were looking for a place to eat near Trafalgar Square and we saw a crowd of people in line in the Corner House, a restaurant on the Strand so we tacked ourselves on and stood for a while; eventually a lady who was standing in front of us pointed to the sign above the door that we were to enter, and I was never so embarrassed before - Ladies Washroom! You line up for everything when in England! Queue as the English say!

I just figured out my pay and it seems that I am short paid roughly $5.00 per month; I shall see about that in short order! It is strange, but from all the Canadian men I have seen in this Club, not one have I known. The majority are Airmen and I have been here for some time as you know and this is no small place. Some, or most of the Air Gunners that I came over with are on Operations now; I guess I was fortunate to be posted to my present station because I still have ten weeks to put in when this leave ends, if it does! I kept the telegram they sent me, saying to stay on leave as it will fill a space in Ye Olde Scrap Book, don't you think?

I saw an officer in the R.H.L.I. yesterday but he was with a woman, so I didn't ask after Norv. I may bump into him anytime, you never know.

Love,
Jim.

Monday, September 13, 1943

I went out with the boys yesterday for some fresh air and that accounts for the new date. I had my first ride in a London Taxi last night and they are queer looking vehicles; they have a big roomy backseat and the rear part of the roof folds down like the cover of a baby carriage. I got caught in a sudden thunder storm and there were no busses handy so I hailed the cab. They are quite reasonable.

Tomorrow I return to the station and I hope there are some letters from you. I am going to get some more Air Mail forms as soon as I get back too. I wish I could send you some good news about Jim Melrose; I often think of him and I hope he is safe because Margie is swell.

Say hello to your Mom for me, and Bob, and don't forget Bon, [Elaine's sister, Bonnie, ed] Cec [Bonnie's finace, ed], and your Dad. Which reminds me; how are the furs?

Love,
Jim.

Jim in the Rear Turret

Wednesday, September 15, 1943

I am writing during an Air-raid and so far I have heard one bomb, and our ack-ack is quite active. I have received an extension to my leave, of seven days, and that gives me till September 21st.

I visited Pay Accounts today and was only able to get 2 pounds, 10 shillings from them so I am not leaving London. Eddie had to return to the station yesterday as his telegram failed to arrive, but he is back tonight, and was fortunate enough to get paid while he was away. He was very thoughtful as he brought my mail with him, letters #1 & #11, plus two that you wrote and mailed with #1. Those are perfect letters and they took some reading. I see the other two are #2 & #3.

The all clear has just sounded so everything should be well, except for those places that were hit. I think it was more or less a "nuisance" raid— anyhow, I am still here!! You would be surprised at the number of men, women, and children that still sleep each night in the tube stations, mostly elderly people, though. Everyone scrammed for the shelters tonight, but I wanted to write. I will answer your other letters tomorrow, as this just covers number one. Your letters sound so much like home, that I can just see you, and everyone else as though I were with you. We have the best country in the world, if only Canadians would realize that. A lot of the fellows are wild over here, but then a lot of those same fellows were at home too.

Love,
Jim.

Friday, September 17, 1943

Well here goes my last Air Mail till I report back on the station. I wish I had as many as I wanted. I suppose Bob's chin is all healed up now, and he has forgotten all about it. That's sailors for you!!

I am going to the Hippodrome at Goldersgreen this evening to see a Variety Show which I have heard good criticisms of. I'll tell you about it tomorrow, and what I think of it. Your letters sound as though you had a very profitable birthday. I wish I could have been in one of your presents.

By the way, there was no dancing or anything like it at that entertainment I wrote about, it was singing, drinking, eating, and speeches.

I am pleased that all of the pictures turned out, and I would like some of you, as that is almost the same as seeing you yourself. I don't know when I shall be able to get mine done, but I will as soon as I can.

It is about time I got cleaned up and sauntered down for supper. I am leading a terribly lazy life here in London I am afraid, but I may as well while I have the chance, as we will be worked hard once we get going, both day and night. I may visit Ailyn on my next leave, only thing is I like to be with the fellows I know, because there are so many strangers you sort of hate to go anywhere by yourself. I will get over that though, I guess.

Love,
Jim.

Sunday, September 19, 1943

Here I am again, still well, and two more days before my leave ends. I had my picture taken yesterday with a group of Airmen in front of the Club. One of the fellows was being congratulated for receiving a decoration for gallantry by the Superintendent of the Club and we were asked to pose too. We were eating dinner today and a photographer came to our table and asked us to have our pictures taken again for a story he is writing!! Just a bunch of Play-boys, that's us! Both shots will appear in the Canadian papers, and also in Canada's Weekly, next week's issue, I think. I will get it if I can and send you the photos.

Eddie and I went to Mass this morning at a very old and poor church which was built by French refugees during the French Revolution. Most Catholic churches here are very small and not at all prosperous. I like ours much better.

Did you know the Hill twins? I met them yesterday and they are staying here. I also met a friend, Ed Armur, whom you do not know.

If I receive more leave on Tuesday I will return to my unit and get a travel warrant for Wales and some money and visit Ailyn as that is not too far from here. Then I can tell you about her and Port Talbot. [Elaine's father's birthplace in Wales, ed]

It is rumoured that we are to be raised to W.0.11, but I will believe it when I see it.

Love,
Jim.

Tuesday, September 21, 1943

I am writing this just before I leave for the railway station to return to my unit and begin three months training. I was to see "Stage Door Canteen" last night at the Odeon in Leicester Square. It was a good picture and I enjoyed most Yehudi Menuhin playing Ave Maria and Flight of the Bumble Bee on his violin; you would like it very much, tho very sad. The Variety Show that I saw at the Hippodrome was not extra good; more on the burlesque line.

All of the fellows that I came over with have finished their training and I am only beginning. The weather is growing much colder now and I wish I had a long sleeved sweater, especially at night. Our barracks is like a barn and I'm not kidding; give me a Canadian Station any time. I think it is going to be a "Hard" winter even if we don't get snow.

Love,

Jim.

Thursday, September 23, 1943

I arrived on the station Tuesday evening just in time for supper which was a sort of hash. I have started my course and this evening I had the first P.T. [physical training. Ed] that I have done since June and luckily it was not strenuous.

Last night Eddie and I went to the station theatre to see "Priorities On Parade", a musical comedy which was fair. Eddie was not placed on our course and therefore he will be on a course two or more weeks behind me. I think he goes on leave again next Thursday.

I am definitely a Tail Gunner and I should have at least seven days leave about three months from now. All of us Tail Gunners had our picture taken in a group by the R.A.F. photographer and I hope to get a print for you.

I received the parcels that my mother sent to Halifax and they seemed intact. I have also got your letters, numbers 18, 7, 21, 20, 23, 17, 26, 24, 8, and the two snaps of you, and the airmen, and also the clipping regarding my arrival over here.

I doubt if I will be flying for two or more weeks yet, so don't worry too much. I have received a very affectionate letter from Lawrence this week, and a short note from Mary M. as well as a letter from my Aunt Ve. Your new clothes very nice, and from what you write, you are going to be very busy knitting.

My letters, I seal myself so if they are censored they will show it. Yours have all arrived untouched so far. I will leave this station a week from this Sunday, to stay on a satellite station for four weeks, where I will crew up, and then return here for another four weeks. January 9th I am due to be promoted to Flight Sgt. but they are sometimes tardy.

Love,
Jim.

Friday, September 24, 1943

I have finally started my course here, and will not have any more leave for about three months.

I was feeling fine till I broke a tooth on a piece of bone that was ground up in my supper, so I must see the dentist tomorrow morning.

I am enclosing the clipping that was in the Wings Abroad with my name in it so you can put it in the Scrap-Book.

So far I have been having refresher lectures on sighting, armament and turrets, as well as Security lectures, P.T. and more lectures! I mailed an Air Mail letter to you last night, but not through the regular post box as I was told that if I took it to our Orderly Room it would be sent to London, R C.A.F. Headquarters by despatch rider and would go faster, that is letter #20 so see how many days it takes; it may be just a way to check on how many Air Mail letters I write! I shall send the next one by ordinary mail in any case.

The English people have not the same standards of living that you and I have. I feel sorry for them as they seem to be so much the under-dog. England is pretty as in regard to the country and resort towns, but London is dirty and drab in every way, not half as nice as any of our Canadian cities. It has some pretty parks, with miniature lakes in them, and many statues and most buildings are very solid looking being constructed of stone. I can't see that they have much to brag about at all. Our railways are better, our cities are laid out better, and everyone lives too close together. Give me Canada where you can be alone if you want to, and and everyone isn't crowded around you.

You and I couldn't have our pretty home in the suburbs, with the lawns and trees and gardens if we lived here, our house would be split in half and another family in the other half!

We have terrible barracks, there isn't any heat, and lately we have been going over to our Mess to shave because there has been no hot water. We don't get any heat till October 1st, and then we have a tiny stove for a room that you could put half your house in! No sheets either—oh well, we won't be here for ever, and when we get on Ops the food and everything is better—so they say!

The English radio programmes are corny, one that just finished seemed to have been taken from August's Readers Digest!

It is growing late, and I must shave before I go to bed, or I won't get on sick parade in the morning, in order to see the dentist.

Love,
Jim.

Sunday, September 26, 1943

Well, I didn't get to Mass today as there are no Catholic Services on this station and we work on Sunday, as on every other day. I didn't write last night because Eddie and another fellow, and myself walked to the village of Upper Heyford with our laundry. There is a woman that does it for us, for a price! We are only allowed to put one shirt a week in the station laundry so that is no good.

We spent all of this afternoon at the four hundred yard range at Otmoor, and it was pleasant there as we had good weather.

I was highly amused this week, one evening, by the spotless table cloths and special dinner and desert, and the hand and foot service given to some crews who were leaving on a little job that night; a sort of "last meal" for the doomed man idea, it struck me, because any other day of the week, those same men have any old hash thrown at them by the same W.A.F.'s who were giving them such good service. Some day, soon, they will be feasting me, and running for my tea and dessert, and I wonder how I shall feel, a little worried, disgusted, no doubt excited. I'll let you know when I can.

I have had a few test jumps similating parachute jumps, on a cable gadget hanging from the girders of a hangar, and it was fun. I am not worried about the future, not yet anyway, perhaps when it draws closer, I will. I never think of it very much, and I know you are praying for me, and as long as I am sure that you believe in me, I have a certain assurance that gives me confidence, and I know I will return home. About eight months from now, with luck, I should be through one tour of operations. One week from today I leave for the satellite station and I hear we are issued with bicycles there because everything is so spread out, some fun, cycling for miles for meals no doubt!

Love,
Jim.

Wednesday, September 29, 1943

I am writing this during my lunch hour, as I have a few minutes before my next parade. I have not been doing very much of interest since I wrote my last letter, the same old routine, and I will be spending this afternoon out at the 400 yd. range again. They are making sure that we know our jobs before we get into things, and they are concentrating more upon the A.G.'s than they ever did before; it seems they are realizing that our job is very important, and they are also teaching us a little of everyone else's jobs too.

I have not had any mail for almost a week now but I hope to get some before the end of this week. I saw "No Time For Love" at our station theatre last night, and it was very amusing, starring Fred McMurray, and Claudette Colbert.

It is still cold and damp here, and I believe it is like this all winter, only colder. I will eventually become used to the climate I suppose. Tomorrow is pay day, am I glad of that! There is not an awful lot to spend money on around the station, but it manages to go, in one way or another! I wish I could get into Oxford to have my film developed. I haven't been able to so far as I have P.T. from six till eight every night, and the bus leaves at five.

Love,
Jim.

Saturday, October 2, 1943

I have just finished packing all of my kit this evening, in readiness for shipment to the Satellite station for which I leave tomorrow morning. I sure have a large kit and will be glad of the extra kit-bag that I am to be issued when I finish O.T.U. In eight weeks time. I'll be four weeks on this station that I am leaving for tomorrow, then I come back here for a final four weeks, then I go on leave. A pilot asked me to be a member of his crew today; he is a W.O.1, and an Englishman named Fraser. There is another Canadian; the Bombardier in the crew and I think there is an English Wireless Op. Air Gunner, and we still need a Navigator, front gunner, and a Mid-Upper Gunner. This Fraser may be a good pilot as he was an instructor for some time in Canada. I hope so! If he is bad, I can leave him, and he can do the same with me. I shall be flying with him during the next four weeks so I shall have a much better chance to assess him in that time.

Your letters #28 & 30 arrived today, and gosh they were good letters; it made me feel swell when I read them.

What is Earl; fighter, or bomber pilot? If you can get me a lighter—one that works, please do, because I have now had my other one stolen! Or perhaps it fell from my pocket. I got my last leave as far as I know, because they had several men ahead of us to go on course, as it was. They just use Lorries to transport us to and from the railway stations, out to ranges, or as they will tomorrow to a neighbouring aerodrome.

We were out at the four hundred yard range again this afternoon. It's good practice! I got the photographs of our course of Tail Gunners, today, and they are not bad; I will send one to you as soon as I can.

I'll have to make up a dictionary of Limey [British, ed] slang and Canadian equivalents for you; I think it would amuse you.

Love,
Jim.

Jim in London

Monday, October 4, 1943

I arrived on this station yesterday morning, and I immediately started to work; lectures before dinner, and then my first flight in a Wellington, after dinner. It was the first time that my pilot had ever flown a heavy bomber, so we practiced landings, and take offs; after the third rough landing, he landed very smoothly, and of course we had a Staff-Pilot along, just in case! These kites [slang for airplane, ed] are not bad to fly in, but the tail turret is somewhat draughty. I have been walking a great deal since I arrived, as they ran short of bicycles and we are bunked almost two miles from the classrooms, crew briefing rooms, etc. and about a mile from our mess. We are quite near a town which is 3 1/2 miles away, and there is a fair sized village about one half mile from here. My pilot may be posted from here two weeks ahead of schedule, and if that happens I will probably have to re-crew because my course cannot be shortened. The Wireless Air Gunner is a Scotsman named MacKenzie, and the Bombardier, a Canadian named Peebles. We are to get a Navigator in about two weeks, and a Flight Engineer when we go to Conversion Unit to change over to censored.

The Mess is cleaner and a bit more pleasant here, but the food is not better. We do get the odd good meal which surprises us. It is rather amusing that the Tea Wagon that serves us in the mid-morning belonging to the Y.M.C.A., was donated by the Bundles For Britain Inc. Albany, N.Y.!

I shall be here for four weeks, then back to the other station for a month; then leave. The countryside is very pretty and the weather has been quite cool and windy. I must leave now, to help polish the floor. It's only a few minutes later, and I have success-fully dodged the Joe Job, so here ah [slang for I, ed] is agin. I am going to sew some chevrons, badges, etc. on my R.A.F. uniform and wear it while my other is being cleaned, so I will be busy for some time doing that; wish you were here!

I am leading a very quiet life; I eat, sleep, listen to lectures, walk, fly, and then the same all over again; I shall have to visit the town and take in a theatre some night, when I get a bicycle.

The Churchill Tanks roar by here all day and they are very large, and noisy too. I am looking forward to Operations, because once I begin them I will finish a tour in five months.

Love,
Jim.

Joking around in training

Wednesday, October 6, 1943

How are you; well and reasonably happy, I hope? I am very well, and as happy as I can expect to be under the circumstances.

It has been raining most of the day, a drizzle with intervals of heavy precipitation. I haven't received a bicycle as yet but I have hopes of getting one tomorrow. I don't mind the walking so much, but it is the time that it wastes, and then my crew all have them and I am sort of left, as it were. I was flying again yesterday, and I am gradually gaining confidence in my pilot, who is, by the way, Scotch, not English. I am due to fly all day tomorrow if it is not scrubbed because of bad weather.

There is not much to say in a letter these days, and as you know I am no journalist. I have not received mail for a week, but there will come a day, I hope!

I am learning to tolerate the Englishmen more, I suppose I am becoming familiar with their ways, and understand them a little better. I used to get into some murderous moods sometimes because of the mere sight of them.

The lectures that I have been having are complete with the latest "Gen" [information, ed] on all types of aeronautics concerned with my job. "Gen" means, information of the very newest, and is very common here. I am going to take a film to the Photographic Section of this station, to see if they will develop it for me. There is no place that does that work in the town.

Love,
Jim.

Thursday, October 7, 1943

I finally received some mail from Canada and six of the nine letters were from you, one from Lawrence, and one from Philadelphia, and one from my Aunt Ve. The numbers were #12, 16, 31, 32, 34, 35, and they were all extra welcome to me.

It was really beautiful this morning, viewing the countryside from 4,000 ft. up, with the sun still rosy and the morning haze still clinging to the hills. The fall foliage on the trees, mingled with those that are yet green, make quite a colourful carpet beneath you. Oxford offers an exceptional treat, with its beautiful colleges, crowned spires glinting in all their architectural perfection; a sight worth seeing from the air. The Wireless Op treated us to a few minutes of recorded music, which featured Bing Crosby, and the Ink Spots. We flew all morning, until one o'clock and then we landed for dinner. The turret was not a very warm place to be this morning, as it was cold on the ground, let alone up there with the slipstream whipping about you, and believe me, that amounts to a fair sized gale. The turret shudders so much when I turn it into the wind sometimes, that I feel that it is sure to topple off into space, but that is foolish, as they are securely attached really. Sitting out there on the edge of nowhere takes a lot of confidence and self-assurance, and it is somewhat lonely too, because the rest of the crew are all up forward.

One crew had to bail out today on my course and they are quite the centre of interest among us. They landed without mishap and the pilot brought the aircraft in successfully. One chap said that he missed a cottage by about two feet, and felt sure that he was going to enter via the roof, in time to join the inhabitants for supper! All in all, it has been a good day, including the weather. I am very well, and am learning more each day.

Here are a few English expressions- Wizard, meaning super; pavement—sidewalk: Sweets—dessert: T.T.F.N.—Ta ta for now: Prang—smash, accident: Duff—wrong, Gen—inside information: Pukka Gen—positive inside information: Book—error: there are many more, which I can't think of at present, but when I do, I will send them along.

It is cold out tonight, and there is a nice moon, not full of course, but bright. You are suffering under the illusion that I have the most dangerous position in Air Crew when actually we all stand the same chance. If I go for a "Burton" (die) the crew have little chance of returning, so if I am as smart as I am trained to be, we will all be safe!

Pilots were trained in a greater number than gunners, because they did not realize how much they were needed on bombers, and they are using more on each kite than they had before. Thanks for the snaps, they are very nice.

Love,
Jim.

Friday, October 8, 1943

Today has been very nice, as to weather, and I have been Skeet Shooting with a shot-gun, and practical work with guns and turret, as well as lectures on meteorology, etc. I am flying tomorrow, and I shall dress a little warmer this time.

I am still without a bicycle, darn it, but I will have one before Sunday. I have the "Canada Weekly" that has my picture in it, and I will send the picture along. I found out that if I tip an airman enough, who works in the Photographic Section on my other station, he will do my films for me. So I will surprise you and send some next month, at last!

Love,
Jim.

Monday, October 11, 1943

I should be flying this morning, but it has been much too foggy for it, but it should be quite clear this afternoon. I was night flying, for the first time on Saturday, and from the taste of it, I would rather stay on the ground in weather that we flew in; it was very foggy and visibility was almost zero. There was a perfect moon, but it only made the fog worse and we had to approach for a landing three times before we successfully touched down. One time we were sailing toward the runway, and I felt the nose of the aircraft pull up sharply and a nice big tree loomed up out of the fog, just under my turret, naturally all flying was cancelled for the night, and we stayed down. The last few mornings have been very foggy, even though you could see a round disc of the sun through the haze. It will prolong my training indefinitely if it keeps up this way.

I have a bicycle now and do not have to walk so much. The walking must have been good for me as I picked up a ravenous appetite (no cracks). I have just come from having my fourth haircut since I left home!

Last night I was speaking to some tank Corps Soldiers, Englishmen, and they have invited my pilot and myself over to their camp for a cross-country run in a General Sherman tank, U.S.A. I would like to go, but I don't have the opportunity to leave the station during the day.

We have no restrictions in regard to jewellery except that they must not have any military information, such as Squadron number on them, other than your rank, personal number, and name, and then you only worry about that when you are going out on an Operation.

I must go and get my dinner now, as my pilot has just informed me that we fly in an hour's time.

Love,
Jim.

Tuesday, October 12, 1943

I have this afternoon off, we were scheduled to have P.T. but the instructor dismissed us and told us to go on a seven mile bike ride, which none have bothered doing. It is another of those foggy days, and if it is the same tomorrow there will be no flying, and as I said before, our course will be definitely delayed. I had a bit more Skeet-Shooting this morning with the 12 gauge shot-gun, and I am improving each time I practice.

A parcel was forwarded to me from my last station, and lo and behold, Laura Secords from you.   They were an extremely welcome present, and I am very grateful, I am being extra careful of them, as candy of any sort is really scarce, especially on R.A.F. Stations.

I was flying yesterday for about two and one half hours and it was pretty up above the fog, and clouds, with the blue sky overhead and the sun shining brilliantly on the snow-white clouds below. The clouds look so downy and white, that you would be tempted to expect them to be as thick and cotton-soft as could be. When you go hurtling earthward through the clouds, nothing is visible in any direction, and they come in the turret like fog and you can feel them damp and cold, especially while breathing, then you emerge below them into the dismal grey fog which shrouds the land and descend until the earth comes to view—if it does. It did yesterday and we returned to base with little difficulty and made a good landing.

Gord Frazer, my pilot, and I cycled three and a half miles to the town last night, and saw "Hitler's Children", which was showing there, starring Bonita Granville. A good propaganda picture, but it made me mad, because I don't believe the Germans are as brutal to their own people as our government.would have us believe. Naturally I am no Fascist, but I do think the barbarity of the Germans is exaggerated.

Harry Venn has done several operations over enemy territory so I hear, and I could have been with him if I had tried to go when he left Bournemouth. I see by the "Wings Abroad" that we will receive gold wings when we complete a tour now. It is a very good idea as it will stop a lot of people from claiming that they have done so, when they haven't. As far as I can tell at present, I will operate from England, or Scotland; the abilities of my pilot are the deciding factor in that matter, so I can't say definitely what to expect.

I must write to Don (Valentine) again soon but as yet I have not heard from him.

The box you speak of in letter 32 sounds good to me; when I go to Ireland I will get as much linen as I can, and if it requires coupons, I hope to be able to acquire the odd coupon from some of my officer aquaintances. All the Air Crew officers and sergeants get along as though they were of equal rank, and that is swell.

One of the lads was going to this afternoon so I asked him to buy me some large envelopes so that I can send the photograph of the Gunners to you. My friend has just returned, and he was not able to get an envelope for me, so I will have to try for myself.

Love,
Jim.

Wednesday, October 13, 1943

I was flying this morning with a pilot other than my own, for an hour, and did we ever have a rough landing! I was up again this afternoon, shooting at a fighter kite, with a camera gun, for the first time. The pilot again was not mine, and the more I fly with others, I realize how good my own is. I will not be flying tonight as it is foggy again, with a slight drizzle. I just this moment met our navigator, a Canadian from Toronto, named George Collins who seems O.K. on first impression. We only need two more now. It doesn't matter what brand of cigarettes you send, as a cigarette is a cigarette over here.

It's funny but when I receive mail from you, it makes me feel good all over, and I could sit right down and write right away, but when I haven't heard from you for awhile, letters are not so easily written; I imagine you find it that way too. You have been very good about writing to me, and I hope you don't tire of it. I will tell you all I dare, and make my letters as interesting as I can so that you might not become bored.

No, I didn't see Madam Tussaud's Wax Museum in London, but I will next time. One thing I did notice in London's restaurants was that the waiters gave you excellent service if you have Canada on your shoulder, as they visualize a handsome tip! Most of the decent restaurants have very good orchestras that play dinner music. I believe I told you about the Turkish dinner I had in a restaurant in notorious Soho (murders, etc). It was 90% rice and spice, and I didn't care for it. It is a section of the city that you stay away from after dark, and the same goes for Picadilly.

My pilot is engaged to a girl in Moose Jaw, Sask. and seems very partial to Canada, and Canadians, something rare in one from the British Isles.

Love,
Jim.

Jim on leave in London

Thursday, October 14, 1943

It as been a wet and foggy day, very miserable and uncomfortable. Today has been wasted in my opinion, as I was on sick parade this morning, having a festered sore treated on my face, and there has been no flying, or lectures. I must report on sick parade at six this evening, as I have to be treated three times today. I am very pretty now, wearing the latest thing in gauze and adhesive plasters, on my face! Very charming, I assure you!

I have procured a few large envelopes, and I will enclose the photo I spoke of in previous letters, along with this letter.

It may be March of next year before I begin operations if this weather continues. I am ahead of most of the fellows in total flying hours, because they have had the misfortune of being scheduled to fly on days that the weather was unfit, like today. I fly tomorrow, and the weather may clear by then. At this rate I may get more leave than is usual, or I may lose what leave is due me; I must wait and find out.

I am writing this in place of an Airgraph because I want you to have the photos.

I must go for another treatment now, so I shall end with this page and mail the letter tonight so that it will be collected in the morning.

Love,
Jim.

Friday, October 15, 1243

I received an Air Mail from you at noon today, and it took fifteen days to reach me; it was number 36. I don't mind the typing as long as I hear from you. Got writer's cramp? I got four letters from home today, and all written at the same time, one from Mother, one from Aunt Ve, and one from Aunt Theresa; they must have heard me wishing. I wrote a letter to you, ordinary mail, last night, and enclosed a photo, and the one from the Canada Weekly for you.

I think the R.C.A.F. Women's Auxilliary supply the cigarettes, I'm not sure. You can buy English cigs here but they are .60 for 20, and poor quality. I have not had to buy any as yet.

No flying again today; it's this cussed weather! All Canadian Personnel must report in a lecture room at 4:30—I imagine it is in connection with the "V" [Victory, ed] Loan.

The hostesses just chatted with us, and many were married and all were very uninteresting; they served sandwiches and cakes, and saw that we had plenty to drink. I believe I told you that we left early. There was a Sing Song, and recitations, and speeches. There were too many men there because a draft of Navy Officers came uninvited. They were strangers, fresh landed in England.

I'm afraid I must answer your letter more fully in my next, because I am short of space.

Love,
Jim.

Sunday, October 17, 1943

I bought a few of these in the post office last night, to see how well they travel, as I can buy as many as I like. (Grey Air Mail) I was in the town to see "The Meanest Man In The World" with Priscilla Lane and Jack Benny & Rochester; a very amusing picture with no propaganda for a change; "Girl Trouble" with Joan Bennett and Don Ameche, was good too; I enjoyed them both very much. Before the show I bought a card and mailed it to Bonnie ordinary Air mail; let me know how long it takes. After the show, we went to a Canteen which is situated in the basement of the Catholic Church; we were rather late, and there were no more sandwiches available, but you should have seen the fuss the priest made of us, he wouldn't let us pay for our tea, and he dashed out to his house and returned with his own personal larder of cakes and cookies, which he insisted we eat! We, Gord Fraser, and myself, know him but slightly as we have only been there once before, but you would have thought that we were long lost friends.

We have decidedly interesting conversations with the priest and I thoroughly enjoy them. I am not an active participant in many of the discussions, but I like to hear the padre and Gord, quote Omar Kyam, Tennyson,

Kipling, with some very well chosen verse, to prove a point. I'm sure you would be interested also. The canteens over here are not the same type that we have in Canada and U.S.A.; these are Snack Bars where you may buy a sandwich, tea, coffee, and perhaps a cake; there are no hostesses other than the elderly women that serve behind the counter, and there are a few chairs and tables to eat at, so when I say "Canteen" don't visualize alluring bonds, etc!! Which would only be natural.

I am supposed to be flying today but it is raining again, and the visibility is bad; perhaps this afternoon it will be better. I am still visiting the M.O. for treatment for the sore on my face, but it is much better now, and should be gone in a few days.

Love,
Jim.

Monday, October 18, 1943

Gosh I was lucky today; I received #39, 37, 40, 42. All Air Mail from you, and they were swell. I am trying to get this letter off to you tonight but I may not, as I am flying till around 6 A.M. tomorrow morning. I work day and night now, you see. I was flying from 6 P.M. till 12 A.M. last night too! It was 5:30 when I wrote the last sentence, and now it is eleven, and flying has been cancelled due to the weather again. We got in a few hours before it was scrubbed so we aren't too disappointed. I am supposed to fly all day tomorrow, but the weather will decide that. I also received the invitation to Bon's [Elaine's sister, ed.] wedding today, but the C.O. would not give me a "forty-eight" so I'm awfully sorry, I find it impossible to attend! Gee, this Saturday Bon will be Mrs.

Love,
Jim.

Tuesday, October 12, 1943

Sorry but the Germans decided I shouldn't finish last night by sending over some kites which caused a black-out. I was flying all morning, and all afternoon today, and thank goodness the weather is bad tonight; I have had enough for today. There is no fun attached to flying all day and night, I can assure you. I am tired out and intend to retire early because I may be up tomorrow.

Sometimes if you are lucky you can get on a program broadcast from the Beaver Club in London. I'll let you know if I ever do. I am catching up to you in this letter writing business but I'm afraid flying holds me back, against my will.

I get mail from you approximately every seven to ten days. I don't mind so much being a tail gunner, I am more important than any other gunner. I still write to Dave; he owes me a letter at present. I wrote to your mother this week. I would rather receive ordinary mail but they are too slow and two Air Mail are better than one ordinary; don't you agree?

Love,
Jim.

Thursday, October 21, 1943

This morning at 4:30 when I arrived at the barracks to go to bed, after flying all day and night, I found six letters from you; I was soooo tired but when I saw them I felt one hundred percent better. As we cruised about in the cold moonlit night I was thinking (Elaine's Editorial Note: Sorry this part is censored by yours truly, the typist).

Your letters were numbers 19, 22, 23, 25, 41, 45 which I can't answer tonight as I must dash off for supper, and then I am flying again until the wee small hours of tomorrow morning. I'm afraid that as long as the weather is reasonably fine I shall be very short of time in which to write; I carry my writing kit with me a great deal, and try to dash off a line whenever I can, so I hope you will understand. I must go now, finish later!

I am in our Mess now, after eating supper, and I have a few minutes before I collect my harness for tonight's duties. As matters stand at present I am to be assigned to the best Bomber Group in England with the lowest record of losses, and the highest standards of efficiency, so I am well off. That should make you feel better, and I am not writing this to kid you along; it is the truth. Also on the best bombers in the world.

Love,

Jim.

Saturday, October 23, 1943

I am writing you a letter while I have the chance, and I will try and make it long enough to please you, so that you will not mind waiting longer for it. I flew all Thursday night, until seven Friday morning, and I slept from that time until three-thirty Friday afternoon. My crew and myself had tea, and boarded a train for where we had supper at a hotel before seeing "Flight For Freedom", starring Ros. Russell and Fred MacMurray. The hotel was very nice; we were asked to sit in a room and wait until the supper hour. The room had dark wood, panelled walls, a huge fire-place that one could almost walk into, and very low, comfortable chairs, with a short legged tea table in from of the fire-place. The floor was constructed of polished hardwood blocks, and covered with small carpets. The Dining-Room was very large and it had an even larger fire-place than the first room; in the centre of the room stood a large highly polished table of very dark wood-mahogany, perhaps, I wouldn't know, and on the table stood pieces of very heavy silver candelabra glittering in the light of a chandelier. The waiters were very proper, dressed in tails, and their service was excellent. We had pork chops, mashed potatoes, and cabbage, coffee, and the dessert was an excuse for apple pie, covered with custard. Fruit in this country has none of the rich flavour of Canadian fruit; it is flat tasting. The meals sound good, but they are inferior, because of the smallness of the portions, and the scarcity of butter and milk. This morning I was supposed to fly at 8 A.M. but the weather being "Duff" it was cancelled, and I attended lectures. This afternoon the weather cleared and I flew from 1:30 till 5:00 and then had tea, and from there to here! In England you have breakfast, lunch, tea, (4 to 4 P.M.) equivalent to our suppers, and supper, which is anything that is left over and they haven't had time to throw out!

Thanks for the picture of Bill Baggs, and the one of us; as soon as I return to our main station I will be able to get you some prints. Thanks heaps for the snaps that you enclosed in letter 23; they were, and are swell. I was very pleased to get them. Thanks also for the snaps you enclosed in letter #25. I don't write to Harry Venn, but I know where he is and I intend to contact him. He has done a few Operations. I know, as one of the fellows corresponds with a lad on the same Squadron.

I was soaring about the blue this afternoon, about one mile up from good old terra firma, when Bon & Cec were married, and I mentally wished them all the good wishes I could think of. I sure hope they will be terrifically happy. Did the wedding go through well? I'll bet your mother will miss Bon, and hated to see her go.

I received the parcel that was sent on Aug. 30 yesterday, and everything arrived intact. The film carton soaked up a good deal of moisture from the cookies but I expect it will be alright. The socks are perfect, even when they are a little hard on the toes from "bits of paper" I found; that was sweet of you, I got a big kick out of it. It is many moons since I have seen so many chocolate bars, and packages of gum, candy and peanuts. The gum is really something, as I appreciate having some, especially when I have been flying a lot, and often passed mealtime. I will thank you now for being so good to me, and I shall write and thank your mother tomorrow. An Australian, Englishman, and a Canadian, sampled the cake, and the Englishman couldn't believe his eyes! All of the fellows (most) share what they get to a certain extent. That was definitely a box of "gold," and I am storing the gum and candy for future reference. I am going to retire now, as I may have a hard day tomorrow, and believe it or not it has taken me all evening to write this, with interruptions of course!

Love,
Jim.

Sunday, October 24, 1943

Flying all day again today and I am due up in an hour's time, I have just returned from briefing, and I doubt if I can finish this now. There is a rumour passing around that we will have a few days leave, before returning to the main station, and if it materializes I will visit Ailyn so that I will have that matter off my chest! I expect to finish my training on this station, weather permitting, in another two days or so, then the leave, the approximately one month on the main station and perhaps a month's leave. The weather was fine today, but very cold last night. I was not flying last night so I stayed in barracks and wrote you an "ordinary mail" letter.

I haven't been doing anything interesting that I can write to you about. I am well, although I have a feeling that I have a head cold coming on as I have had a slight headache for the past few days, and that has made me rather irritable and fed up in general.

They tell me that all Air Gunners have been granted a raise in pay effective last September lst, of .25 per day; not that we didn't have it coming to us. It will make a difference of $7.50 per month and it all adds up! That is about 15s. 10p more per pay.

One of the fellows was saying that it would be a good idea to visit an American Squadron that fly Liberators between here and New York, if and when we get the month's leave and go home! Nice work if you can do it. It might be worth a try. I heard of a fellow that did it, and he arrived back on his station a month late because he couldn't get a trip back when he needed it. I will see what I can find out on the matter. I imagine that hundreds of fellows would do it if it were possible.

Love,
Jim.

Tuesday, October 26, 1943

Here I am, waiting for some ground fog to lift so that we may fly this afternoon. It is a nice bright sunny day so I expect to go up within the hour. I hung around all day yesterday, expecting to fly at any minute, and no dice! We flew last night instead.

I received two Spectators [Hamilton, Ontario newspaper, ed] on Saturday, Sept. 13 & 14. It was nice to read a newspaper for a change instead of the rags they print over here, even though the news was old. The comics are nice to see too, as they have very poor ones here. It was 1 P.M. when I wrote the beginning of this letter, and now it is 10 P.M. We did take off alright, and intended to drop some bombs on a target from 10,000 ft. but we were not away from the station five minutes before a dense ground fog rolled over the target, aerodrome and surrounding countryside; we attempted a landing but were advised to land at a station not yet enveloped, which we did, along with several other kites from our base, and an American Liberator. We were not down long before that drome was also smothered in fog, so we left our aircraft and had tea while we waited for transportation back to our unit. The ride back in a truck was fun, as there were twenty of us and we sang all the songs we could think of, but the going was very bad, and we just crept along. At one time the W.A.A.F. driver stopped the truck on the doorstep of a house. When you mix fog with blackout, you have something to cope with; I still can't go the English people; they think they are so superior when really they are miles behind America. I hope the war ends soon; Then I can live with "white" people again,. This is my last "blue" Air mail, but I have bought some grey ones. I haven't heard from you since you received the first Grey Air Mail form, so I have no idea how well they go; perhaps I will hear from you tomorrow.

I should finish here before, or by Sunday. I just have three day-light trips to do now I believe.

The socks you knitted for me fit very well; I wore them today and they are warm and comfortable. I owe several letters now, because of this flying.

How are the "Newly Weds"; happy as larks? I heard from Frank D. last week, and he is still breaking his neck to get into Air Crew, the dope!

I don't know what time I fly, if I do in the morning, so I had better get ready for bed.

Love,
Jim.

Wednesday, October 27, 1943

Hurrah! I made it tonight, I'm actually writing to you tonight instead of flying! I was afraid it was becoming hopeless, but I see that it is still possible now and then. I did not fly this morning, but I'll have been flying around at ten thousand feet all afternoon. I have only one more trip to do here, then I return to the other station, and aside from getting my mail sooner, I shall also be able to get some more blue forms; aren't you glad!

One of the lads that was on course at Macdonald with me has gone for a "Burton", dead, in other words; his name was Evans. He was one of those that went straight from, and onto an operational squadron without O.T.U., so it is well that I missed that parade when I was there.

There are so many Canadians here now that they are beginning to refer to this as a Canadian Station! Every new course that comes in seems to be ninety percent Canadian, so we have an even chance of getting a Canadian Mid-Upper Gunner, and it is my responsibility to get a good one, and if I have anything to do with it he will be a Canuck, especially when the Flight Engineer is almost certain to be an Englishman!

Love,
Jim.

Thursday, October 28, 1943

I haven't been flying today, due to the weather again, and I won't be up tonight either. My crew left this afternoon to spend a forty-eight in London, and I unfortunately have one more Air Firing exercise to do, so I must remain behind in case the weather clears. We go to the main station on Sunday and from all indications we probably will receive a few days leave before resuming course. My Navigator received a promotion to Flight Sergeant today but mine is not due for a few months yet.

A Canadian Gunner that is on course with me, a kid about eighteen years old, met a little Scotch lass in Edinburgh when he was on leave, and apparently he shot her a terrific line about marrying her and taking her to Canada, because she was writing to him continually; well, he decided it was time he disposed of her, so he had a pal write and tell her that he had been shot down over the Rhur. She promptly wrote to our Station Adjutant and requested my friend's home address so she could write to his family!!! The officer sent for my friend and demanded an explanation. Incidentally, she is still writing! Did you ever hear of such a stupid trick? The girls over here all want to marry Canadians, and return to Canada with them, and from what the boys say, they don't beat around the bush about it either.

We flew all yesterday afternoon, and when we decided to return to base, the pilot and navigator were completely lost, as the nav. had not bothered about our courses because we had been in the vicinity of our base all of the time, but we got playing around in the clouds and got off our course. Believe it or not, I, the lad in the back seat, pinpointed our way back; I'm quite proud of myself!

Love,
Jim.

Friday, October 29, 1943

I was very fortunate indeed, that I did not receive a "48" [2 day leave, ed] yesterday with the rest of my crew because if I had, I should not have received the six letters from you, that I got today. Numbers 29, 33, 43, 46, 48, and 49. I also got four other letters, one from Bill Grewar, Don V., my grandmother and one from my cousin Mickey in R.J.V. I am the envy of the camp! I was hoping for mail today and was almost afraid to look.

I stayed in last night and wrote letters, and this morning I awoke around 10 A.M.—lazy sod aren't I? The weather-was bad, foggy and grey, to be exact and all of the lads were still in bed. One or two got semi-dressed and made toast at the ridiculously tiny stoves we have, so I was treated to toast and marmalade in bed, very good too! The bread, butter, and marmalade had been pilfered from our Mess last night! I got up in time for dinner, received my mail, read it, and returned here to scribble this off to you. The weather is trying to clear, so I may fly this afternoon yet.

Thanks heaps for the snap of Earl, and the other. There is no such thing as Christmas leave over here, so I expect to pass Christmas on some station, unless I am on leave between units.

Conversion Unit is the next step between O.T.U. and an operational squadron, so named because you convert from the aircraft you have trained in, to the type you will operate with.

The weather is getting much clearer now, and I may go up today yet. Did I tell you about one of the chaps that bailed out a while back? It was rather amusing, because he lost his boots from the jolt of his chute when it opened, so when he landed he was in his stocking feet. He went up to a farm house with his chute draped over his back and inquired after a telephone, the lady of the house asked him if he had his automobile outside as she had no phone! Some people are dim!

I am trying at the moment to interest an Australian friend of mine to visit town this evening with me, as I would like to purchase some Christmas cards if I can. I think he is weakening, so I must hurry in order to catch the train, as well as eat first.

Thanks ever so much for writing so often, and for such nice letters as well, they are the high spot of my life these days.

Love,
Jim.

Saturday, October 30, 1943

I have just figured out that I have been in these British Isles for 79 days now, and this is my 42nd letter, so all in all I haven't done too badly as that is an average of one letter every 2nd day, which is not as bad as I thought. I imagined that I was further behind. I think you will agree that I have done fairly well, when you consider that I have moved around a lot in that time, and service routine does not allow much free time in which to write. I hope to get down to a steady letter-every-night routine when I am definitely settled down somewhere. I do my best anyway.

I received another letter from you today, #47, which was a surprise. I think it came over with the others and must have been held up.

I went to Banbury last night, and bought some Christmas cards, such as they are. It is difficult to buy good ones because of the shortage of paper. I went to see "Strip Tease Lady" for the second time, and it didn't improve any on second sight; I had even seen the cartoon before! The other picture, Jacare, a Frank Buck production, was interesting.

I was up flying in fog with another crew today, and we were unable to do our bombing exercise because of it, and of course we had trouble finding the drome on our return. We landed safely, and in time for dinner so everything turned out alright. That song, "Coming In On A Wing and a Prayer," must have been written by some fellow over here! Our mid-uppers arrive on this station tomorrow and I hear they are all Canadians, which is a "good show" as far as I'm concerned. We will outnumber the Limeys in our crew 2 to 1 then.

We had to march four miles, the distance around our aerodrome today because we were all late for flying this morning. The whole course had to do it, officers and all, and they even sent a W.O. [Warrant Officer, ed] after us on a motorcycle to see that we went completely around. We wake up in the morning and if we are scheduled to fly, and it is foggy, we just roll over and get up when we feel like it; well this morning they made us fly, fog or no fog!

We were due to leave here tomorrow, but I am told we shall be here for another few days, perhaps a week. When we finish with Germany we still have the Japs, and naturally the Australians expect us to do our share there, but if I have done a tour, I will return home for a few months before going down there, and I think myself, that the Japs will pack up when, or shortly after Germany does, so that is a minor worry at present, and crossing bridges before we come to them. At present, operations in Italy, and the far East are, and always have been much safer than from England, so never worry about me leaving here, as it maybe for the better if I did.

Love,
Jim.

Sunday, October 31, 1943

My crew are all back from London now, and they have been given another day off as there is nothing for them to do here. I am still waiting for the weather to clear so, that I can finish my last exercise and complete my course here. It is a muddy, wet, and very grey day, but perhaps tomorrow will be different. I wonder what we would do if it were not for the "tomorrows" that we look forward to; it would be hideous without them I'm afraid. This is a dull life, nothing to look forward to at the end of a gruesome day such as this. I used to always have your company to brighten up the day, and oh how I miss it now.

Below is a partial view of our barrack site, the first one mine, and all buildings are painted a nice cheerful black!! Behind the buildings runs a paved road which is very muddy because tanks have ploughed up the grass at the edges and traffic and rain have spread it on the road. Across the road are the huts of some of the ground staff, and instructors, as well as our wash-rooms where we shave. The huts are not wooden, they are constructed of some sort of weather-boarding. Our hut has a cement block to the right of it, in which are moulded crevices to place the front wheel of the bicycles in to serve as stands. Also on the right of all of the huts are Air Raid shelters. Now you know what the exterior of our "happy" homes are like!

I think that I will go to Banbury to a movie this evening, as the features change tonight, and my pilot is going and wants me to accompany him. I think it is a good idea as it will be something to do which will take my mind off things for a while.

A new course has just arrived outside the barracks and there are Norwegians, Canadians, Australians, and what have you, among them. I haven't seen anyone I know yet. I will return your type-written sheets in this letter, and a clipping that I took from the Spectator.

It is about time that I cleaned my shoes, had a shave, and got out of my battle-dress, in readiness to leave for Banbury after I have tea. There isn't anymore that I can write about, I'm just wondering how many of my other letters were chopped up by our friends, the censors. They always catch a few letters, and once they catch you being indiscreet once, I believe they watch for your mail. I don't believe I have made any grave error though, at least I hope not. Your letters have all arrived intact. I hope they don't take Bob, and I also hope that they won't need to when he is eligible. It isn't a great deal of fun for anyone.

Love,
Jim.

Monday, November 1, 1943

Another day of loafing around the station, doing nothing but travel between the Mess and our barracks at meal times. It is a very wet and muddy day, with no possibility of flying, and my crew are all away in London again today, the lucky stiffs. I pedalled to Banbury after tea yesterday with Gord Fraser, my pilot, and we saw Rosalind Russell, and Walter Pidgeon, in "Design for Scandal." I think you and I saw it together at home, quite some time ago. I enjoyed it for the second time, and after the show we went to Whately Hall for supper; that is the place that I described to you before, in one of my past letters. We pedalled back soon after eating, and retired for the night. If this keeps up, I shall be both very lazy, and quite bored, even more so than I have already been.

Boy was I surprised this afternoon, a parcel arrived for me, and it was a one pound family package of Smiles'n Chuckles, from the 119th Bomber Squadron. Am I ever lucky; As you notice, I ran out of ink and have refilled with blue.

I wrote an ordinary mail letter to you last night, and enclosed your typewritten sheets, so you should receive it by Dec. 1st. I also mailed some Christmas Cards to Canada today, and that allows them almost two months, so they should make it. I don't know whether Ned is still at that address you sent me in one of your letters, or not but I will drop him a line tonight in any case. I haven't written to him for some time, and I believe he owes me a letter. Have you heard from him? I didn't send Peg or June a card because you usually attend to that.

Love,
Jim.

Tuesday, November 2, 1943

Yet another Air Letter. I do hope that they are making good time, I believe I will write an Air Graph to you, and mail it at the time that I mail this, so that you can compare their merits, if this has any!

The Tank Corps Pipe Band just marched by our barracks; they must be practising, as it is the second time within the last half hour that they have done so. I'm going to see "International Squadron" in Banbury this evening with my Australian friend, Brian Joyce. He is the same height as I and he has fair hair and blue eyes, and smokes a pipe. A rather quiet fellow, twenty-six years of age, engaged to a girl named Betty in Melbourne, and he has his Batchelor of Arts degree. He is a Sergeant, Bomber. Now you know almost as much as I do about him. How does he sound to you? My Navigator is back from London, and he brought a small portable battery radio with him, which he paid 8 for; strictly speaking it is not worth it, but in view of the scarcity of radios here, he was fortunate. I am satisfied anyway, as now we can have music once in a while, and that makes a great deal of difference around here.

We have a.new C.O. [Commanding Officer, ed] now, and he is creating a good deal of disturbance around the station, discipline is becoming more rigid each day, and we are losing one privilege after the other. T'ain't good! Just another New Broom sweeping clean, I guess.

I opened a Post Office Savings Account this morning by depositing 7, a sort of "Leave Fund," you might call it. Oh yes! When I am able to visit Ireland, I know where I can procure some linen for you in Belfast; it seems you must know someone! I'll save all I can so that I will be sure to have enough money when it is necessary. I hope I don't get rooked! In Eire you can buy Ice Cream, and everything else that is unheard of over here, but there is a tremendous amount of red tape in connection with visiting the place. From this Post Office Account I have, you can only withdraw 3 per day, but there are 18,000 branches throughout the British Isles.

Love,
Jim.

Jim and Gordon Fraser

Tuesday, November 2, 1943

I have written an Air Letter to you today as well as this Air Graph, so that you may compare their efficiency. I shall mail them at the same time. I have written all that I have had to say in the Air Letter so that leaves me with nothing to write now.

I have just had tea, and am feeling somewhat better for it. The weather shows some signs of clearing, so I wouldn't be surprised if we were flying tomorrow. You should see me these days running about the station with a short pair of rubber boots on, which you need with the muddy roads around here. The first clear day we have and we are flying I shall get a snap of the crew taken in front of one of our kites, me included, of course. Would you like that? It will have to be a day that there are no Staff Instructors with us, as then we are in too much of a hurry to be able to do it.

Love,
Jim.

Wednesday November 3, 1943

Today is clearer than the days have been for the past week or more, but as yet I have not been flying. There is a possibility of it, later on this afternoon.

I have just finished writing a note to the Secretary of the R.C.A.F. Women's Auxiliary, to thank them for the chocolates that I received from them on Nov. first.

This morning I spent playing Darts with some of my crew, in the Crew Room, while I waited for a chance to fly. I am becoming quite a good player, as it is the main pastime in England. I'll have to teach you how to play when I come home. The Crew Room is approximately 35' long and 18' wide, and is furnished with wicker, and leather easy chairs, three tables, a stove, and a locker in which an assortment of games are kept. The purpose of the room is to supply the crews with a rest room and recreation room in which to await orders to fly, night or day. When they want us, they know where to find us— sometimes!! At present the Canadian boys are avidly consuming a Toronto Star Weekly, that someone must have received today. You have never seen a quieter nor more absorbed group of men in your life, till you see the boys reading letters from home; a high powered cannon could not interrupt them. The Group Capt. is around inspecting the station today, and I am supposed to attend a lecture at 3:45 this afternoon, if I am not flying. Perhaps the new C.O., the Gr. Capt. has something to say to us, I have no idea but I do know that there will be several fellows absent.

I hope to receive some mail from you by Friday, or perhaps Saturday at the latest. I hope they don't get held up. Shucks, I hear there are certain customs snags in regard to bringing linen from Ireland, so it may not be as simple as I had imagined. I may be able to overcome that obstacle too, I hope.

Love,
Jim.

Wednesday. November 3, 1943

I told you in the Air Letter that I wrote this afternoon that I would write you an Airgraph this evening, but I find that I am without one, therefore you are receiving this instead.

As you may have guessed, my crew are all on the station now and three of them are going to the theatre this evening, but as I was in Banbury to see "The Desperadoes" last night, I am staying in now. It was a good picture, filmed in technicolour, a Western, but a good show all the same.

My wireless operator and myself have the whole billet to ourselves so far.this evening as those that have not gone to town are up flying; quite peaceful around here for a change!

Love,
Jim.

Thursday, November 4, 1943

Well it looks as though we will be on this station at least until Sunday, as we have yet another day of fog. This is some weather I must say! George Collins, my navigator, has gone back to London on a thirty six hour pass so he is making the most of our prolonged stay; I wish I were with him, as it is not so dull there. I'm so fed up with every and all Limeys that I don't trouble to speak to them unless I have to—what a race!

This has been just another day of loafing around, waiting for the weather to clear. I had hoped there would be a letter today, but they won't be overdue until Saturday. It was Friday that I received my last mail.

I am thinking of going to Banbury to a Cinema this evening and I may go with Brian. If I hang around camp much longer I'll go stir-crazy. I think "Heaven Can Wait" with Don Ameche is playing at one of the theatres there, or,"Watch On The Rhine", so I'll see one of them.

I have an Australian stamp and two from India for you, so I will send them along in my next ordinary letter. How are my letters arriving these days? I hope you are getting some every week. The Yanks really gave the Germans a pounding yesterday, something like 500 Fortresses took part, so the papers say.

My Wireless Op, whom we all call "Mac" went to the village with me this morning and we returned with much treasure, a small cake with one or two rasins in it. We are saving it for this evening when we know we shall be hungry as wolves, as usual!

Did I tell you that I received a very nice letter from Bill Grewar last week? He has promised to send me some snaps of his family, so I shall send them to you. Have you heard from Ned; where is he now? I wrote to him the other night.

I may visit the Tank Corps tomorrow and see if I can take them up on their invitation for aside; that is if the weather is the same as usual. I hear there is a free show on in camp tonight and if it is any good I will see it and go to Banbury tomorrow. It is almost time for tea now, so I will be heading for the Mess as soon as Gord returns with my bicycle.

I think I will write you an ordinary mail letter tomorrow, and if I have a lot of free time, I shall see what I can do about some sketches.

Love,
Jim.

Friday November 5, 1943

Last evening I visited the camp library and borrowed a book entitled "Code of The West" by Zane Grey. Brian and I then went to the Mess for supper; cold jellied meat, cheese, bread and margarine, a brew they say is Cocoa, After devouring this feast we went to the Airmen's Mess where the movies were to be shown, and saw a corny picture, starring Flanagan and. Allen, two rather poor English comediens, a Popeye Cartoon, also not very good, and last month's News Reel! It all helped fill in the evening and was free so I can't really complain. We returned to our billets and I read about half my book before retiring. It is fair reading, and passes the time; I am almost finished now, and shall probably complete it before I retire this evening.

This morning I arose at about 8:30 and as the weather showed signs of clearing, I made my way on my trusty bicycle down to the Crew Room, carrying my novel with me. On arrival there I noticed some crews preparing for their anticipated flights and found that I was not scheduled to fly at the moment. I took my book, and made myself comfortable in an easy chair and read, with sundry interruptions till eleven, when I made a dash for the Tea Waggon (mobile canteen) and managed to bribe a friend who was at the head of the queue to purchase tea and cakes for me, as well as himself. We always welcome the Tea Waggon as we invariably have not risen in time for breakfast—lazy louts, are we not! After enjoying the tea and cakes (wads) I returned to my book until 12 P.M. when I decided I had better make tracks for the Mess to eat dinner, a kind of stew, and poisonous ersatz coffee, as I was due to fly at 1 P.M. While at the Mess I found that there was a parcel waiting for me at Ye Olde Poste Office, 300 cigs, to be exact, and from your mater. They were certainly a welcome sight, as I had been suffering various convulsions from smoking the native herbs, sold here under the guise of cigarettes. There was a card enclosed, which I will post to your Mother so she will know that they arrived safely. They are well wrapped these parcels, covered with a sort of tar paper. After dinner I dashed back to the Air Field, changed clothing for flying, drew my chute and harness from the store-room and waited patiently for orders to take off. We got airborne around 2 P.M. and I finished off my exercise and also my quota of training on this station; now our crew is waiting to return to the main station with the rest of our course, when they also complete their details. Many of them are up tonight taking advantage of the fair weather, and we have a very good chance of leaving here on Sunday. I have been reading for a while this evening, and when I finish this letter, I shall probably finish the book, if I don't retire first. Incidentally, no mail again today, but tomorrow has its possiblities.

I am enclosing the poem that I spoke of in letter #49, and some Australian stamps, as well as two Indian ones, and a few Canadian ones that you may have use for, also two Edmonton street-car tickets! Some collection eh. You will also find my embarkation leave form enclosed.

Love,
Jim.

Jim, Collins and unidentified airman

Saturday, November 6, 1943

Just another day of loafing around trying to look busy, but not a bad day as far as the weather is concerned. This afternoon reminds me of the very pleasant days that we used to go to the double headers on Nov. 11th of years gone by, at the H.A.A.A. grounds. Sunny, a trifle cloudy, and a cold wind, but how I did enjoy those games. We will have to take them in next year.

I haven't heard from Canada since a week yesterday, but my navigator has gone to our main station this afternoon and he will bring me any mail that there may be there for me. I hope he has some letters from you!

I told you in the ordinary letter that I wrote last night, that I finally completed my last flying detail yesterday, and I am finished here, just waiting for the other crews to finish too, then we will return to the main station, and go on course there, or receive some leave, one or the other. I don't care which so long as they keep me busy. I'm not at all interested in leaves on this side of the Atlantic.

Love,
Jim.

Monday, November 8, 1943

Yes, I am back on our main station once again, and have managed to secure four of these forms. Saturday night, on returning from Banbury I found that Collins, my navigator, had brought me some mail, letter #50 from you, one from Mother, and one from John. I saw "The Battle of Britain" and "Nine Men" in Banbury, both stories of the war; the former being quite interesting.

We arrived here about noon yesterday, and we were flying last night, therefore I was forced to forego writing to you until this evening. The barracks that we are quartered in now, are the best I have been in since leaving Bournemouth, and I am sleeping between sheets for the first time since leaving London. This building even has steam heat, admittedly on a small scale, but it is warm enough so far.

Did I tell you that my pilot is going to teach me to fly so that if and when I remuster I will have had more flying experience and on the biggest night bomber in the world? The papers optimistically say that Germany will be finished in six months, and if so I will not care whether I can fly or not.

Eddie Lehman leaves here tomorrow morning as his course is finished and they have two weeks definite leave and probably will get additional, He has been to Paris, and says that it was lit up like a Christmas tree.

I have only been back for a day and one half, and I like the place better than I did when first here. The food is still terrible, but we are doing something about that. I have just returned from supper, a very thin slice of meat, and a piece of cake and cup of tea. Would you care to join me for supper some evening? All meals are not that bad, so don't think I am starving!

I brought you a little closer today; I was looking at snaps of you with a magnifying glass! I saw quite a good show in the station theatre this evening, "Fingers At the Window", starring Lew Ayres, Laraine Day, and Basil Rathbone. It was a thriller, and quite good at that. These shows only cost sixpence for sergeants, and are always complete with a comedy, newsreel, and shorts. There are two shows per evening.

I found six Spectators awaiting me when I arrived yesterday and I shall begin reading them tonight. They are very nice to have. I am going to write a much different type of letter tomorrow night if I am not flying; I wonder how you will like it! You will be sure to tell me, I'm certain.

Love,
Jim.

Tuesday, November 9, 1943

0730	Awoke and dressed hurriedly.
0750	Dashed over to the Mess for breakfast.
0755	In queue waiting to be served breakfast. Received breakfast consisting of porridge without milk, greasy fried potatoes, and ersatz meat pie, and tea.
0805	On parade with my course in front of our Mess.
0815	Marched up to the Crew Room, and then went with my Crew to be issued with Thermos flasks.
0830	Found out that our Record of Kit was necessary to be produced as well as a chit ordering the Stores Clerk to issue us with the required Thermos.
0840	Went to the Barracks to get my Record of Kit.
0850	Returned with crew and received our flasks.
0900	Put flask in locker with my flying kit, and read a newspaper.
0930	Heard that there was a parcel in the Post Office for me.
0945	Picked up letter #44 and a parcel from you.
1000	At barracks investigating contents of the parcel, and was very pleased to discover a Reader's Digest and a snapshot album, as well as a lovely pair of socks. I shall also be extra clean due to the soap. Thanks a lot; it was very thoughtful of you to send those things along. I have saved all of the Kleenex and will make good use of it. After reading your really grand letter I felt very good and missed you too. I will answer it fully in this letter.
1100	Dashed out to see if I could get some tea and cakes, but Collins and I arrived in time for tea, they were fresh out of cakes. The lady in charge said that she would give us some cakes if we would carry her equipment over to the N.A.A.F. kitchen, which we promptly did, and received 3 cakes each, fresh from the oven.
1130	Returned to barracks and read the Spectator of Sept. 15th till noon.
1200	Made tracks for the Mess to have-dinner consisting of potatoes, turnip, carrots, cabbage, and a slice of meat, and ersatz coffee. Dessert was boiled pears; not so good.
1230	Started this letter to you.
1315	Must leave now to report on parade for the afternoon.

1330   Am now in the Crew Room and have signed the Flying
        Regulations book and checked over my Log Book. I find that
        they have failed to enter about twelve hours that I have spent
        in the air and I guess I will have to let it go that way, but I will
        keep closer check on it from now on,

0200   Writing to you while I am waiting to be briefed for tonight's
        flying. I am due to be up from 6 until 12 tonight, so I will have
        to finish this letter tomorrow. I am going over to the
        Navigation Section now to draw some maps that I will need
        while here.

                    Love,
                    Jim.

Thursday, November 11, 1943

Well due to the exigencies of the "Service" I'm afraid there has been a
terrific gap in this letter. Believe me I have done my best to finish this sooner,
but I have been flying every night, and will be tonight as well. These are not
small trips but long cross-countries, and by the time we hit the deck, and have
a meal, it is past time for bed, as we still have a program of lectures for our
daytime "leisure". I received letters #38, 53, and 54 from you today, and have
just finished reading them, but I will have to interrupt this letter again before
I answer your letters as I am briefing now, and must pay full attention. Tea
follows briefing, and then I expect to utilize some of my time before flight to
finishing this letter. Au revoir.

Here I am, back again for a few minutes then I must dash off for Pay
Parade. Someone robbed me of 1.10s since I arrived back here, about $6.75,
which they must have removed from my wallet while I was sleeping. I am more
shocked, and disappointed than anything, as I thought I knew the lads and
that they were all decent fellows. It is fortunate that I put the bulk of my cash
in the Post Office account or I would be out that also. I will never give them a
second chance, I'm sure of that. As well as letters from you today, I also got one
from Mother, one from Bernice, and one from Bill Woolcott which was quite a
surprise.

We have one Air gunner (Can.) in hospital with pleurisy and another
received a burst eardrum last night, so it is doubtful whether either will be

flying for months to come, if they do at all. I have found that my navigator is quite good, because when he told us our base was directly below us, we dived through several thousand feet of cloud and sure enough we were only a half mile from base—darned good navigating, especially when one considers that our compass was haywire, and we had a few other difficulties.

Thanks for the pretty maple leaves; I like them very much. Rob sounds as though he has a head on his shoulders; does he like Motor Mechanics? The poem that you wrote out for me is very good, and no doubt quite true. Your account of the weekend you spent at Cedar Springs with June was really good; I could picture all of the places you mentioned, and my memories of them are so vivid I was almost there beside you. Have you finished Paul Revere yet? I imagine you will have by the time this letter reaches you.

When we fly at night, we are entitled to a meal when we land, and every station has a small Mess near the hangars, which is invariably referred to as Smoky Joe's. The one on this station serves the best meals that I have yet eaten in the R.A.F. and even the coffee, which is ersatz, is good. This particular Mess has been decorated to resemble the sea bed; its walls have murals painted on them depicting colorful fish and other marine life swimming in and about under-water vegetation. From the rafters hang fishing nets, and lobster traps, and the rooms are lighted by ornate sea lanterns. In a corner stands an old anchor and rope, and also a pile of coral. The ashtrays are pretty sea-shells. We all like to eat there, and the thought of a good meal after spending several hours cruising around the cold night skies is very gratifying. There is a sign with a painting of an old seaman and Smoky Joe's lettered on it, suspended from a sign post reminiscent of an old Inn, standing in front of the Mess.

I must go for my pay now, I'll finish this afterwards. I have returned once again and have received my pay which they have not started to make any change in. I wonder when they will get round to it! I will answer the letters that I received today in another letter else I shall not be able to mail this tonight before I take off, and for all I know, I shall be flying tomorrow night.

I am enclosing a telegram for our scrap book, and I did have another but I seem to have misplaced it. I am also enclosing a clipping from the Spectator! I will have to stop writing soon, so I had better let this page end the letter. I will be out over the Channel for my first time tonight and I will tell you about it later.

Love,

Jim.

Friday, November 12, 1943

I am doing my best to get this letter off to you this afternoon as I shall be flying again this evening. I am in the Breifing Room at present and have just been briefed for tonight's exercise. We were out over the North Sea last night, at 12,000 ft. and it was so cold I nearly had one finger frozen. I could not see the water, or tell when we crossed the coast because of cloud, and fortunately we did not meet any enemy aircraft. We did have an excellent meal when we landed though, and I did a little better than the rest of my crew, as I ate ahead of them and there was only a Squadron Leader and myself in the Mess; he and I had liver, and then were treated to some lovely stewed steak, and potatoes and vegetable. I sure had a large appetite too: I got to bed at 4 a.m. and arose at eleven this morning, and will be flying at five thirty.

No mail from you today, but then I had some yesterday so I shouldn't be so piggish; I mailed an ordinary letter to you last evening. Thanks for the snaps that you enclosed in letter #38 along with the leaf.

The socks that you enclosed in your parcel are very comfortable and sure kept my feet warm up there last night—temperature zero! One of these nights they will be going with me to pay Adolph a visit-on business.

I find that I am not short paid as I had thought; they pay us every 14 days over here and it was every 15 days in Canada, so that made the difference. This letter is not as nice as I would like it to be but I am pressed for time, and I would rather you received a hurried letter from me than none at all. Did I tell you that the fellows refer to flying as dicing (dicing with death)? If someone says he is going dicing tonight, we know what he means; just a little R.A.F. terminology.

Love,
Jim.

Saturday, November 13, 1943

No flying for me tonight, but I'll be dicing tomorrow morning. I had lectures all day, and my briefing for tomorrow's flight. I was all set to write to you earlier this evening but I found that my, navigator had bought reserved seats for our crew to see a Variety Show that was held in the station theatre. It started at six and we were out before eight, The show was a mild sort of burlesque, and had one or two funny instances, but the women were corny. I came back to barracks and as there seemed to be plenty of hot water for a change, I took advantage of it and had a shower. I also gave myself a shampoo.

I chiselled four more of these forms today, and I will try again next week. I'll be flying over London for my first time tomorrow and it should be a very interesting sight; I am rather looking forward to it. It gets quite monotonous stooging all over England in the turret, especially at night, and you daren't leave the turret at any time as you never know when you will be attacked by some German intruder kites. We have had a Mess meeting and our food and the manner in which it is served, have improved a great deal.

I am very well, and I hope to remain that way, so don't worry about me.

Love,

Jim.

Sunday, November 14, 1943
Well, I was all ready to take off this morning but fortunately flying was scrubbed as ice was forming on the wings at two thousand and there is a great deal of rain, There was ice on the ground when I went for my breakfast. We had eggs and bacon but they were ice cold so we didn't enjoy them.

Casa Blanca is showing in the Station Theatre tonight and I may go and see it; I saw it when I was in Belleville. I found the photo of the lads receiving their wings, that I was at I.T.S. with, in the Spectator and I will send it to you for our Scrap Book, in case you didn't get it. I am listening to Guy Lombardo now and one night at the satelite station we got Glen Miller.

There has been a gorgeous full moon the last few nights and I had an excellent view of it as we were up 12,000 ft. above the cloud, and at one time half of the cloud was beautifully rosy from the setting sun and the other half a blend of blue grey tints from the moon, and shadows. When the moon is full and there are no clouds below, the lakes and rivers stand out like platinum ribbons and pools. Flare paths are very pretty from the air at night with their double row of multi-coloured lights stretching out straight and listening in the dankness below. These sights are really nice the first few times but after that they are taken for granted and you are much more interested in keeping your eyes open for other things, and in keeping warm. You should see all the clothes I wear; first of all my every day clothing plus a huge woollen crew-necked sweater that stretches to my knees, the fur lined leather trousers and coat which has a big fur collar, suede flying boots, fleece lined, a pair of silk gloves, woollen gloves, and leather gauntlets, a May West (Life-jacket), a parachute harness, and my helmet with radio & oxygen attachments When you have all that on you can hardly move, and you are no warmer upstairs than you would be in ordinary clothing on the ground. Later I shall be issued an electric suit, gloves, and socks.

Love,
Jim.

Monday, November 15, 1943
I thought I would be able to drop you a line last night, but I found that I couldn't by the time I had cleaned out my kit bags and repacked them and my locker, as well as dug out my Great Coat and cleaned the brass on it; a tough job too, as it had not been cleaned since early last Spring. You see we had a full ceremonial parade pulled on us this morning by the Group Captain, the first I have been on since July. After parade I had to dash over to the Control Office for last minutes briefing on the flight that was to have come off yesterday morning, but had been postponed till this morning. It was a cold windy morning and we took off quite early, climbing to twelve thousand, where the temperature was twenty below. We switched on oxygen end set course. We had a rather disappointing view of London because of cloud, so I can't describe it to you. We flew along the South Coast on one leg of our journey, and it was beautiful over the white cliffs of the mainland end of the Isle of White. It was so cold in the turret that vapour from my breathing formed on my oxygen mask, dripped

onto the steel of my turret and froze into a chunk of ice about four inches square. The trip was a navigational success, and we touched down safely. After Interrogation by our Intelligence Officer, we headed for the Mess to eat a much belated dinner as it was close to four in the afternoon. After eating we went to our barracks and cut cards to see who was to take our laundry into the village on the bombardier's bicycle, and as you may have known, I was Joe! On returning from that chore I went with my crew to have supper, which was not bad for a change. That accounts for today to the present time of writing, so now I shall answer your letter #54.

I have written your mother a letter; I wrote it about a month ago and I also posted the card to her that came with the cigarettes. I would have written to her several times since I arrived in England, but I was bashful about it, don't ask my why. I'm screwy I guess, that's why I asked you if you thought she would like to hear from me.

My navigator, whom I shall hereafter refer to as George, talked me into taking an Ultra Violet Ray treatment with him yesterday, and now I have a slight "sun" burn on my back. We can have these treatments at any time and all you do is strip to the waist, put on dark glasses and sit in front of the Tay-tubes, for a few minutes; I was only there eight minutes. You have to be very careful about being overexposed as you can seriously injure yourself. I found out that thirty percent of the R.A.F. are Canadians, but you never hear the Limeys [Englishmen, ed] giving them credit!

It is drawing near bed time and I am ready for it too, but I shall have to shave first. I wrote Don V. a letter yesterday, but I owe many others, and darned if I know when I can answer them. Time seems to really zip along now that they are keeping us busy again. I am going to try again tomorrow and see if they will do my film for me, and if not, I will leave it in London and have it sent home when it is finished. I have had a pair of shoes stolen from me since I told you about the move; I wish I could catch the louse. I hope the Yanks are right about the War ending in six months; it would be a God-send to everyone, as well as me. I will put my snaps in the album as soon as I get the opportunity. A few fellows brought large ones from home, but they are getting damaged from carting them around.

Love,
Jim.

Tuesday, November 16, 1943

I was very fortunate today, I received four letters from you, numbers 56, 57, 58, 59, as well as one from my Aunt Ve and my mother. We were all ready to take off this morning, but first I reported my Turret Doors unserviceable as they failed to lock; that was fine as we decided to keep the turret stationery so that I couldn't fall out, but then the pilot discovered our starboard engine was also unserviceable so we gave up end returned to camp for dinner. That ended my flying for today but I am afraid I may be Joe'd to go up with another crew tonight, as their gunner is sick. I hope not as I shall be flying tomorrow morning with my own crew. I had an Aircraft Recognition examination, one on turrets and one on tactics this afternoon, and I did very well on each of them.

Love,
Jim.

Wednesday, November 17, 1943

Yes, I elected to fly with that other crew all right, and I didn't get back to barracks till midnight, and I was lucky to arrive then. It was very, very cold up there, and there was little to see but the cold grey shafts from search-lights feeling through the dark, like ghostly fingers, now and then grasping our aircraft and reluctantly releasing us as we identified ourselves. The flash of practice bombs bursting on ranges all around us, intermittantly illumined the sky and completed the panorama, with of course, the usual flashing beacons, and flare paths. I am not flying this morning and I have taken advantage of the fact by finishing this letter. Be sure and let me know how these letters go won't you, so that I will know whether to use them or not.

An English girl over here has just married a soldier whom she has waited for for seven years; there was quite a piece in the papers about it. I hope we don't have to wait that long. He was serving in India.

I did burn one or two of your first letters, but I have kept all the others; I haven't the heart to burn them, and one of these days I shall read them all in sequence. My Aussie friend Bryan, has all his fiancee's letters and when he hasn't received mail for some time you can tell, cause there he is sitting up in bed, reading all the past ones; he must know them by heart now.

I had a very tasty meal in Smokey Joe's last night, bacon, chips, and beans; I even managed to scrounge a second serving. You can really eat after several hours in the air.

Love,
Jim.

Wednesday, November 17, 1943

If things had progressed as planned, I would be dicing at this moment perhaps ten thousand feet above the Isle of Man. We were given rations for the trip, a bar of bitter chocolate, four candies, a cube of chiclets, and two sandwiches, but the weather grounded us and we gained on the deal. I had managed to get electric moccasins to wear inside my flying boots, electric gloves, and a full electrically heated suit; I have never worn one before and I was anxious to test the clothing as I will be wearing the same on Ops. If it works as well as they claim, it must be wonderful. However instead of freezing upstairs I am writing to you as I wanted to be able to.

We have a mid-upper gunner now, a friend of George's named Don Moffat who lives a few houses from George in Toronto. He seems quite young; the wireless op is 26, the pilot is 28, and the rest of us are all under 25. I found out today that Brian is a Catholic; I wish he was in my crew, as we get along very well because our ideas are somewhat alike. Perhaps he will be on the same squadron. I got two more Australian stamps from him for you, and I will send them in my next ordinary letter along with the second telegram that I had mislaid.

I was thinking today of the day that I will arrive home and how wonderfully happy I will be, and I wondered if it was possible to be so overwhelmingly happy as I expect to be.

This flying business sure makes a guy tired, I guess it is caused by all the fresh air, cause I'm ready for bed around nine every night unless I'm dicing. I got an Airgraph off to my Mother today, and one to Bernice, and if I get the chance tomorrow, I shall write one to my Aunt Ve.

Poor George, a couple of Christmas parcels arrived for him last week and he has been saving cake and other foodstuffs for Christmas and tonight he descovered that mice had been helping themselves inside his locker! He lifted out one parcel and a mouse skittered across the floor; so now he is investigating much more cautiously. I'll have to remember that! Time for bed again and I must shave so I had better get cracking.

Love,
Jim.

Friday, November 19, 1943
Dicing again last night so I could not write to you. I was all prepared to go out on an all-day trip this morning, looking for survivors of last night's bombing of the Occupied Territories, over the Channel and North Sea, but through a change of plan, and error, they Joe'd someone else in my place which didn't hurt my feelings any. I have been doing very little today as my pilot was out searching until this evening and therefore I could not fly, I exchanged the uniform that I was issued at Bournemouth for a larger one, and I got a good fit and was very lucky too, as the one I have now has the chevrons, Canada Badges, and Canadian buttons already on it so I have been spared a chore sewing them on.

I received the Christmas parcel from you and your mother today, and I am restraining myself from opening it with considerable difficulty. It got here in good time, didn't it! It looks very interesting from the outside, and I have it locked in my locker. Thanks heaps, I'll have to wait and thank you and your mother more fully on Christmas Day, I received the sweater from my mother yesterday, and a cake. All of the lads are getting parcels now and they are very pleased.

One of the fellows has been snooping into our Course Records, and apparently another chap and myself are marked as the keenest pupils on the course! Nope! I haven't got a swelled head!!! I'll have to be careful and keep that record up. My pilot has confidence in me and that is something.

I got a couple more Australian stamps for you and I am enclosing them all in this letter along with the other telegram and clippings that you probably already have. We expect to be held here longer than we should because of foul weather, so that means at least another three weeks before we get any leave. One of the lads has just returned from a few days leave in London and while there he saw "The Army Show" and apparently was sitting near the Royal Family; he says he was surprised at the amount of paint Princess Elizabeth wears! He also said that someone had left a message for me at the Canadian Legion Club while he was there, but he doesn't know what it was. Probably someone trying to find me. I haven't seen "This Is The Army" yet, but I may sometime. That was awfully nice of Mildred to give her father my name; did you thank her for me?

I was in the Decompression Chambre with my crew yesterday afternoon and we went up to 25,000 ft. so fast that Mae and I temporarily were inflicted with the bends (stomach pains). Apparently Gord, my pilot, has exceptional ability to go without oxygen as he did very well in the Chambre. We had a very heavy frost last night; the ground was perfectly white this morning when I went for breakfast and it stayed well into the afternoon.

You should see this room—two separate groups of men playing poker, some dressing for a dance being sponsored by the Sergeant's Mess, Brian and I writing to our sweethearts, and one fellow stretched out on his bunk sound asleep. Of course the air is filled with tobacco smoke and quite stale too, and of course we will be sleeping in this stuffy atmosphere because of the windows being blacked out. Of course the only reason I am not going to the dance is because I have a nasty large corn on my little toe which makes me lame!! If you believe that you're being hood-winked cause I'm not going because you are not going to be there and that is sufficient reason for me. I m perfectly content without associating with the "gentler" sex. The [identity deleted, ed] has a philosophy all worked out that suits him; he has a girl friend in London who has an apartment and he goes there every leave, a "home" away from home, as he puts it! He is young but should know better; I guess he thinks I am a prude but I don't care. He's happy and I guess that is enough for him; for myself I want something much better.

Love,
Jim.

Saturday, November 20, 1943

I mailed an O. L. to you last night and forgot to enclose the Australian stamps that I said I did. I received four parcels today, cigarettes from you, Mr. & Mrs. Dwyer, and mother, as well as the Halloween candies from you. Thank you ever so much it was darned sweet of you to think of the candy, and your thoughtfulness made me want to hug you and tell you that you are the best girl anywhere. I wish I could do something for you, but according to a notice in our Post Office we can't even send cables for Christmas. Your letters are very good too, and I will answer them one at a time.

We were supposed to fly tonight but it has been scrubbed due to weather so we are going to the station "Cinema" instead—if tickets are available. It sure looks as though the weather is going to hold us here for a while, so I will be that much longer finishing my course. It is a chilly grey day, and we had a heavy frost again last night. Thanks for the snaps of you and June; also for the pretty place-oard and the V nickel. I'll keep them till I come home. You are progressing like a house an fire with the printing aren't you? It sounds very good! Besides the letters from you today I got one from mother, George, Aunt Ve, cousin Mickey, Uncle Harry, so I didn't do badly at all. My cousin sent me a snap of her husband and some of her home and herself, dog, and daughter; they are very nice, and it was good to get them. I'll have to be careful of them or send them to you! She says she is expecting a visit from us when I get home! Your Airmail letters were written on Nov. 8 & 9th and that is good time as today is the 20th. I have been given a good idea for the making of sandals; I have an extra pair of insoles for my flying boots and they are leather on one side and sheepskin or fleece on the other, so now all I have to do is fasten-straps on them then I will have a good pair of "Slippers". It is almost time for "tea" now so I will have to go and eat soon.

Love,
Jim.

Relaxing between raids

Sunday, November 21, 1943

A fog smothered damp day again, and of course no flying because of it. Don't faint from the shock but do you know what I did this morning—give up? Well I was at Mass this morning at 8:30, the first time I have been able to attend since leaving London; Brian and I went together and now I feel much better. I thought I would be flying at 10:00 this morning or I would have gone to Communion too. If we go, we can't get breakfast afterward.

I spent most of last evening writing letters and then I went with one of the lads to get a cup of tea and a jam sandwich. We returned and after chatting with George for a while I retired. The news continues to be very good, thank goodness; let's hope and pray that it does not change. I haven't been doing a darned thing since I wrote you yesterday so I'm afraid I haven't much to write this time.

Your failure to receive letter #33 has me worried; I wonder could I have put the wrong address on it, if so someone will enjoy a laugh at my expense! I hope it turns up alright.

It is some time later now, and I have just returned from tea, which was very inadequate. I met a fellow from Hamilton on the station today, George Bates, and he is a W.O.2 but I don't know whether he is in Air Crew or not because he had his great-coat on. He used to go to Central, and has been over here for some time. I don't believe you know him. I stuck several of the snaps that you have sent me, and ones that I carried with me into the album and those corners look swell. I have started another moustache and I shall keep it until I land in Canada, then I'll hack it off—maybe I'll grow a nice handle-bar type!

Tonight George and I are going to see "By Candle Light" a three act play being put on by the Station Personnel. It will no doubt be corny, but there is nothng better to do. We are scheduled to fly tomorrow morning and this fog is supposed to lift by then, so we may at that. The boys are gambling again, in fact it goes on all day! Good thing that is not one of my vices. I was supposed to fly over Aily's home on a course the other day and I would have had a preview of the town, but then again you can't see a heck of a lot from 10,000! My pilot has invited us to his home in Manchester for Christmas if we are on leave then. I don't care whether I go or not actually, but we have a very good chance of being on leave then if we are not in the middle of a Commando Course or something.

Love,
Jim.

Monday, November 22, 1943

It was very grey and dreary this morning when I awoke and we were scheduled to dice too. I met my crew in the Crew Room and we all meandered over to the Control Office for a final briefing before preparing to takeoff. After that we went and signed for our chutes and harnesses, and May Wests, and began changing into warmer clothing for the trip. It was a comparatively mild day and we were not going up to any great height so we didn't have to bundle up as much as usual. We were assigned the "Jinx Kite" of the lot, and we all took a dim view of the fact, but fortunately the old crate performed very well considering its reputation! We flew over a portion of Wales and out to sea along the Welsh coast, and the sea was quite calm and rather pretty too, as it was several shades of green due to the mottled effect of sun beams striking it through breaks in the clouds. The odd white cap unfurled and crested the calm swells as we flew by, and that alone was the only sight to be had other than the distant shore and the cliffs of islands off point.

When you skim close to the tops of the clouds the propellors whipped them into whispy curls. It is quite depressing after being up above the clouds flying in blue skies and bright sunlight to descend below and invariably be surprised by the unpleasant greyness of the world beneath, like passing from day into night. We landed around four in the afternoon and were from the kite back to the Crew Room in one of those snubnosed half truck and jeep affairs that are used for the purpose, and was I ever hungry as I had missed breakfast—first time since leaving the satellite.

Now as you notice I am writing to you. The inevitable "Black Jack" game is in progress again, and we are settled down to the usual evening here. The end of a "glamorous" day in the Air Force!!! Mac's brother mailed him a Saint Christopher medal on a crocheted string, and the people over here call them "Good Luck Charms", a very fitting name, I don't think! We have just returned from having a "spot of tea" in the Padre's canteen, and I am ready for bed too; shucks it's almost ten o'clock!

There is a rumour that we will be doing something special tomorrow night, so I may not be able to write. I'll tell you about it later.

Love,
Jim.

Tuesday, November 23, 1943

I am not going out on the special trip that I expected tonight, but we will be dicing for approximately six hours on another project. We expect to take off around one tomorrow morning and hope to be back by five, then tomorrow night we may do the other task. According to the meteorologists the weather will be extremely cold, and I am not looking forward to five or six hours of freezing.

I have bought tickets for my crew, and we are going to see "Thunder-birds" which is showing at our Station theatre this evening. It is supposed to be quite good. We are going early in case our flying schedule changes.

I was lucky today as I received a large oval tin of hard candy from my cousin in New Jersey; about two lbs. I guess and there was a very nice Christmas Card enclosed. It was quite a surprise. I'll try and enclose that letter that she sent me in this letter, so that you can read it.

Today I came across the N.B. [special note, ed] in the Reader's Digest that you marked, and I am walking around laughing to myself all of the time; a little while ago I was crossing the parade square, chuckling to myself and I turned around just in time to catch two M.O.'s sneaking up on me with a straight jacket!!!

If I do this trip tomorrow night my course here will have been completed and my crew and I shall be all set to go on leave. I didn't want to finish here quite so soon, because I would have a much better chance of being on leave for Christmas if I were to remain here another week or two. However we shall see.

One of the lads just passed me two delicous Marshmallows—mm-mmm, they're good!

I haven't been doing very much all day; this morning I had to hang around the Crew Room, and with the help of the mid-upper, "Don" and the wireless Op "Mac", I swept it up and made a bee-line for dinner. After dinner we were briefed for tonight's flight and here I am after briefing. I am going to dash over for "tea" now, so I'll finish this afterwards.

Back from tea now, and it was not too bad; we had some excellent crisp green celery, and it was really good. We had some the other day too! I was thinking of you as I ate it, and of how much you like it too.

It is quite an experience taking off from this drome, as it is terribly hilly, and as your know, the ideal airport is as level as a billiard table. I turn my turret to face the port side of the aircraft, the pilot revs up the motors, we receive permission to take off and the throttles are opened.up, a great wind rushes all round the kite and we leap forward, hurtling down the runway, my turret bouncing up and down the rolling terrain like a roller coaster, then a final lurch and our clumsy steed becomes airborne, groaning from the effort as we slowly gain altitude with our load of bombs and ammunition. We circle the field, set course, and we are off on another trip, dicing as usual.

I am going to the show now, and will finish writing to you before we take off tonight,

I have just returned from the show, and it was so-so; a few good parts but it seemed to end rather abruptly. We dashed over to Smoky Joe's to draw our rations, just in case our trip should be cancelled tonight; they consist of three sandwiches which are decidedly poor, more like six pieces of bread and butter! An orange (real one too!), four candies, a bar of bitter chocolate, four chiclets. At present the weather is bad, being cloudy, extra windy, and raining as well. We are sitting about waiting to hear whether our trip is scrubbed or not, and it is now nine and we shall probably have to wait until about one before we know. I must report to the Crew Room now; good-night!

Love,
Jim.

Wednesday, November 24, 1943

I received two letters and a box of Laura's [candy, ed] from you today, a letter from your mother, and the cigarettes from Rob; I believe they are the ones that you mentioned some time ago. My crew and I reported at the Crew Room last night at ten, and received our final briefing, after which we had supper at Smoky Joe's. After supper we were driven out to our aircraft of the night, T-Tommy, and prepared to take off. After inspecting the instruments, etc. we roared down the run-way and became air borne. We set course and began climbing to get above cloud and we were at 12,000" and still in cloud, rain, sleet, and ice on the wings, when we discovered that we had no oxygen so we descended a great deal and continued on our way. At one time everyone was complaining of the cold except for a change, Jimmy; I had an electrically heated suit and was it ever good. We completed our detail and touched down very tired and hungry, and I rolled into bed around 7:15. I got up at 12:30, had dinner, and found out that my crew had been excused from a trip over France because of last night's flying, and as I am definitely tired, I was glad to hear the news. We have been kidding the lads all day that are scheduled to go tonight, requesting the keys to their lockers so that we might help ourselves should they fail to return! Which brings something important up; would you rather that I destroy your mail after a short period, just in case? I'm not being morbid but it just occurred to me that you never know who will be going through your belongings, and when we expect to go over enemy territory we are not allowed to carry papers of any description; just your rations, cigarettes and jewellery, and of course identification discs.

I wrote you an ordinary letter last night and mailed it just before take off. We did not observe Nov. 11th in any way over here, in fact I didn't re-

member it till I read your letter today. You appear to have gone in for printing in a big way; I may return to find you managing quite a large business
I may be here another week or two yet, and it will be at least two months
before I am working regularly. I am going to retire early this evening as I
am not flying, or going to a show, and it won't be too soon either. I have
just heard a rumour that we are to leave here this coming Sunday, but it
may be just another story; they are plentiful in the Air Force. I have been
exceptionally lucky in regard to parcels and letters and that is mainly due to
the goodness of you and your mother, and don't think that I don't appre-
diate it. You have been very good to me, guess I'll have to marry you and
make my miserable life happy. What do you think? Well, tomorrow is Pay
Day again and I wonder if they have started paying me my raise, or started
deducting for the cash I signed over in London.

Brian just gave me a piece of a cake his fiancé baked for him; he got
one from her before which was her first attempt and it was lousy; he wrote
and told her how wonderful it was and lo and behold he received this one,
which really is good! He was peeved with me because I woke him up when
I came in this morning but it's O.K. now. I wish he was my Bomb-aimer.

Love,
Jim.

Friday, November 26, 1943

I was not able to write to you last night, due to flying duties, and
tonight, or I should say, this evening, we are to dice for six and one half
hours, as we are going on a 1,000 mile jaunt, so I am dashing a few lines off
so that you will be sure that I have not forgotten.

I received a blue form from you, and one from my Aunt Ve yesterday,
#51 to be exact, and they both took over one month to reach me; they sure
must have gone astray en route. Early or late, they are always welcome. The
boys all returned from France in one piece last night, and the night before,
although one pilot got his foot frozen and is grounded for a short while.

We expect to touch down around 3 A.M. tonight, then we are to be
interrogated, then eat, and roll into bed, then we shall most likely have to
rise in time to be present at another briefing for tomorrow night. The

moustache is coming along fine (much to your probable disgust!). I'm afraid I must dash away now and finish tomorrow.

Love,

Jim.

Saturday, November 27, 1943

That long jaunt was cancelled last night but we did fly until 10:50 on another course. Five lads lost their lives that were two courses behind me, last night; I didn't know any of them. It is very foggy and wet today so there is no flying, and I doubt if there will be any tonight; I believe I shall take in a play in the station theatre. I have made arrangements to have my film developed at long last, so I hope to be able to send you some pies in about a week. The play turned out to be an Orchestral Concert which was excellent; they played Sleeping Beauty and Ravel's Bolero which I enjoyed very much.

I owe Mary Martin a letter from over a month ago, tsk! tsk! I received letter #66 from you today. Brian's brother slept here last night; he looks much like his brother, same build, and height; he is a wireless operator and was on a short leave. If the weather clears I shall leave here within a few days. Eddie is still on leave and I forward his mail to him. Did I tell you that your mother's letter was swell? Here I go again, but I will write again tomorrow.

Love,

Jim.

Monday, November 29, 1943

Yesterday was another of those cold, wet, grey, days, and I managed to attend Mass in the morning again which was fortunate. I didn't fly at all during the day,.but sure enough the weather cleared as the "Met" people had claimed it would, and we were dicing shortly after tea, until about eleven. I was not accompanying my own crew, but was a sort of "guest" of another crew for the night. The trip was not very eventful and we landed safe and sound after completing our details. I am going with my own gang tonight though, and we do not expect to touch down before midnight; the weather forecast is not a very encouraging one but it could be worse I know. If the weather continues as it is now, we will leave here, probably Sunday or sooner, as we are more or less finished now. There are things that I should like very much to tell you but I'm afraid it is best kept till after the war, for military reasons, naturally.

I am very well, aside from having the common slight cold, so you have no cause for worry in that respect! Gosh! Every time I start a letter to you someone comes along and tells me I'm due for a lecture or something; wish they'd buzz off and let me finish! Back soon I hope.

Love,

Jim.

Tuesday, November 30, 1943

Not as soon as had hoped, but at least I am back! The flip was not too bad last night, except of course that our own Ack-Ack tried to shoot us down at one time.

I received a swell letter from you today, #55, with the snap and news clippings, and air forms enclosed. Thanks heaps. That was the party all right, that I was at in London, although it sure sounds nicer by the paper's version! Perhaps I'm prejudiced.

I was at the dentist's today and he is not through with me yet, so he says! I slept until eleven this morning and was supposed to fly this afternoon but it was cancelled, after we had been waiting for hours. I am going to the show tonight with my crew as we are not dicing until tomorrow morning. This flying business is beginning to get to me, but I guess a good leave will remedy that.

I shall answer your letter tomorrow in detail; one of these days I will be able to sit down and write you a real letter, with no interruptions and bags of time to say all I want to. Just when I feel I have oodles of things to say to you, that is exactly the time they decide that I am to do something else.

Love,

Jim.

Wednesday, December 1, 1943

There was no flying last night, so after finishing a letter to you, I went to the show with some of the boys. The picture was very poor but for the part played my Monty Woolly. Ida Lupino co-starred but the lines were awful.

We were scheduled to fly this morning but that was scrubbed as well as a special trip that we were to do tonight; we have only around ten more flying hours to get in and then we shall get some leave. There are some very discouraging rumours floating around to the effect that we will get only a few days leave, and then take a one month Commando Course at a God-foresaken hole in the north. It is to be hoped that it is only a rumour!

My crew and I spent part of this afternoon practicing ditching, (landing in water and climbing into a dinghy as quickly as possible) and abandoning the aircraft via parachute. A very good thing to be adept at!

I received a cheque from my Dad today for 1-2-4 which is $5.00 in our money, as a Christmas present; I think it was very nice of him, don't you?

Two letters from you arrived today #70 & 71 and it was a pleasure getting them too. They were really nice. I received a Christmas Card with a letter from my father's cousin (formerly Mrs. Copeland), I know you did meet her, if you will recall, and she says that she has sent me a Christmas cake! Very good, methinks! I'm awful aren't I!

I intend to visit all of the places that I missed on my last stay in London, and I shall write nice long letters about them all for you. The fellows I was with last time were not interested.

I still like to fly, but since this week, I have lost much of my enjoyment in it. I like flying in daylight, but too many things happen even over your own territory at night, and then it is much colder too. We fly at heights that require the constant use of oxygen from take-off to landing. In Canada it was fun, over here it is a grim business and even I did not fully realize just how grim, until recently. Some pilots are only suitable for certain types of aircraft, while others can handle more complex and larger kinds, and as in the case of my own skipper some are more experienced. I have not actually been over enemy territory as yet and the time that I was supposed to go it was cancelled so now I will not until I go on Ops. Eddie was changed to a mid-upper gunner and their course being shorter, he was crewed up with a course ahead of me, and is now at a Conversion Unit after having about three weeks leave. I really was due to visit Cambrai one night but someone else got Joe'd because we were flying till 7 A.M. that morning. The only thing that happened was that one chap, an Aussie, got his foot frozen and is now on crutches recuperating.

They were chiselling us on our rations and we checked up and now we are dealt with more fairly, and we decided to spy more Mess Fees in order to allow them to buy us unrationed food, extra messing.

I was in the Intelligence Library when I read your letters and there being a large magnifying glass handy that is used for perusing target photos, I thought, bang-on, I'll bring you closer, and presto, it worked. Of course I had to do that rather surreptitiously as the Intelligence Officer would take a decided dim view of the practice, I think!!

I have been over to see the Dentist this evening, and now I have only one more tooth to fill—I hope. Most of his work has been removing old fillings and putting in better ones that are more suited to rarified air that we breathe at high altitudes.

I seem to have arrived at the end of my rope now, and not a very long one at that, but it could be worse. We are going to dash over to "Holy Joe's" (the padre's canteen) and get a sandwich before it closes, then I shall retire after writing my mother a letter; guess she thinks I have forgotten her but I haven't; everyone but you, I owe letters to, and at that you have suffered too.

Love,

Jim.

Thursday, December 2, 1943

I received letter #68 from you today and it was very nice. I wrote an O.L. to you last night so it should arrive around Jan. 1st 1944. I also wrote one of these letters to Rob today and possibly it will arrive with this one.

One member of the crew generally lags behind the others due to minor breakdowns that compel him to repeat an exercise or two. East would mean Italy or possibly India, I couldn't say. I won't have to worry about that for at least another two months or so.

I am going to see "The Crystal Ball" starring Ray Milland this evening as I am not flying. I am to go on a Cross-Country tomorrow morning if the weather permits.

Love,

Jim.

Friday, December 3, 1943

It has been a very foggy day so therefore we have been grounded and also tonight. I visited Pay Accounts Office during the day and have succeeded in having my Pay Book adjusted in regards to my assigned pay as well as the two bit raise per day in pay.

According to the latest "Gen", we will be here at least until next Wednesday as we have a flight like Eddie's to do before we can go on leave. An American "Lightning" spent the night here last night and we all gave it the once over this morning; it is a trim looking aircraft; very streamlined.

I have to clean out my locker, and generally tidy things up around my bunk tonight because the Group Captain is inspecting the barracks tomorrow, worse luck! I shall shave off my embryo moustache this evening before retiring as someone made the insulting crack that it makes me look like an Englishman! Actually, I had decided I like my puss minus the bush anyway, so there too!! It really is doing well too; the bush I mean. Did I tell you that the dentist yanked one of my teeth yesterday? He drilled it till it was 9/'10 cavity, then found out it was impossible to fill it. I was passed as being fit, but last night a filling fell out of another tooth, so I'll have to see him again.

You must be quite an expert with your printing equipment now; how much will you charge me? Do I get a discount? One of the lads received a mickey of whisky concealed in a loaf of bread, from Canada! What next! The picture "Crystal Ball" starring Paulette Goddard and Ray Milland was very good, and I was laughing aloud most of the time. It was a real gloom chaser but for the clinches. I am going to get cracking on my locker shoes, brass, etc. now before it's too late as it will take some time; you know me, slow as ever!

Love,
Jim.

Saturday, December 4, 1943

I have Just finished checking through all my correspondence from you that I received since landing over here. I find that the only letters I have not received from you between #1 & 71, are numbers 27, 62, 64, 67 and 69. The last four have most likely been O.L. and still are not overdue, but #27 must have gone astray.

Perhaps I have never mentioned or written this following paragraph to you, but I started a letter on the boat, and because of the crowded state of our Canteen on the boat, I never did finish it; I did save the page, and here are its contents:

Since I have left you days pass by monotonously, each day identical to the preceding one, till I wonder why I am here wasting my time. Nothing has made me feel so far away and separated from you before, as this great and powerful expanse of water does; it is unimaginable until you are in the centre of it, then you feel it and feel very much alone and insignificant, and you realize how much man must trust in God because after all, large as the ship may be, it is but a chip on this colossal body of water. We are alone, unescorted, with but an occasional view of a protecting aircraft; we joke about it, the subs, the surface raiders, and the possibility of attack from the air, but deep down every man realized his peril, and shows no fear. I think it is because none of us really dwell upon this in our minds or perhaps it is ignorant confidence in our own destiny and the arms of our ship which make us careless, but then we have come for Peace and Liberty, and war has not introduced itself to us in its true colours yet.

That has been kept in my writing kit for quite some time, ever since I wrote it at sea, in fact. Not a very good effort and I also had a great deal of respect for the censors at that time.

I am enclosing three clippings from Wings Abroad, the one about the Warnicks was dated Nov. 24. A program from the play that I saw here, and the clipping of Jim Melrose which you must have already from the Spec.

I have been flying most of the day, in fact I had my dinner at four, so you understand how hungry I was. The very latest information is to the effect that we are leaving here on Monday, but that may be a duff-gen too. I also heard today that we don't have to take a trip like Eddie's. Tomorrow morning I will be flying at 0830 so I guess I miss Mass unless the weather is unsuitable for flying.

I am also enclosing the envelope and message that I received with the cheque my father cabled—I hope the thickness of this letter has not been disappointing, I don't intend it to be. Another rumour that is circulating here is to the affect that our Conversion Unit Course has been lengthened from four to six weeks, so I should be O.K. till February at least.

I shall try and have my mail forwarded to me while I am on leave, by a friend of mine on the course behind me so that I won't have to wait too long to hear from you, because I wouldn't like to pass a month with no mail.

This is not as lengthy a letter as I would like to have it for the simple reason that I have no news to convey to you since last night, and nothing exciting has happened today, as usual. Perhaps it is also because I am tired from flying all day, and my mind is not over active—could be! I have to rise early tomorrow for briefing as we have to be at our aircraft at least one hour before take off, and briefing comes before that, so I shall try and roll in by ten and it will be at least that time after I wash and shave.

We were listening to Dina Shore sing "Give Me Something To Remember You By" on the kite's [plane, ed] radio.

Love,
Jim.

Sunday, December 5, 1943

Last night I wrote an ordinary letter to you, not a long one I'm afraid, so don't be disappointed when you open it because it is quite bulky due to clippings enclosed. I had to miss Mass this morning I'm sorry to say, as I was supposed to fly at that time. I was up for an hour at noon, testing an aircraft that we are to use on a special detail tonight, and since then I have had dinner and am now waiting till 3:30 when we are to be briefed for tonight's detail. I didn't get to sleep as early as I hoped to last night because some of the lads had come in tight from a farewell party that was held in our bar for an instructor that has been posted. The lugs woke me up and it seems that they took a dim view of my not joining them. I shaved the hair off from under my proboscis last night, and you will never have to put up with a "beastie" as they are called over here. Glad? It is quite definite that we are to leave here on leave tomorrow, but at what time I have no idea. We will be in bed till mid-day, I do know that.

A formation of at least one hundred Fortresses passed over here this morning, so I guess Adolph received another kick in the pants today; it was quite an impressive sight to see, and noisy too. They are playing "Silver Wings in the Moonlight" on the radio now, and that will be us tonight I guess. I must go to briefing now.

Love,
Jim.

Tuesday, December 7, 1943
We had the briefing alright and I was all set to take a trip over France but as usual it was cancelled, and now all of my course but three or four crews, are going on leave tomorrow but we must remain here until we do our little trip; what night it will be now, I have no idea, but there is a fair chance that they will excuse us altogether and let us go on leave too

I received a letter from you #73 yesterday and one from your mother.

This morning I received #62 and a card from you; thank you very much, the card is grand and the letters swell. I have just mailed the film to Bournemouth to a Photo shop that a chum tells me will do them in two days; he says he sends his there and they are very good, so here's hoping. The other arrangement I had fell through. The regular poker game is in swing on my right, and so far my bomb-aimer is winning, but then he usually does. I may make that letter tonight an O.L. "The Moon is Down" is showing in.our cinema this evening but I saw it at Macdonald so I won't see it again. The weather is very ropey so don't worry about that flight as I am almost certain we will leave without carrying it out. I won't be flying again unless it is for that purpose, until I report to my next unit.

Love,
Jim.

Tuesday, December 7, 1943

I am at Holy Joe's endeavouring to write you this letter with a minimum of interruptions; our barracks being filled with gamblers and the air foul with tobacco smoke and there being no table on which to write.

I mailed an Airmail letter to you earlier today which I hope and trust that you have received before this epistle: I am very much afraid that my coming leave will be a disappointingly short one and will be insufficient to cover Christmas as I had hoped. If it is only for a week or less I will not go further than London because travelling would eat up almost three days if I were to visit Wales as I would like to. You would be surprised just how necessary a good leave is after you have been flying for three months; your nerves require the rest away from service life to say the least; to say nothing of your morale.

None of my crew drink at all if there is a possibility of flying that day or night. If anyone did, the remainder of us would soon tell him off, never fear!

That month's leave is, or was, only a dream as to date I have lost over a week of my leave due to the weather, and the crews that leave tomorrow are only receiving ten days so I will be lucky if I get a week, didn't get any leave between the satellite and this station, as you must know by now.

I generally read several days of the Spec at one sitting as they arrive very erratically and in bunches, but I usually get through them before the next bunch arrive.

Briefing is pre-flight planning and all crews engaged in a certain excercise are briefed together. They receive their navigational details such as the course and aids, the weather and winds to be expected at different heights, as well as cloud conditions and temperatures. We also receive instructions as to how many guns or fighters are to be expected where, and when, and all the "gen" in connection with the detail. Everyone is made familiar with the route and what to look for and we all discuss the trip before from every angle. We are usually briefed several hours before take-off time as the navigators have so much work to do beforehand. If a flight is postponed for a day we have to be rebriefed as the weather and winds are different, naturally.

When we are forced down on a strange drome [airfield, ed] we usually stay there till the weather clears and then fly back, but because of the nearness of the station we landed on, we returned to our own base and another crew was flown there the following day to pick up our kite. Strange aircraft are always landing on our drome during bad weather and it is quite common to find a Liberator, Mitchell, or Lightning sitting in front of our Control Tower of a morning. Did I tell you that the crew of the Liberator that was forced down in the fog with us, carried their bicycles in the fuselage of their aircraft? These Yanks sure hate walking; it was comical to see them unloading the bikes and riding away to the Mess for tea. I guess they have been diverted due to bad weather before and were not going to be stranded if they could help it. We could do that too—if we had bicycles!

Here are some things listed below that suit certain song titles!

You are My Sunshine	Pay Parade
Coming Through the Rye	Pay Nights
Why Not Take All of Me	War Savings Certificates
We Three on Town Patrol	Service Police
I've Got You Under my Skin	Innoculations
Playmates	Army, Navy, and Air Force
I'll Follow You	Station Warrant Officer on Parade
You Walked By	Morning Inspection
Once In a While	A 48 hr. pass (in Canada!)
You Are Always on My Mind	Annual leave (in Canada!)
Night and Day	Security guard
Come All Ye Faithful	Duty Watch
Beautiful Dreamer	Night Guard
It All Comes Back to Me now	Pork Pies in the Canteen (in Canada!)
You Do the Darndest Things	Medical inspection
Never Took a Lesson In My Life	New Arrivals

They are not overly amusing and you may not undertand all of them but I have taken a chance on it.

Now I must go to bed because the lads want to turn out the lights. I am back at the barracks now, and ready for bed myself.

Love,
Jim.

On leave in London with a friend

Wednesday, December 8, 1943

Well I'm still on the station and will be indefinitely; most of the lads are leaving tomorrow and I believe we will end up at a different station than they, if and when we eventually leave this one. We still have our trip to do, and the weather is impossible at present for any kind of flying, mush less a long trip. We are all rather "cheesed" due to our predicament and take a very dim view of the situation.

How would you like a prize English Bulldog as a pet? I was talking to a Squadron Leader this afternoon, and he has a Champion Bull which he hopes will have pups by Christmas; well, we want a mascot, and what would be nicer? Of course on this station and the next we will not be allowed to have pets, but on a Squadron I think they are more lenient. If I could get one like his dog I would like to bring one home for you if possible. They are ugly alright, and I imagine you would not be keen about one though. We might get one as a mascot in any case.

I received a letter from you this morning #75. "Sing You Sinners", starring Bing Crosby and Fred MacMurray will be showing here tomorrow evening and although I saw it quite some time ago, I expect to see it once more. Before we go on leave we have to receive some of those lovely needles that I had at Manning Depot, and some of the lads passed out as usual! I'm not anticipating them in the least.

They tell me I am the most level-headed member of my crew outside of my pilot; someone is looking for a quarter no doubt! A pal of mine, Leonard Spenoley, says to say "hello" to you for him.

Love,

Jim.

Saturday, December 11, 1943

There has been a considerable gap between letters this week, but I'm afraid it was unavoidable this time. We have really finished our course now, and must hang around getting final medicals and clearances for equipment we have been using; we are stalemated at the moment because many of the officers are away for the week-end and we will be unable to leave till Monday evening at the earliest unless a miracle happens. Last night we were

up dicing for approximately five hours and it was a grand night, clear as a
bell due to a gorgeous full moon. It was extremely cold though as freezing
level was two thou, and we were travelling at ten thou. One hundred miles
or so of our trip was over the North Sea and we were flying above a solid
mass of pure white cloud, a perfect silhouette against them too, because
of the moon. We were warned of intruders over England while we were
out there, and that did not make us feel any happier, as we had been seeing
bags of flares and unidentified kites all over the sky, as well as streams of
tracer arcing above the clouds now and then; however we returned to base
without mishap and had a good supper at Smoky Joe's. We arose in time
for dinner, and now I am writing to you. They have had us standing by up
at the Crew Room the last few nights, but it was a waste of time as the fog
did not lift.

I received a letter from Eddie and he is on leave in London now, after
completing a ten-day Commando course, which we will probably have too.
At present I have no idea how long or short my leave will be. I heard Frank
Sinatra sing "Sunday, Monday, or Always" yesterday afternoon on an American Forces Programme. Gosh it was good.

This afternoon I received a Christmas parcel from my mother, which
was very welcome. I must drop her a line or two today. Next week I hope to
receive the prints from that shop in Bournemouth and as soon as I get them
I shall send them along, with the negatives in an ordinary letter.

We will have thousands of things to talk about after this is all over, and I
wish we could start now. I dreamed the other night that you met me in
London to spend the week-end there, but unfortunately I woke up too soon!
I don't want to meet you there though, I want to see you in Hamilton.

Love,

Jim.

Sunday, December 12, 1943

We had our innoculations this morning so now I have a rather sore
deltoid muscle in my left arm, cuss it! I wrote an Airmail to you yesterday
and was going to send you an Air Graph today but this will have to do as I
am out of graphs. We should be leaving here tomorrow afternoon as we are

almost cleared up concerning the red tape, and we are to be paid tomorrow morning again soooooo!

I hope there are some letters from you tomorrow morning so that I can take them with me. I guess I'm greedy, I'm always looking for mail from you, twice a day in fact, even though I know that the mail comes but once per day.

I wrote Lawrence, and Bill Woolcott a letter yesterday, and I am gradually catching up; I still owe five or six! As you say, it's sure nice to get mail.

At present I am planning on staying in London for a couple of days with part of my crew, and if I have enough time I may see Ailyn too. There are some friends that my family want me to see and I probably will as I can reach them very easily from London as they live in the suburbs more or less.

The way I feel right now, I've got to get away from flying and have a real good time to forget a few things more or less. We have lost some of our friends and for the third time in two weeks, so I don't feel very cheerful, in fact I am very glad to be clear of this unit.

I got a course average of 75% which is not bad, and as I told you before my assessment was quite good. The top man had 80% (The Englishman).

I have all of my kit to pack yet, and my arm feels as though it had been wrenched from its socket, but I will get it done somehow. I hope it feels better in the morning; otherwise I am very well. I am going to have my uniforms cleaned, and my shoes repaired while in London, I hope! How has the printing business been progressing? Are you still staying up all night at it? How is the weather; much snow? We had a couple of flakes here, and it is quite cold too, but of course snow never stays for more than an hour on the ground around here, at least it hasn't yet! Do you think you will be doing much skiing this winter? You should receive some very nice letters from me next week if I do all I hope to do, so let me know how you like them.

Love,

Jim.

Thursday, December 16, 1943

Well here I am in London again, and as usual, taking life quite easy. Please excuse this pen it is terrible; I had to borrow it in order to write, as mine is at the Waterman Co. Office having the nib changed, and I will get it back on Wednesday. I am back at the Canadian Legion Club, and feel very much at home here, as everyone remembers me from my last stay, which is quite pleasing. I am staying here with my Navigator and another two lads (gunners) and so far I have not seen much outside of visiting Head-quarters, hunting up a Cleaning Establishment that cleans uniforms in less than two weeks, and the same for a shoe repair shop, and also locating the Waterman Office. I saw "The Dancing Years" starring Ivor Novello tonight, and it is a very good play; the costumes were gorgeous and the dancing and scenery and lighting were really quite marvelous. The play, being English, was of course suggestive in several places, but very enjoyable all the same. I have kept my programme and shall send it along via ordinary mail. I have also received my snapshots from Bournemouth, and will enclose them along with the programme so you will have them at long last. The letter that I shall enclose them in was started on Monday, but due to the fact that I was not well, and also having had little to write, I did not complete it at the time. You just can't write very well when you feel as though your arm and shoulder have been mangled due to inoculations!

I hope to get out to Middlesex to see an elderly couple tomorrow, so as to sort of pacify my mother and grandmother and when that is done I hope to get around the town a bit more, which is rather difficult when one sleeps in most mornings! I was rather unfortunate as I arrived here the day after Eddie left for Conversion Unit, so I don't expect to see hime for awhile.

I am beginning to feel better for my leave, and should be all ready for the old grind again when I return to the station. You see I must return, as they do not know where to send us yet.

Love,
Jim.

Tuesday, December 28, 1943

I am back on the same old station again after what seemed a very short leave, and believe me I'm not glad to be back. I received letters #28, 30, 69, 82, 88 and I will answer them as soon as possible. This is my new pen nib and it writes much easier than the other one.

You will be disgusted with me I know, but from your point of view I didn't do much on my leave; I doubt if you would understand, but just to

CHRISTMAS GREETINGS

I might write down a score of things, ✶ ✶
As others many times have done, ✶ ✶ ✶
And yet this little message brings ✶
One simple wish — and only one :✶ ✶
We cannot meet this Christmastide,
But we in thought can yet draw near,
And may the Peace of God abide ✶ ✶
Within your heart through all the year!

MARJORIE CROSBIE.

Apart this one, but together next!
All my love,
Jim. Ⓧ

Christmas card to Elaine

laze around and take things easy was all that interested me. I tried to get tickets to see The Lisbon Story but I couldn't get them except for today and I am not on leave now so I had to forget it. Perhaps I shall see it another time. I was hoping for an extension to my leave so that I could travel to Wales but as you know it was not forthcoming. We were not allowed to travel all last week because of the heavy demand on the railways, so I was glad that I was in London and not stuck in some small town. This is the wrong time of the year to visit the coasts as the weather is so miserable and it is the same in the North. I met a lot of the fellows while at the Club that I was on course with in Canada, and one lad that I was at Belleville with. Most of that bunch are over here now, he tells me. I also met a fellow that I was at Cathedral, Jim somebody or other, I don't know the last name, but I think you know him to see. I had Christmas dinner at the Club, and it was excellent, turkey and all the trimmings. They had a variety show for us in the evening which was quite good too. I missed Eddie a great deal as he was always full of fun and kept things lively and the ladies at the Club liked the both of us very much it seems, because they are very good to us when we go there. (Incidentally these ladies are old enough to be my mother!) It makes you feel good to walk into a place over here and have them say, "Hello Jimmie, glad to see you back, and how are you!" and then wish you luck when you leave, especially when thousands of fellows are coming and going from there every month. Gordon stayed with us the first two days and then left for home and I don't blame him as I would too if I were anywhere near. I like going to London because if you know where to go you can get most anything, and you can always find several friends at the Canadian Clubs. I saw "Flesh And Fantasy" and it was very morbid and I did not enjoy it. "North Star" was a very good show about Russia and of course the war, but it was much better than the usual tripe, although it was quite sad. I saw a couple of other pictures too but darned if I can recall the titles! My memory is really hopeless I'm afraid; I'll have to smarten up or I'll be a sad mess! I have never been over Fritz's "Domain" [Germany, ed] and my pilot and crew are quite competent; it should be a few months yet before I am doing anything unless our schedule changes.

Love,
Jim.

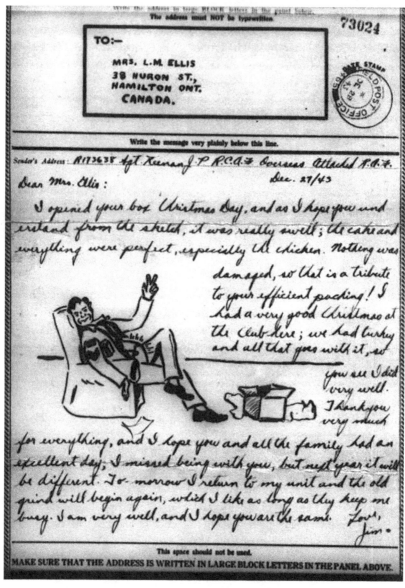

Thank you card and sketch to Elaine's mother, Mrs. Laura Ellis

Wednesday, December 29,1943

Today 1 received letters #67, 64, 78, 79, 81 and a box of Laura's from you, as well as a box from mother & George, and one from Aunt Ve, and one from the 119th Bomber Sqdr. Ladies Auxiliary, as well as cigarettes from The Saturday Night Club. Apparently all of those arrived while I was on leave in London.

We all arose this morning rather reluctantly and began a programme which is to carry on for the next two weeks, a refresher course on which we will do about five more hours flying on this station, along with lectures and physical training; what we do after these next two weeks I have no idea; I may get another few days of leave or I may report to Conversion Unit. I was very glad to hear that Harry Venn was still alive today, as I had heard in London that he was dead. Many have gone since I started my course here and my leave could not have come-at a more opportune time, my nerves were much the worse for wear. We never did visit France; the weather was not satisfactory so we were excused from the trip.

I have not heard from Ned for months but I will drop him another note as soon as I can and see if I can contact him. God knows where he is now. I hope he is O.K. I am still with Gord Frazer; he is my pilot and will always be, I hope.

If I think too much, as I have been the past two weeks, I shall be a nervous wreck, and I'm not fooling. Thanks heaps for the chocolates I sure am glad to get them. I am in exeellent health and I hope you are the same; I will answer your letters day by day until I have covered them fully.

Thursday, December 30, 1943

Last night I went to the Station Cinema and saw "Marked Woman" starring Bette Davis, a picture that I saw in Canada years ago. The fellows have all returned to the station now and they all look rather worn out and haggard. We had P.T. yesterday and again this morning, and this afternoon we saw some Intelligence Films. They were quite dry, as we have had the subjects pounded into our heads for months.

I can readily understand why Rob had a good time at that dance in Toronto. I'll bet it was fun; I shouldn't be on Ops before the end of March according to my present calculations. Thanks very much for the Airmail forms and much more for the five snaps. Thanks also for the two snaps and A.G. Form that you enclosed in #67! Also the three snaps and forms in #69. I'm sorry to hear about Bill Mayo, and I know how you must have felt. We, the lads over here, are becoming callous in that regard, we have to be, because we just couldn't continue if we dwelt on such happenings. They are quite common occurrences, and I have lost many friends already. Barney Redmond, one of the lads that I spent my last leave with, went on Dec. 11th. You must be hard, don't let these things weigh on you, and for goodness sake if something does happen to me, don't go off the deep end, tomorrow will always bring a brighter and better day, and things always happen for the better.

I hope Earl does get a Commission and stays in Canada, it would be a swell break. On my final results here I find that something is radically wrong; whereas I know, and the other lads know, that I have almost topped them in every phase of this course, I have ended it with not much better than an average mark, and as one lad said, I must have an enemy among my instructors; perhaps one of them heard me voice my opinion of the R.A.F. and Englishmen in general, but I have been treated definitely unfairly. That sounds like I am making excuses, but I'm not and I needn't have mentioned the situation at all if it was my fault. I have never missed a parade and I have always known more "Gen" than the average chap, so see if you can figure it out, I can't! Why I knew more when I arrived here than the other lads did, and the instructors remarked about it! One of these days I'll get a break, so help me.

Tonight I believe I shall see "Tarzan Triumphs", at the Cinema before going to bed, although I have oodles of letters to answer. Give my love to your mother, and remember me to Cec and Bon and your brother and Dad. I am going to try and write another letter before I leave for the show, so I had best get crackin!

Love,
Jim.

Friday, December 31, 1943

Here we are beginning a new year and ending an old one that saw many changes in your life and mine and the first New Year's Eve that you and I have not been together.

Here is the start of a letter that I began on Dec. 13:

"Believe it or not, I have received the prints of my film, and I will enclose them in this letter, so here's hoping you receive them alright after waiting all this time! They all turned out fairly well as you see. I will send the negatives as soon as I get some prints of them for the lads. How do you like them?

I am all cleared now from this station and I was supposed to catch a train for London this morning at eleven, but being the guy I am, I missed it because I didn't have all of my kit packed. My arm was terrifically painful last night so I couldn't pack then, and it was not much better this morning. I believe I shall stop here until tomorrow morning now, and catch the train then and meet the lads in London.

Last night I saw "Get Crackin" starring George Formby and I wasn't very keen on it. I don't care for him very much do you? Someone should stick a pin in me I think, 'cause I don't seem to have any pep or energy, and if I don't get going, I'll be here for the rest of my leave!

It is extremely quiet here now as the majority of the fellows are away; out of 21 lads that did sleep in our room there are only about five left, and they are leaving with me tomorrow.

I can't get over the snaps; I'm very pleased with them!

Not having heard from you for the last couple of days, I have very little to say, so please excuse me if this letter is not awfully long. I haven't been doing anything to write about, to tell you the truth. That sounds like a lame excuse but it's a fact nevertheless."

Besides enclosing the prints in this letter, I am enclosing the Programme from the play that I saw in London; I think you will be able to picture something of what it was like when you read it. When I come home we will see some of these really good stage plays; I have always had the notion that I wouldn't care for them, but that was an impression that I received from amateur performances, these are much superior. In the shows over here the usherettes come down the aisles and serve tea at intermission time and for those that desire other beverages there is a bar.

You can also smoke in every theatre in England, from what I have found out. There are ash-trays along the backs of the seats in front of you. In some of the shows, between pictures (showings) the lights come on, as at home, but a large electric organ rises out of the orchestra pit and is lighted much like a Wurlitzer, and the organist plays several selections until time for the next show. It is very nice, and quite fascinating to see the organ appear out of nowhere; I am going to bed now, so until tomorrow, au revoir!

Love,
Jim.

Saturday, January 1, 1944

As you see, I have followed your suggestion and have started over again at #1. The O.M. that I wrote last night was No. 80 and I enclosed snaps and a Programme for you. Today, I was most fortunate as I received #76, 84 and 85 from you which I shall answer as soon as I catch up on your previous letters.

Sometimes the other lads get passes when I don't because they are further ahead due to my encountering bad weather when it is my turn to fly and they have had all good weather. How did your billiard lesson come off? I can't play the game myself! You will have to teach me. Helen's Billiard Room sounds very nice, it must be well. When I arrived back from leave there were several "Specs" waiting for me. Your socks haven't paid Adolph a visit yet and they won't for a while. By the way the Ronson was a terrific surprise, expecially as you had written that you couldn't get one. Thanks heaps and heaps, I watch it like a hawk! The letter that you enclosed with it was very sweet too, and as I had not heard from you since arriving in London, I really liked it. I was sure glad to get the lighter cause I hate cadging lights from the fellows all the time. I like the Crest and initials very much too. The whole parcel was perfect and couldn't have been better.

At present I must do 30 Ops and then I can remuster or have 3 months "rest", usually staff instructor on some station over here; or else if we get on Pathfinders as Gord would like to do, we will do 45 Ops and then be through for the duration. Don't worry about that, anyway.

We get rations for every trip of five hours or more and often we collect them before a trip is cancelled and then we are way ahead of them! By the way, the box of Laura's I received was #3, I am certain that I wrote and thanked you, Rob, and your Mother for the cigs. I always wear the electric suit if I am to be upstairs for more than an hour, and as long as I have it I am never too cold to do my job; it is really a marvelous suit. I have four guns, not just one. I have decided to keep all of your letters because they are not very bulky when they are tied up as most of them are Airmail. What course is Jack O'Neill on? My navigator is the best one on our course and that is saying something!

Thanks for the snaps that you enclosed in #76. My gosh, so you are even learning to play poker, tsk! tsk! I know a little about that myself but when the lads play it costs cold hard cash, and lots of it. I must thank your Mother very much for the Masses; it is darned good of her and I am sure they will help. The moon doesn't look much bigger from the air but you can see it better because you are usually above the clouds that ordinarily obscure it.

I doubt if I will be on this station later than next week, or the end of this coming week I mean; that is if the rumours are true. I have no idea where we will be going though. How do you like the size of my writing? I think it is quite an achievement, in fact almost as long as an ordinary letter, don't you? I find this nib much easier to write with too! Well, that is about all I have to say this time, I guess I'm plumb written out, so to speak.

Love,

Jim.

Sunday, January 2, 1944

I have been out hiking across country since nine this morning with Gordon, and all we had with us were three vitamin tablets each. We travelled over ten miles before we finally arrived back on our station at 3 this afternoon. It was a practice excercise to give us experience in travelling to a certain point, undetected, in the event that we are forced down in Europe. We were hunted by the Home Guard, and the R.A.F. and we eluded them all until we were within two miles of our station. It was fun walking in the fresh air all day, especially as the day was much like any fresh, exhilarating day in the Fall at home, and I enjoyed it very much. We ran across several tiny little villages with the usual winding narrow main street and thatched roofed cottages with dormer windows, but we avoided them as most were closely guarded. We had a meal on our return, and here I am dropping you this line.

I received letters 89, 92 from you this afternoon, and I was both pleased and surprised because as a rule there is no mail for us on Sundays. Your apron made from handkerchiefs must be very pretty, I would like to see you wearing it. I have seen some of the Christmas Airgraphs from Africa myself, and they are good at that. I was growing the moustache to look older, but as you know now, I have removed the pesky thing. The Commando course usually takes about ten days, but there are longer ones too. I may never take it. I like "Dance of the Hours" from Fantasia too, and many others that I can't remember at present. The Bank must have a guilty conscience or something when they start handing out bonuses, but I'll bet it was nice to get.

I hear we are flying in the morning, but it is rather fantastic as we have returned most of our equipment and Gordon has left his at home. My wireless operator, Alex Mackenzie, has invited me to spend our next leave with him in Glasgow, and as he is a "good scout" and by the way he drinks little, and not at all at home, so I figure that it would be a wise thing to do. I will refer to him as "Mac" from now on so you will know who I mean. You would like him, he is very good-hearted and best of all I believe he likes me! Another thing, it won't cost me a fortune. I spent about $135.00 this last leave, but then I was overly generous here and there, although $10.00 a day is nothing in London. Can you imagine me with that much on leave in Canada? We sure could have had one glorious time, we two. I have just returned from seeing "Air Force" starring John Garfield, and I liked it very much; have you seen it?

Love,
Jim.

Monday, January 3, 1944

Much to my surprise, I did get in a little flying this morning and I enjoyed it very much although it was a trifle bumpy. We are leaving for the Commando Course on Wednesday as I had guessed, so I am expecting another short leave at the end of that.

Well, did this letter surprise you at the Bank [Elaine worked at the Royal bank of Canada, ed]? I hope so anyway. We passed this afternoon looking at instructional films and tomorrow we will be dashing around getting clearances again. I received a letter from your mother yesterday, and forgot to tell you. My crew are all visiting a local Pub this evening with the rest of the crews from our course, and I may drop in for a while as it is a sort of farewell good riddance to this station. At present the boys are all playing poker. I don't play. You should see the stack of letters that I must answer- - like a job? It will be swell to get home and have a wife to look after such "trivialities"! Don't hit me. I'll write them myself! I was only fooling.

Love,

Jim.

Tuesday, January 4, 1944

We have had a very quiet day today attending to various bits of red tape relative to leaving, medicals, etc. and of course good old Pay Parade! I did join the boys at the "Three Horse Shoes" last night, but due to a slight rain and the finances of some, there were not many there, just four Flying Officers, W/O Fraser, and another sergeant as well as myself. One of the F.O's is very comical at all things and he related several amusing experiences that he had while he was 2nd Mate on a Lake Steamer, and also when he drove a tractor trailer up in Northern Ontario. I received a letter from Mary the other day. She mentioned receiving the odd letter from David now and then. I never hear from him anymore, perhaps my letters bore him these days. I don't seem to have made many lasting male fridnships in Canada during my civilian life. I hope I have better luck in the Service, I guess it has been my own doing. I have been reading several of the "Specs" and now have only four more to peruse, and then I shall have read them all.

We leave here at 1 P.M. tomorrow and I may spend ten days in Lincolnshire, which may be interesting. Gordon is engrossed in the ever present poker game, and he has me sitting beside him for luck. I hope he wins. Right now I am going for supper, so see you anon.

Love,

Jim.

Thursday, January 6, 1944

Well I didn't expect to be away so long, but now I am in Lincolnshire and may be here for the next six weeks before I go to Con Unit, then I doubt if we will receive any leave between here and there. Tomorrow I go on a twenty-four hour pass and I may go to Nottingham with Mac. This is a combined course of lectures and commando exercises, with no flying. I have to have an additional course when I complete this one, but I don't know where, and I will meet my crew at Con. Unit. You shouldn't have to worry till April sometime, so this should be good news for you. All the lads I came over with will probably have completed a tour by then, and I am just starting, if I ever start. We are just killing time here as far as I can gather. The Mess is very much better than the last; we actually are served at our tables by the W.A.A.F.'s. The food is good, and the place is clean, large, well furnished and warm, so it won't be too hard to take. I'll try and write again this evening. Au revoir.

Love,
Jim.

Sunday, January 9, 1944

I left here for Nottingham on Friday afternoon, and stayed there until eight o'clock Saturday evening when I caught a train to Lincoln and so back to Ye Olde Grinde here. We didn't do very much, I saw "Stage Door Canteen" again because the other lads had not seen it and we had a lovely supper at the King's Hotel in Nottingham before we left for the train. There is a splendid big Cathedral in Lincoln that was built hundreds of years ago, and the architecture is magnificent; there are portions of the old Town Wall and some of the ancient stone gates are still standing. I would have taken some pictures but the weather was unfit for it, so I hope to get some in future. They treat us here, much as they did the first month I was at Manning Depot, you know, lots of parades, roll calls, marching, and all the red tape that goes with it. This morning I had a real old fashioned egg for breakfast, you remember the type, the kind we used to get out of a shell! I even had my first "cup" of milk since I arrived over here on Friday, why, we even had a small tin of orange juice apiece! What is this world coming to! Don't answer that.

I tried to get some decent Post Cards in Nottingham, but was only able to get one that had a picture of the city on it, so I shall send it along today. I get rather "cheesed-off" with life over here but I can always hope that it won't be long now. Gordon has volunteered for an early posting but doubt very much if he will succeed because there are too many ahead of us with much more influence because of rank; I believe we will always be in this country.

I think we get a twenty-four hour pass every week, and if that is true I will have to spend the odd one on the station because it costs too much to travel and hotel bills on top of that are rather expensive. The Squadron Leader did not bother to let me know about the pups, so I will forget it as one might be an awful lot of bother anyway. Technically I am supposed to be a Flight Sgt. Now but I must wait until it comes out in orders, and that may take a couple of months.

Love,
Jim.

Tuesday, January 11, 1944

Yesterday I received letters #72, 74, 90, 91, 93, the first that I have received since arriving on this unit, one week tomorrow. Yesterday we had lectures, and we saw a new Security film and last night I retired early because for some unknown reason I have been very tired the last few evenings. Today I missed my morning parade, as Gordon and I overslept, but I believe we have gotten away with it as nothing was said this afternoon.

This afternoon we did nothing but have our teeth inspected by the dentist, and this evening I am writing letters. Last night, it snowed and we actually have about an inch of snow still on the ground and it made me feel good just to see it there, even if the sky is very dull. Just a touch of home I guess.

Yesterday parcel #4 arrived from your mother and she couldn't have packed it better, it is well, and a perfect birthday present too; everything arrived undamaged. I also received a box from the Grewars, a late Christmas present, and it was very nice. I'm an awfully lucky guy if you ask me.

Thanks for the forms and the cute snap that was in #72. You don't seem to be doing too well with your cooking, I wonder how my first

breakfast will be. I heard about Evelyn & Mickey from Mary. I actually
received a letter from David today, and now that I have moved away from
Oxford he has sent me the address of a friend of his there! He recommends
Britannia Lodge, Lake of Bays, as an ideal place for a honeymoon. He was
planning on Philadelphia for Christmas.

Love,

Jim.

Wednesday, January 12, 1944

Another day drawing to a close, a miserable day, wet and grey, and a
day of lectures for me, but not a boring one. Gordon wanted me to go to
town to a show with him this evening, but I wanted to write to you, much
to his disgust. He has gone with our navigator, so he has company now, and
should be satisfied. I wrote no less than seven letters yesterday, so you see
I was quite busy. This is my first for today, and I have learned today that it
is impossible to procure these forms on this station at the present time, so
I am awfully glad that you have sent me some. Thanks for the cartoon and
forms that you enclosed in #74, the cartoon is cute.

I hope to be through before fall, I hope, I hope. I saw "Dixie" and it
was very good, and in technicolour too. You would like it, I think. Don't
ever complain about my Luck, because as long as I am alive and healthy, I
shall consider myself most fortunate. There is luck, and "luck".

Love,

Jim.

Wednesday, January 12, 1944

Don't ask me why I am writing this letter to you, I have written you an
Airmail letter earlier this evening and since then I have had my supper and
I just want to see you, and talk to you tonight.

Love,

Jim.

Thursday, January 13, 1944

Well, I received a very cute birthday card from you today and another very good one from your mother. I also got your letters #83, 86, and #95 today. Letters number 83 and 86 are really grand, and I enjoyed them very much, they were certainly nice and long, and needless to say, they hit the spot. Thanks for the bulletin on Julianna, the forms, and for the lovely perfume.

I can imagine the Carnival very well from your excellent description and it must have been extremely beautiful to behold. You and I shall attend it together this year.

They are playing Dance of The Flowers from The Nutcracker Suite on the radio now and it is quite nice isn't it.

Thanks for all the snaps, and the clipping of Bill Baggs.

When you fail to return from a trip the Orderly Officer and Service Police open your locker and take all of your kit to the Guard Room, and eventually all letters, etc. are sent to Canadian Headquarters. Of course cigarettes and anything edible is confiscated and anyone is liable to get them. Sometimes personal things, lighters, and stuff like that disappear and there is no way of tracing such things as they can always claim that you had such articles with you. Usually, or always, the Orderly Officer lists everything that is found in your locker and kit and a close check is kept until it reaches headquarters. There everything is sorted out and all personal belongings that are non-issue, are sent home. Now you know as much as I do.

I haven't got a picture of my crew as yet, and Brian is not in my crew. He is a friend in another.

I received a letter from mother today and it is quite a coincidence that she remarked about your new dress too, and your earrings, so it must be a lovely dress. Sure wish I could take you out in it.

The only way that I find out that there is mail for me at the Post Office is by going there to see, or by having a friend who has been there tell me that he saw some for me. Then if I hear that there is I make haste, and pronto! The others find out in the same manner.

Gordon has asked me to extend to you his best regards, and that he thinks I write to you too much! Personally he has been writing almost as much this week himself. Which reminds me, I won't be able to write to you on Friday or Saturday nights as I am on pass then and don't have the opportunity but that is just while I am on this unit.

Fortunately we have never been attacked by enemy kites and the closest that I have been to them so far is when I saw one go down in flames not far from us, over the North Sea. Incidentally a Canadian pilot accounted for it and two others that night.

The electrically heated suit is not very bulky and I manage quite well now that I have become accustomed to working in a confined space. The shoes that I had stolen from me were R.A.F. issue, and I still have my Oxfords, needless to say they need repairing at present, even though I just had the heels fixed in London, now the soles are going. Whenever a letter is censored let me know to what extent so that I can be more sure of what not to write. I can get into serious trouble if I make too many boners. And I am being very careful these days. Yes, the painting is of an identical kite to that which I shall fly in. I never did find out who left the message for me at the Canadian Legion Club, but I think it was a sergeant that I palled around with at Bournemouth.

As far as I can tell, your pictures are as good as any that I have seen of Thompson's. Well, that covers both #83 and #86, and they were sure swell letters, and I think the best I have had from you. I can't thank you too much for them.

Gordon and I are just about ready to have supper now, and I doubt if it will be very good, as tea was not so hot today. They are playing "More Than You Know" on the radio now, know it?

Don't forget to give Bon & Cec my best when you see them, and Rob and your Pop too! I'll write to your mother, and do that myself. We are going for supper now, and in fact I have just returned; it was not good, as I had expected, one slice of spam and two jam sandwiches, and cup of fair cocoa. Of course I could have had beets, but you know that I dislike them. I believe I shall buzz over to barracks now, and if there is any warm water I shall have a shower, shave, and after cleaning my boots and brass, retire.

I wonder what you are doing right now, it is 8:45 over here, so I imagine you are still at work. Don't tell me this is page eleven, I can't have written that many, but then I have, at that, or so it seems. It is so nice "talking" to you though. I must stop now as I am using Gordon's table, and he has to write a letter to a friend; you see, I have been using his room as a writing room as it is quieter and he is the only one to bother me there.

Love,
Jim.

Sunday, January 16, 1944

Sunday again, and they seem to roll around and pile up so much time that we have been apart, but never mind, next fall will see us together or very soon afterwards.

I was in Nottingham again this week-end, and I had my camera along but as luck would have it, a heavy fog settled over this part of England on Saturday morning, and I could hardly see more than two feet in front of me, in fact it has been foggy all day today too, therefore no snaps. I went to see "Thank Your Lucky Stars", starring Eddie Cantor, Alexis Smith, Ann Sheridan, Bette Davis, and many others; it was pretty good as it was a musical comedy.

This morning everything was covered with a heavy frost, all the shrubs, trees, grass, and buildings, and it was really cold, but very pretty. We had lectures all day and we sat in the lecture rooms with our great coats on, and our hands thrust deep in our pockets trying to keep our knees from knocking and teeth from chattering. I have a cold in my head but that is to be expected, and I am using the Vatronal, thank you. This is my second week here, and I have four to go, and I don't mind saying that I am getting rather bored on this station. I have seen reconnaissance photographs of our targets after our bombing, and these raids have been so completely effective, and equally so in every German city that you can't help but pity them and wonder how they live; in some cases of cities ten times as large as our own, there is nothing but walls standing, if that; I fail to see how they keep on, or that they can at this rate.

Love,

Jim.

Monday, January 17, 1944

I received one letter from you this afternoon #97 and I was glad to hear from you.

Excuse me for a few minutes as I am going to dash in for supper. Be right back! Hey ah [I, ed.] is back on the job again after being gone for almost an hour,

Did you hear about the Nazi war broadcast that went like this, "Terror

Bombers of the R.A.F. were over Germany last night; one of our cities is missing". Kinda cute I thought, don't you agree? Quite true in some instances too. With Eisenhower's arrival in England this week and the general tempo of all the war news, one has reason to hope for peace in the not too distant future. The latest conjecture as to the second front is that it will get under way within the next forty or one hundred days. No doubt I shall have a share in the episode if it holds off that long.

I hear by the radio this evening that I am eligible for a service ribbon plus a Maple Leaf on top of it for different reasons. Guess you know all about it.

Last night I wrote a letter to Mr. & Mrs. Grewar, and one to Jack O'Neill. He says that he gets his wings on the twenty-ninth of this month, and I hope he receives a commission as well. I haven't heard from Frank for some time now, and that is rather surprising I believe. I mentioned receiving a letter from David last week which was quite unexpected. I heard from Lawrence today and he always asks after you. He is very well and all wrapped up in a lass in Scotland, with whom he spent his last leave which was for New Year's. He had a swell and economical time, so I guess it pays to meet some local belle and live at her home on leaves!!! Don't say it, I'm not inclined that way and will be most happy to evade all such situations at all times. I would much rather spend the money.

I received a carton of cigarettes from St. Ann's Catholic Women's League today and that was a welcome surprise too. I am really most fortunate.

I liked your letter #86 so much that I read it over again and I never get tired of reading it.

Today I got myself into what may mean a slight difficulty as I skipped parade this afternoon after roll call, and apparently they had another later in the day, so now among several other names, mine is conspicuous for the lack of a check against it. I guess the old Wing Commander will tell me a thing or six tomorrow.

I must trot off and have a shave now and totter into bed, so until tomorrow when I shall write again.

Love,

Jim.

Tuesday, January 18, 1944

Your letters 96, 98, & 99 arrived today and they were swell; you are very, good to write so often and I shall never forget it. I wish you wouldn't worry so about me, as I will be home just as surely as any Joe Erk in ground crew, especially as you say so many prayers for me. I may be home much sooner than you expect so don't fret about it, and keep smiling.

I heard from Bill W. last week, and I guess I didn't tell you. So you had an airman for company on New Year's Day! I'm green with envy, tsk, tsk, never would have thought it of you Elaine. Remember how jealous I used to get? I hope I have cured myself of that by the time I return to you as it is very unpleasant.

I had a little skeet-shooting this afternoon, and I managed to hit six out of seven, so I'm not too bad. I appeared before the Squadron Leader today for skipping a P.T. period yesterday, with several other Canadians, an Aussie, a Newzie, and a few R.A.F. He gave us an hour's drill as punishment which took place at seven thirty this evening, and they only kept us ten minutes so we got off lightly. Thursday is pay day and I am rather glad of it as I had to draw 2 from my account last week-end and I would like to deposit it again.

What is the situation between Peggy and Jack, is she engaged, or have they forgotten about it for the duration. There don't seem to be many single gals left at home now.

We are still killing time here and becoming more tired of it every day, and there are the usual rumours of seven days leave, floating around. If I get it, I think I will go to Glasgow with Mac or in any case some place that won't entail too much travelling. I have promised him that I will go though, so guess I shall end up there. He has no sisters, so don't worry!!! As if you would.

Love,
Jim.

Wednesday, January 19, 1944

I am sitting here listening to [name deleted, ed] and trying to write to you, or rather, quite the opposite. He tells me of one or another of his affairs d'amour every now and then, and of course I must be duly attentive!

Today has been a typical English winter's day, wet, drizzling, and very grey, and we were in the hands of the R.A.F. Regiment all day. This morning I wrangled my way out of being on parade by Joeing myself as barrack warden to supervise the cleaning of our rooms, and thereby I missed a route, march and managed to get a cup of tea and a bun at 10:30. This afternoon I ran two and one half miles through the country in running shoes, sweat shirt and a "cute" pair of shorts, and consequently became quite mud spattered and generally dirty and overheated. I had a lovely hot shower when I returned to my quarters, and gave myself a shampoo as well, so now I feel very well but for a certain stiffening of my lower leg muscles. It seems I have done little or no strenuous exercise since last June, and not much then! I intend to get back into shape from now on at every opportunity. Shucks, I walked six miles last Friday evening with Mac and two friends in order to get into town to catch the train for Nottingham as we had been unable to get on the bus as it was overcrowded.

I wrote Frank a letter this evening so I hope to hear from him sometime next month, or the following month. I go by months now instead of days you see! I am going for supper now, see you later!

Back again and all ready to talk to you again; now what was that you were saying before I so rudely interrupted you? You weren't saying anything? Sorry, my mistake: (no, I'm not wacky!) Did you know that I have gained at least fifteen pounds since joining the R.C.A.F.? I now weigh one hundred and sixty-two pounds with my clothes on, and I estimate that I really weigh about one-fifty five stripped; I could do with more though as you already know.

I am enclosing two stamps for you, one from Eire and one from Australia, so you see I haven't forgotten you during the day.

Tomorrow is lecture day, and I hope they have some interesting ones so that I will not be bored. Guess I'll miss this life for a while after the war, no lectures, parades, flying, but they will be replaced I hope by you, a family, a good job and your very charming company, so I shall be extremely happy. I'm afraid you will have to get after me now and then as I waste so very much time as you know.

Now I must prepare for bed as I have to be ready for an earlier parade than usual in the morning, so I beg you to excuse me.

Love,
Jim.

Thursday, January 20, 1944

Just another of those damp grey days over here, but it was brightened by a lovely letter from you #80. Thanks for the snaps and the forms. So that is your new dress, and the furs; you look very purty and I like the dress. I received a letter from Don & Ella and one from Bon & Cec as well today, and I liked Bon's letter very much and was very glad to hear from her. It was nice of Ella to add a note to Don's letter, did you see it?

I received the overflow of box number four, which as you know is #5. Thanks ever so much for the socks, handkerchiefs, film etc.; that was some overflow, almost another complete box. Oh yes, I received a very cute card from Norv & June today!

When I got up this morning my calf muscles were so stiff and sore that I could scarcely walk and they are not much improved at present; these 2 1/2 mile cross-country runs are not so good! That will teach me to make P.T. regularly and keep fit.

Bon seems to be very happy now and that is swell; she tells me that you and June have a little rivallry in regard to who gets the most letters; I'm afraid I may have let your down now and then, but I shall do my best.

By the by, don't pay too much attention to these war strategists on the Home Front as they seldom if ever know the score, though they have an air of "knowing" something! Those that talk most know the least.

Gordon cannot get us an early posting as there are too many men of senior ranks ahead of him, so we shall be here as long as anyone else. To illustrate that, a Wing Com. arrived yesterday and was posted today. Understand? Today was pay day, so there is a large crap game in progress as usual; yours truly is not interested of course.

You should see the pile of laundry I have to do, for the first time since entering the "soivice" [service, ed]; it's going to break my heart, and probably my back! I am sending my "good shirts" to Mac's mother with his laundry so that they will get done properly. I wrote a letter to the Education Officer at headquarters last night to make enquiries about courses that the Government has to offer for any service men that care to take them, and if they have one that appeals to me I shall take a stab at it; Gordon was also interested when I mentioned it to him so if he decides on the same course it will be swell, and we might get somewhere.

Don't let anything worry you as I am very well and 1 hope you are equally so. Give my love to your mother, and remember me to all and sundry.

Love,
Jim.

Monday, January 24, 1944

I am still on the same station and bored as usual, but I broke the monotony a little by travelling to London with some of the boys for the week-end as I had tired of Nottingham and also we had just been paid so we could afford it. We arrived just in time for the large air-raid that London has experienced for many months, and the biggest I have ever been through myself; it was quite a sight and I stood in the street and watched the multitude of searchlight beams search the skies for aircraft and trap them and then there would be a great barrage sent up by the big guns and the sky looked much like a huge display of fireworks on the 24th of May. Very pretty, but as I watched I thanked God that I was not up there in the thick of all that deadly beauty. While in London I saw "Sam Demetrio" a naval story of the Merchant marine which was much like the one that Noel Coward played in, not very cheerful, and I wouldn't recommend It to you. Since returning to the station I have had a session with the Dentist and horror of horrors, he removed another of my dwindling number of molars!! You will be having a toothless husband if this goes on and I'm not sure that you would like that. What about it?

I received letters #100 &102 today. Now I fully expect a proper earful from your next letters, and I am ashamed to admit that you have every right in the world to throw every mean word in Webster's at me, but could a guy really write a cheerful letter home at Christmas time? Skip that, I'm just a heel and I may as well admit it; I wish you were here right now so that you could tell me off verbally and completely as I so richly deserve. All I can do is promise you that you will never lack letter from me again if it is humanly possible for them to be written, no matter where I am in future. I wish this damned war would end so that we could live a normal and happy life together, instead of this long-distance stuff that is no good for either of us. I have figured out that my next leave should come in the Spring, so I will be visiting Wales as it should be nice there then, and I will describe it to you as accurately as I can. I don't mind travelling by train over here so much now that I am used to it.

Love,
Jim.

Tuesday, January 25, 1944

Boy, oh boy, oh boy, did I ever get a super present today. I'd say it is the best one I have ever had, and it was a swell surprise too. You couldn't have thought of better gift, or one that I would appreciate more than I do your photo. It is so natural, so much like you that I just sit and stare, and stare some more, Thank you, and that thanks has all my heart in it. I have your picture in front of me as I write this and I can't help but stop and admire you often as I sit here. The card you enclosed is very pretty, and thank you also for that. You are too good to me. I don't think you can really understand just how much your photo has pleased me, nothing else could do so, except yourself.

I went to see 'Trade Winds" starring Joan Bennett, Frederick March, Ralph Belamy, and Ann Southern last night, in the station Cinema and it was good even though rather ancient. There was an extremely old comedy with it which must have been one of Bob Hope's firsts! This morning I did nothing, and this afternoon was largely taken up by our Liaison Officer from Canadian District Headquarters. He gave us a lot of information regarding commissions, promotions, and transfers to R. C. A. F. and ways of going about any inquiries we wish to make. This officer struck me as being a rather good head and I expect him to be my source of information as long as I am over here as I will be in his district from now on, I believe.

If I get a pass this week-end I think I shall spend it in Lincoln at a nice little hotel called the Saracen's Head and I hope to get some snaps—if the weather permits. Gordon may accompany me, and I would like to have a leisurely time for a change instead of dashing for trains and spending hours on them. I am very well, and I trust that you are also. Things are going along well over here, so don't worry about me.

I'll be seeing you soon I hope; so keep smiling, and don't let things get your down.

Love,
Jim.

Wednesday, January 26, 1944

I received three Airmail letters from you this afternoon #103, 104 & 105. The first one made me feel very bad, and that one was too good for me at that. It's so inadequate to say that I'm sorry, and at present there is only one thing that could make me feel worse than I do, and that would be for you to say that you are through with me altogether.

George didn't tell me why he stayed at the Club; I think it was because the girl's family were in town, and spent Christmas Day with them at their home in a village somewhere. I have never met the girl, or have I been with George other than at times when we were out with other lads as well.

Your letters #28 & 30 did reach me on Dec. 28th and they are both Airmail; they must have been lost for a while. I received a letter informing me to tell Eddie that his brother was killed last Sunday night, but he is not with me and I have written to him some time ago and he has not answered; I feel almost as badly about it if I were he. I am answering your letters rather sketchily in this letter I'm afraid because I feel pretty rotten and just can't settle down to it as I usually do.

Love,

Jim.

Thursday, January 27, 1944

This morning I had a very boring lecture on hand grenades, the purpose for, and the method of using them. I managed to scrounge some time from that to get my hair cut, and these English barbers are a menace; anyway my hair is shorter now and that is the main thing. As long as you can't see it, it matters not how it looks really.

This afternoon we went on a Route March and they took us through the country and one or two quaint little villages. It was quite windy but fortunately we never were marching into it, and I enjoyed the fresh air and scenery a great deal. You would laugh to see the farm horses over here, they are stout, thick legged, short, and have hair all over them that is three or four inches long; Very shaggy beasts. We returned at five o'clock, very tired and warm, and of course ready for a good meal. My legs are somewhat tired too, and all of this fresh air has had its sleep inducing effect, so I will be wise if I retire early this evening.

I put your picture on top of my locker every night and it is right in front of my bed where I can lay and look at you; I like your smile and eyes, so much that I am tempted to carry the photo about with me during the day. When I awake in the morning there you are smiling at me, and gee it's good to see you. I don't think you will ever realize how much I appreciate your picture. The fellows say you look swell too, and one Aussie said that you looked like a clean wholesome girl that a fellow would want to marry! I promptly informed him that it was my intention to do that very thing, (You've got to watch these Aussies!) By-the-way, Lawrence wants to came to our wedding, in fact he would like to be Best Man. We must remember to invite him.

Love,

Jim.

Friday, January 28, 1944

I am writing this instead of an Airmail because I have a few stamps to send you that I am sure you haven't got in your "collection". Five South African, one Eire, and six Australian.

How'm I doin? I will be sure to enclose them all this time and not forget them as I did before, I have a pass this week-end, but I am not travelling anywhere, and am staying on the station tonight; no, I'm not broke, I still have about three quid, so I could travel if I wanted to. Tomorrow I shall go to Lincoln and send my Grandmother a telegram to wish her the best for her birthday on the third, and if it is a fair day I will get some snaps while in town, to send to you of course.

This morning, I had a lecture on morale, and discipline from an R.A.F. Regiment Wing Commander, and a lot of what he said struck me as being quite true but somewhat impossible to practice. You would have agreed with him as well because much of what he said fits snugly with our own ideals. After his lecture we went to the Station Cinema to see an American propaganda film which portrayed the brutalities of the Hun in no uncertain fashion in order to show us why we are fighting this war. Quite a horror picture and very interesting. After dinner we had a talk by a decidedly insulting and unlikeable R.A.F. Wing Commander, in regard to N.A.A.F.I. (Navy,

Army & Air Force Inst and P.S.I. (Public Services Inst.) two organizations that are supposed to cater to the general welfare of Service Men and supply them with entertainment and canteens on each station. The N.A.A.F.I. published a profit of 3,000,000 for last year! I strongly distrust this organization and so do my friends. However they make little money from me so I should worry! After that we had a gunnery period and so to tea.

One becomes tired of seeing camouflaged buildings, sinister dark things day after day in their drab war-paint, each station different only in its layout, but always the same hangars and billets, wherever you are. The cities are much alike, all have numerous Pubs and Hotels, all are strange and not very friendly and all are like empty houses during the blackout. A few people hurrying along in the dark, no friendly lamp lit windows that you like to peek into as you walk along, and even the restaurants and cafes close shortly after ten-thirty. The days are easy as there are many places that are new to you, but at night you may as well retire early unless you go to a theatre or stay in a Pub.

From now on I hope to visit a different place every leave, and I think it should be most interesting. I will have to do this on my own because the majority of the lads prefer certain cities and as long as they continue to enjoy themselves in them they won't go elsewhere. I understand their views and you can like one place more than another and new cities are like new friends, strange until you get to know them.

I will amble along now before I bore you rigid.

Love,
Jim.

Saturday, January 29, 1944

I awoke this morning rather tired as the roar of the home-coming bombers disturbed my sleep last night a great deal; there seemed to be large number of them out last night too. However I had breakfast and returned to my barracks to clean my shoes and brass, wash and shave as well as make up my bed. This occupied most of the morning as I took my time (I had plenty to spare) and gabbed to some Englishmen and Australians about how nice Canada is, and you know me, gabby as ever! At twelve o'clock I visited the Post Office but there was only a letter from Eddie so I proceeded to the Mess and had dinner with Gordon and after dinner we went out to the highway to queue up for the one and only afternoon bus to the city. When it finally arrived it was much too inadequate for the number waiting and we were stranded until a dump truck stopped, then a lot of us clambered aboard and arrived in town that way. I sent the telegram to my Grandmother for her birthday, and then Gordon and I saw "Girl Crazy", starring Mickey Rooney and there was a very good English comedy on with it. I enjoyed them both. We ate at one of the hotels afterward and met some of the boys. We ended up by catching the last bus back to the station, which leaves Lincoln at 10:15. And I was sober the whole time. Next week-end I expect to do much the same thing, and I hope to meet Eddie as he is stationed quite near to me, and as I mentioned before, he lost his brother last Sunday night in a raid on Germany. Well honey Child, that is all the news for today unfortunately, perhaps I can do better tomorrow.

Love,
Jim.

Sunday, January 30, 1944

How are you; keeping your chin up alright these days? I am very well and today was bright and sunlit for a change. We had lectures all morning and some instructional films; the lectures were quite mediocre but those in the afternoon were very interesting, and I was only slightly bored with one which was quite dray, and the last one of the day, so I think that accounts for most of my disinterest. At noon I took some snap-shots of Gordon and Mac, and they took some of me so I will have some for you soon; happy now? One of these fine week-ends when I have some dough I shall try and have a photograph taken for you to add to the numerous ones you already have. Tomorrow I am scheduled to play hockey on a team representing my course, against a team from another course. We will play at a place named Grimsby, and where that is I have no idea. Can you imagine me playing hockey; I can't! It should be fun and it isn't as though I had no idea at all;

after all I did play now and then (in my youth!) I hope we play, and I shall be sure to let you know how the game went.

They changed the system in the Permanent Sgt's Mess today and though I tried valiantly and determinedly to remain there, I lost out, and am now eating in the mess that has been created for the overflow of sergeants from the other mess. What a mess, and I do mean mess; oh well, I ate two weeks longer than I should have, so I can't complain!!

How is the mail reaching you now? Frequently and continuously I hope. Well m'darlin, I must prepare to hit ye olde hay again, I can't imagine what makes me so sleepy these days but I seem to be perpetually tired. It is eleven o'clock, and I am with the Regiment tomorrow so I had better get along.

Love,
Jim.

Monday, January 31, 1944

I have had a very nice day today; we left the camp just before noon in an R.A.F. van and were driven to Grimsby, a town on the sea-shore thirty miles away.

We had lunch in a Cafe in the town and then went to the Arena which is situated on the outskirts of the town. The ice was better than I had expected and the rink measured approximately 20' x 80'. All the hockey equipment was supplied by Canadian organizations and although I take a size 10 skate I wound up with a size 12, so you know how well I was skating! Our team wore maroon outfits and the opposing team wore yellow. We had a very good game which ended in a tied score of eight all. The only person injured was our goalie as he stopped a puck with his chin and had it split open. After the game we skated for two hours and civilians were allowed in then and we got some excellent hot chocolate (I had three cups!). At five o'clock we left to return to the station and arrived in time for a late tea that had been reserved for us. It was very nice to get away from the station for the day and we were all anxious to be able to do a little skating in this land of mild winters. Well, that accounts for my day over here, one more day gone.

I may leave here one week from next Saturday, and then I shall be flying again as usual. I am listening to Bob Hope at present and he is pretty good, hmmmm Lana Turner too. The dirty so and so's, they fried a real Porter House Steak next to the mike, and did it sound good! My mouth is still watering, in fact I am drooling.

Love,
Jim.

Tuesday, February 1, 1944

Gordon has just dashed away into town to keep a date with his Canadian "brother-in-law", a Flying Officer in the R.C.A.F. I declined his invitation to join them, truthfully not only because of writing to you but I am not interested in going out; of course if I did go I could always write before retiring and that is why I say "not only because of you".

Today was not very interesting even though we had lectures and a little time on the range, as usual. It has been a very windy day with spasmodic periods of sunshine. I received a lovely box of chocolates from you at noon which bears the number "4". Thanks ever so much, they are very good, and most welcome to say the least.

Your photograph is sure doing good work. I have it on my locker morning and night, and often at noon.

There is a rumour of a posting to India but we have very very little chance of getting it, and I doubt if Gordon will ask for it, and anyway there are too many already after it. I think we shall just sit tight over here and let things take their natural course and sort of go along with the tide as it were.

Love,
Jim.

Wednesday, February 2,1944

Today has been grey and windy and has been a day spent with the R.A.F. Regiment, although I must confess I scrounged most of the day by missing P.T. and an eight mile route march. I visited stores this afternoon and was issued with new inter-communication ear phones and micro-phone. That has been the extent of my labours today, but for an hour spent on the parade square this morning, so you see I have had a very soft day of it; what do you think?

Gordon is in town seeing his "brother-in-law" again this evening, and from what he says, they get on quite well together, which is a good thing. After tea, I went to the Station Cinema to see, "In Old California", a story of the Gold Rush days, starring Wayne Morris and Binnie Barnes; it was not as good as I had expected but it had a few good laughs in it. Have you seen it? After the show Mac and I went over to the Sally Ann (Salvation Army Canteen) and had. a sandwich and cup of tea, and from there to the Mess, where I now am writing.

I have heard nothing new about postings so I am as much in the dark as you are. Tomorrow is Pay Day and none too soon, although I still have about ten bob left. Mac has renewed his invitation to Glasgow and as before, I have accepted it in anticipation of a leave before I start operations.

Love,
Jim.

Thursday, February 3, 1944

I guess this has been the quietest birthday that I can remember, but shucks I'm well and I'm not being mistreated so I have no cause for com-plaint. We were paid this morning and that took up the greater portion of the morning, the rest of which I passed conversing with Gordon. At noon, I received a carton of cigarettes from your mother and they arrived not only in time for my birthday but at just the right moment as I was running quite low, so they are really welcome.

This afternoon I did absolutely nothing but keep out of everyone's way, and I read a western story novelette from n old Star Weekly that Gordon had scrounged somewhere. At the moment I am a bit "cheesed" but I'll get over it by tomorrow, I expect. I will not be surprised if we leave here withing the next ten days too.

Tomorrow we are getting a decidedly unexpected forty-eight, so guess I shall get out of here for the week-end and perhaps see some shows or something in London. Mac wanted me "to go to Glasgow but you spend about two days on the train and there goes the "48". Oh well, I'll do something anyway, and I'll keep my nose clean.

Love,

Jim.

Saturday, February 5,1944

I missed dropping you a line last night as I was travelling and it was quite late by the time that I arrived here in London and secured a lovely room at the Bonnington Hotel on Southampton Row. It is a "temperance" hotel, which means no women, "visitors", and no liquor, so you see that I am in good hands. I tried to get a room in several of the Service Clubs but due to the week-end influx of men, none were available. This is a very nice double room that I am sharing with a Canadian Sergeant from Kitchener, an ex-St. Jerome's student that knows Bill Cauley and the Luntz kid! I met him while on my quest for a room and we joined forces; he seems to be a nice fellow, and he is a Catholic, needless to say. I saw a very good show, perhaps you have seen it; "The Girls He Left Behind", starring Betty Grable, Carmen Miranda, Phil Baker, Benny Goodman, and of course his orchestra. I liked the show a great deal and I know if you see it, you will too. I met a couple of the lads that I was on course with in Canada, at the Canadian Legion this afternoon, and they tell me Harry Venn is still going strong, and I was pleased to know that. They are a good way through their tour now, and are looking very well.

Gosh the last few nights have been lovely due to the moon; I guess you have noticed it too. Tomorrow I shall go to Mass at the church of St. Anslem and St. Cecelia, which is but a few blocks from here, and I will remember you, and "us" in my prayers.

Love,

Jim.

Monday, February 7, 1944

I arrived on the station early today and in style at that! Five of us got an ancient Rolls Royce taxi and travelled in state up to the main gates; I think it must have been someone's limousine in days gone by, and it was fun just riding in it.

Your letters #101, 107, and one not numbered which was written on January 24th, and one #94 which is super and thanks for all the snaps, the clipping, and the forms. I have read all your letters but #107 and I want to write this letter before I do because I'm afraid it may make me feel just about as low as I really am and I don't want to spoil the effect of #94 which was so swell. I've got it coming to me though, so I'll have to take my medicine. I got a swell note from Mac's mother today inviting me to spend next leave with Mac and also insisting that I send my laundry to her with Mac's! She has done a few shirts for me and made a grand job of them, but I won't send her the rest of my clothes as I don't like to. I'll send you the note so that you can keep it for me. It's darned nice of her I think.

By the way, I have brought the letter here to the station to mail, as they are only to be mailed from Camp P.O.; the letter I wrote in London. I saw the Ice Carnival while in Toronto and I know that I told you at the time; You don't like Rye? Well I don't either, nor do I care for Scotch, so let's stay sober and enjoy life! I'm going to read that other letter of yours now, and one from your mother, so until tomorrow evening when I shall write again, au revoir.

Love,
Jim.

Tuesday, February 8, 1944

I wrote your mother a letter today and she will probably crown me 'cause I took the bull by the horns, as it were, and. started my letter "Dear Mom". You will have heard about it by the time you are reading this, and I hope she doesn't mind. I just don't like calling your mother Mrs. Ellis, after all have known her a long time haven't I, and aren't I marrying her daughter? Do you mind?

I read your letter #107 last night and contrary to my apprehensions, it was swell; I was tempted to write you an additional letter after I had read it, and I would have, but for the hour.

I'm glad that Airgraph that I posted to the Bank was a pleasant surprise, and I shall send a letter there now and again if they will help in any way to make you happy. I have received the two books from you, pardon me, the two letters that were extra long, and gee they were swell and they must have taken a good deal of time to write.

Your mother has mentioned that you and she work on the quilt every time you have a spare moment or so, and I'll bet it will be a good one. Frank tells me that he received a lovely card from you at Christmas time and he.told me how lucky I am to have a wonderful fiancée like you. He didn't have to tell me, I know that, and have always been aware of the fact.

Jack O'Neill should be home on leave now; have you seen him? I have sent a film to be printed and although I don't expect all of them to turn out I should have some of myself, Gordon, and Mac. I expect to have them by a week today, but if I am posted they will have to be forwarded and that will take longer.

I have two stamps from India for you and I'll enclose them in this letter tonight. Don't use the above address as your mail will take longer to reach me.

I am going to call it a day when I finish this letter as I have already written one to Eddie, one to your mother, and one to mine, and I think that is good enough for one night, don't you?

Once I start Operations I shall have nine days leave every six weeks, so I shall get my travelling done then, in this order I think; Ailyn, my great uncle in Westmoreland, and I don't know who will have priority after that, but that is what I shall do. To visit Ireland one needs at the least two weeks as it is so difficult catching the boats and bothering with red-tape for such a trip; it takes up a lot of time, I'm told; however I will cover as much as possible before I come home, and then there will be little that I have missed, if anything.

That covers most everything for the present that I can think of so perhaps I had better leave off.

Love,
Jim.

Thursday, February 10, 1944

Yesterday I had some examinatIons, one of which was aircraft recognition and I managed to get 95 marks for that, but as yet I have not learned the results of the others; no one beat me, so I feel quite satisfied at least. Last night I went to see "The Man Who Came Back", a story about the swamps in southern United States, and it was quite good too. I went with Mac and we retired soon after the show. Today has been Regiment day, but due to clothing parades it was an extremely soft day for me, and also a lucky one as I managed to hand in my old battle dress, in exchange for a brand new one, so I am feeling quite proud of myself because everyone was so sure that I wouldn't be able to wrangle it; I fooled them.

Tomorrow morning our crew and two others are scheduled to tour a factory in Nottingham, whether to impress us or the war workers, I have not quite ascertained, but it will be, or should be a nice change. I shall have a snap taken of me in the new battle-dress for your benefit, so that you may see it, as it is smarter looking than the Canadian issue. I wrote you an O.L. and said that I was enclosing two Indian stamps, and as I had not got them with me I failed to send them! I'm one awful fellow, and I'm sure you will agree. I intend to try and see Eddie in Nottingham tomorrow night if possible; it's a long time since I saw him last.

I am very well, as always, and I hope you are the same, and that you do not worry too much about this guy over here.

Love,
Jim.

Sunday, February 13, 1944

Friday morning we left for Nottingham to visit the Raleigh Works and we passed the morning going over the plant; it was not very interesting as I have seen much better things at the National Steel Car, and the civvy that showed us through the plant knew less than I, so I learned very little from it. After seeing the plant I went to see "Saludos Omegos" with Gordon and Mac, after having dinner in the theatre cafe. It was a good show and I liked it very much; after that we caught a train to Lincoln and had supper there, and shortly after that got a taxi to the station. I slept until noon on

Saturday and after dinner Mac and I went to see an English Foot-Ball game between Sheffield and Lincoln, at Lincoln and it was not bad, the score was 0-0, the first of such games I have ever seen. We had supper and then saw a show "The Adventures of Captain Tartu" starring Robert Donat, and it was quite good although another Anti-Nazi propaganda picture. Today we were notified of our posting to Con. Unit and I am going on the ten day gunner's course at another station before I rejoin my crew there. We leave tomorrow, so I doubt if I shall hear from you in the next two weeks although you will be sure to hear from me.

I received your letter #111 on Saturday, and it was swell.

Love,

Jim.

Monday, February 14, 1944

We, the air-gunners, arrived on this station about two hours ago, and I have had tea, been assigned a bed, and have come immediately to our Mess writing room in order to drop you this insignificant line of chatter from me.

You will probably be quite amazed to find five snap-shots enclosed in this letter, and very recent ones too; Harry spoiled the one of Mac & myself by moving the camera a bit but I intend to get some on this station for you as well, and I hope they turn out much better. I hope to keep you well supplied from now on, so I hope they all get through to you.

Eddie is here on this station but I have not been able to see him yet as he was flying today and will not return until tomorrow.

Did I tell you that Mac, Gordon, & myself posed for a photograph of the three of us while we were in Nottingham on Friday? I will be able to get them this week-end if I can get to town; they will not be very elegant as they are not expensive but I will send mine to you as soon as I get it.

Well, Earl & Jack did very well, didn't they; they are both good types though and I'm not surprised that they got their commissions as well as their wings, and no doubt they deserved them. They are doubly fortunate in that they are remaining in Canada; their luck appears to be excellent!

I should be dicing regularly soon, weather permitting, and during the next ten days only in daylight, so it won't be so bad, After I leave here and graduate to the heavy stuff with my crew I shall be flying day and night, as before, and things will not be so boring as they have been for the last two months.

Are you receiving my letters regularly now? I write to you at every opportunity, so you should hear from me often.

Love,
Jim.

View from the Rear Turet

Wednesday, February 16, 1944

I wrote you an ordinary mail letter on Monday evening and enclosed five snap-shots for you of myself, Mac, Gordon, and a friend named Harry Edwards. I hope they get through to you alright and that you will like them. I may be able to get some snaps on this station, and I certainly hope to get others at Conversion Unit with the crew. I met Eddie last evening and as he is to leave here on Friday, for a squadron. We went out together. After he leaves here I doubt if I shall see him much if ever while on this side of the Atlantic.

I don't expect to receive any letters from you for at least another two weeks, if then, as I shall be moving quite often for the next two months, and it will take my mail some time to catch me. I have guarded against some of it by sending my next address to Base P.O. instead of this one and I hope when I get there that my mail arrives soon afterward. This is the largest drome I have ever been on, and it is a good station too. We are getting new eye tests here on night vision and I am not very sure of my chances, but I'll let you know how I make out.

We have had very irregular rain and snow and sunshine-filled days lately, and English weather seems to be always as inconsistent, one moment Spring and the next Winter, and that is why it is miserable. I am very well as usual and I hope that you are feeling well yourself.

Love,

Jim.

Saturday, February 19, 1944

I have had three night vision tests with the lads and I got 32 out of 40 marks, first, and 29 second, and as yet we have not heard about the third test. I was highest among the Canuck's. One of the fellows is on the verge of being grounded as his results were so poor they tested his eyes and they are bad. Perhaps I should suggest they check mine! I have lost all of my kit, all but what I wore to get to this unit; at least the R.A.F. lost it for me as it was on one.of their trucks and no one has seen it since. I don't know what to do now, and I sure hope they find it in a hurry. I went to Nottingham to pick up the photograph of Gord, Mac, and me but it was not ready, so they promised to mail it to me. I was flying today (in borrowed kit) for the first time in almost two months and it's funny how you enjoy it once you are at it again, even though you would be happy not to fly but a moment before you enter the kite. It was a Canadian pilot and he was excellent.

They actually have a Catholic church on the camp, a little tiny building twice the size of your garage at Cedar Springs. I was there this evening and said some prayers for "us" and also went to Confession. I had a chat with the padre afterward and he seems quite likeable, young, and I believe Welsh. I shall go there to Mass tomorrow morning, and of course Communion. It's a little confusing kneeling beside the priest at Confession, no cubicle and about two feet from the seats, but I am becoming quite used to such things and they bother me very little now.

I have read your letter #111 for the "nth" time; it is the only one I have till my kit shows up. I have got your photo with me thank God.

Love,
Jim.

Sunday, February 20, 1944

In spite of all my good intentions as to Mass and Communion this morning, I had to fly and therefore must try again next Sunday, and then I will be at Conversion Unit, but I'll honestly try.

My kit is still untraced and I must make some inquiries by telephone this evening about it. I have started smoking my pipe a little now, and will do so until my kit is located because my cigarettes are packing in the kit-bags unfortunately. The weather has been quite cold recently and we have had slight flurries of snow. We are learning quite a lot of useful information on this station, and the instructors know their subjects very well for a change.

I have not taken any snaps yet because the weather is not suitable, but I expect to get some on our first nice day for you. I am going to start on another saving spree now in preparation for my next leave; I have about 28 in my account at present but it will look better when I add $26.00 to it that I have in my pocket at present. I was paid on Friday and that represents a little more than my complete pay.

Love,
Jim.

Monday, February 21, 1244

Another Monday. I was flying again this morning for approximately one hour. I have had my final Night Vision test and my results are what they term "Average", and so close to being "Above Average" that it amazes me! I did very well. The lad that failed has had his eyes examined and he does not need glasses, so that means he is alright as far as day operations are concerned, so he may be attached to a different crew and squadron. We will be writing examinations on Wednesday I think and our results go to the Air Ministry, so I hope I do well.

I saw "Seven Days Leave", starring Victor Mature the other night, and it was fair. Last night I was at a Music Concert in our theatre given by a Pianist, Cellist, and a Soprano, all women and when they rendered "Ave Maria", my heart was home. There were just a few selections that I really cared for. I can hear "Don't Get Around Much Anymore", on a radio in the building, how true my sweet, how true!

Tuesday, February 22, 1944

Well, can't say I have anything to write about this evening but I'll see what I can do. Did I tell you that I finally received my kit yesterday at noon? Well, I did, and not too soon either. Tomorrow morning I write my examinations, so guess I'd better brush up a little, although I feel quite sure of myself, but all the odd [good, ed] marks wouldn't hurt amy, what say you?

Today has been very cold and late this afternoon it began to rain, and still is, darn it. The photograph from Nottingham should be waiting for me at my next station now, as I asked them to mail it there for me, sooo I'll send it along to you pronto.

The first day I am home I'm going to sleep at your place if I must stay on the chesterfield, and I might even stay for a week!!!!! You're going to have your hands full getting rid of me but you could always have your father toss me out, and then I'd sleep on the steps, so there too!!

I had another short flip today and it was quite cold up thar, [there, ed]tis a fact! Tomorrow's letter shall be the last from here until I return a month hence.

Love,
Jim.

Wednesday, February 23, 1944

This as you know is my last day here, and I have come through all of my examinations today with flying colours. We have our final test tomorrow morning, which is on Aircraft Recognition, and we leave here sometime in the afternoon. This station has been very comfortable as we had steam-heated barracks, and good food, and the routine was not boring in any way, so we shall be sorry to leave. All reports on our next station are quite discouraging in every way as we hear that the barracks are very poor, and as it was on the satellite station of our O.T.U. everything is widely separated, only this time there are no bicycles to be had! So you may take it for granted that I am not in the least enthused about this change, however it is to be hoped that we shall be there no more than a month. I wasn't flying today so I have completed my flips as far as this station is concerned. The lads have all made their way into Nottingham tonight, as usual, and yours truly is behaving himself and remaining on the station as per custom; I have no desire to go on a spree.

Love,
Jim.

No. 106 Squadron,
                                 Royal Air Force,
                                    Metheringham,
                                        Lincs.
                                 3rd September 1944

Dear Miss Ellis,

            I regret to tell you that
your fiance, Sergeant James Keenan, who was
missing from an operational flight on 26/27
April 1944, is now reported to have lost
his life.   He has been buried at Chauffort
in France.

            Please accept my deepest
sympathy.

            Yours sincerely,

            M. M. J. Stevens.
            Wing Commander, Commanding,
            No. 106 Squadron,   R.A.F.

Miss E. Ellis,
38, Huron Street,
Hamilton,
Ontario,
Canada.

Part III
The Rest of the Story

Part II of this book focused on Jim Keenan's letters to his fiancé Elaine Ellis. They tell most of the story of their deepening love during his assignment to Bomber Command in England. The first edition of this book (April, 2014) did not include Part III. Many months after Elaine's death (April 14, 2013), however, I came into possession of some documents and items left to me by Elaine that provide a fuller understanding of the events that transpired before, during and after the war. In addition, a document provided by Ann Collins, the widow of Navigator George Collins, provided a detailed description of his two escapes: from the crippled Lancaster; and then from France. Receiving these documents created a desire to tell "the rest of the story." Some of items from both Elaine and George Collins are personal, but they serve to help relive and enliven those important events from so long ago. They tell the story of ordinary lives caught in the enormous drama of WW II and its aftermath.

This edition also includes a short description and some photos of the Memorials held for the three airmen by the people of Chauffourt. Readers of the first edition often asked me questions about the medals awarded the three airmen. So in telling the story of the medals, I also became intrigued with the correspondence the families following the death of a loved one. The RCAF war records for Jim Keenan has over 150 pages of documents, including correspondence with the family following his death. A small selection (including one in German) are included at the end of the text.

This war story is just one of many, but I realized that I was the last person to know most of the relevant details. I felt strongly compelled to tell as much of the story as I could, lest it be lost like so many others. Schweinfurt

was one of the most important targets of WW II. In fact, it was bombed by
the British and Americans on numerous raids, none more "famous" than
what the U.S. Army Air Force considers the worst "mauling" they encountered during the war – in fact, in their history. It is often referred to now as
"Black Thursday." While a number of accounts provide detailed records of
the event, a short summary and some detailed narrative for the book *Black
Thursday*, give a chilling view of the life and death drama of a bombing raid.
I briefly recount the main details.

So now, here is the rest of the story.

Memories

Important among the documents I received after Elaine's death were handwritten notes and RCAF jewlery from Jim, a rather large scrapbook with
memorabilia and scores of news items of friends joining the forces or reported missing or dead, the one letter Elaine wrote to Jim that was returned
unopened, several pieces of related correspondence, and items collected
during and following the war from returning military. One of the most important was Elaine's diary.

Elaine's Diary and Notes

In addition to letters exchanged between them, Elaine left a record of her
love affair with Jim in a number of ways. Her daily diary covers the period
August 3, 1936 through December 7, 1940, and begins frequent references
to Jim starting in 1939. I excerpted highlights related to Jim (beginning with
the somewhat rocky first references) and other men of interest to Elaine
and women to Jim. Both ultimately replaced these other interests with af-
fection for each other. It appears that they meet in 1936, if not before, likely
at Cedar Springs, where both families had cottages. By 1938, there were occasional references to Jim, and by 1939, there is almost daily entries related
to Jim calling, having dinner, playing tennis, skating, swimming, and dates.
Elaine graduated from High School in 1940, and as her diary makes clear,
she and Jim had been testing their love for each other for several years, and
dating exclusively for more than a year. Jim confessed his love for Elaine on
April 1, 1939.

Elaine Ellis' high
school graduation

April 1, 1939.

I have never mentioned love to you
Since that time that I proved untrue
I have never dared till now
To tell you just how
Much I like you, in three small
Words, you can be sure I wont recall
And those little words are "I Love You".

        I have written things
before that I have been sorry for afterwards and you may have seen some
of them but I honestly mean this, no
matter what your thoughts are of me,
so please believe me. You may think
it funny but I'm sure I dont and if
you think it is, then at least I have
amused you.

Jim's first love letter to Elaine

I added some key dates related to WW II illustrating the growing world tensions that must have, at the time, seemed very remote to the concerns of these young Canadians. Adolph Hitler became Chancellor of Germany in September 1933, and soon consolidated his power as the Fürher (Leader) and touched off the events that would lead to WW II. By 1936, just as high school student Elaine Ellis starts her diary, Hitler had re-armed Germany with the aim of undoing the Treaty of Versailles, uniting the German people, and invading the rest of Europe and Russia to create "living space" for Germany.

1936

June 29	*Went for a ride at night. Bill likes me.*
July 19	*Jim is very much interested in Claire.*
August 1	*... danced about twice with Cliff*
	... Escorted home by Bill and Jim. Cliff's mad at me.
August 4	*Lenore is on a campaign to get Jim back.*
August 6	*... Jim danced with me all night.*
September 22	*... had first art lesson.*
September 14	*Saw Jim Keenan. Jim thinks I'm swell.*
October, 13	*Jack called. He doesn't think I should keep the 2ⁿᵈ Commandment: "Thou shalt not kiss a boy more than twice in a night."*
November 2	*There were 8 boys in my cards for this winter. I am going to do 8 things this winter where I am going to enjoy myself very much (dances, etc.)*
November 3	*Jack called. Everything ok. Didn't know before I liked him so much.*
September 20	*Jim Keenan came down after school.*

1938

January 29	*Jim gave me his decision* [unsure what this references].

MARCH 1938 ANSCHLUS: THE GERMAN ARMY OCCUPIES AUSTRIA AND PROCLAIMS UNION WITH GERMANY.

July 10	*Jim was up this afternoon. Went swimming.*
August 29	*Jim is A1!*

September 2   *Went with Jim to get our fortunes told. I am very undecided*
              ... two boys ... Don't know which I like.

SEPTEMBER 1938 MUNICH AGREEMENT: BRITAIN, FRANCE AND
ITALY SIGN TREATY GIVING GERMANY THE SUDETENLAND (THE
GERMAN POPULATED BORDERLANDS OF CZECHOSLAVAKIA). BRIT-
ISH PRIME MINISTER NEVILLE CHAMBERLAIN DECLARES: "PEACE
FOR OUR TIME."

September 30   *... talked with June. She told me plenty about Jim.*
               He sure has a line.

October 10   *I wish Jim hadn't said what he did. I was O.K. until*
               I read the note ... I still like him.

October 11   *... she [Peg] thinks she would like to go with someone else.*
               Says "it" sort of died away on her part in the summer. If
               she had the chance she would go out with someone else.
               She thinks Jim sort of takes her for granted. Doesn't like
               him to be always on her tail.

October 16   *From what Jack says, Jim seems to think I still have my*
               finger in his pie. Talk about conceit.

November 11   *Jim thinks Peg's through with him.*

NOVEMBER 1938 CRYSTAL NIGHT: 7,500 JEWISH SHOPS DE-
STROYED, 400 SYNAGOGUES BURNT, ORGANIZED BY THE NAZI PAR-
TY WHO ALSO KILL MANY JEWS AND SEND 20,000 TO CONCENTRA-
TION CAMPS.

December 8   *Something tells me I don't like Jim so much.*

December 9   *Jim asked Peg before me and she didn't give a definite*
               answer. Jim had to tell her he asked someone else.
               Did I feel small.

December 16   *Jim didn't dance with me once. He took Peg home.*
               I bet my shirt he told her lots of stuff.

December 29   *Jim and I went skating this afternoon.*

December 30   *Jim hasn't seen Peg since last Club meeting although he*
               gave here a box of candy for Christmas.

1939

February 5	*Jim ... wishes he hadn't given me that note.*
April 14	*Jim asked me to the spring Festival. Jim and I had a sundae in Wood's.*
July 8	*Jim Keenan [came for] breakfast, stayed for dinner and supper.*
August 3	*Jim gave me a lovely set of bookends.*

1939 BLITZKRIEG (LIGHTNING WAR): HITLER INVADES POLAND AND COUNTRY IS DIVIDED BETWEEN RUSSIA AND GERMANY. (BASED ON THE "MOLOTOV-RIBBENTROP PACT" BETWEEN RUSSIA AND GERMANY).
ENGLAND AND FRANCE DECLARE WAR SEPTEMBER 1.
CANADA DECLARS WAR SEPTEMBER 10. APPROVED BY PARLIAMENT ON SEPTEMBER 9. VINCENT MASSEY, HIGH COMMISSIONER FOR CANADA, PRESENTS DECLARATION TO KING GEORGE FOR SIGNATURE.

September 21	*Lenore says JK likes me. I like him too.*
September 10	*Jim seemed so pleased to see me. Canada declared war.*
September 26	*Jim asked me to a show ... we walked ½ the way home.*
October 8	*Jim and I went to the midnight show. "The Women."* *Norma Shearer, Paulette Goddard, Rosaline Russell.*
December 15	*Jim and I went to the Charity Ball at the Cathedral.*
December 25	*Jim, Mom and I went to midnight mass. Jim came for supper.*

1940 OCCUPATION OF EUROPE: GERMANY, IN RAPID SUCCESSION, OCCUPIES DENMARK, NORWAY, BELGUIM, FRANCE AND INVADES ROMANIA AND YOGOSLAVIA.

April 25	*Jim and I went on a scavenger hunt.*
May 29	*Graduation, Jim [gave me] a pen and pencil set.*
July 15	*Sent a letter to Jim.*
July 16	*Still don't know when Jim is coming home.*
July 7	*Jim & Bernice [Jim's sister] ... here for dinner.*
August 11	*Jim sat with us in church.*

September 2   *Jim and I went to Toronto. Danced to Sammy Kay.*
                Had dinner at Martin's.
November 8   *Jim and I went to see North West Mounted Police.*

WWII. EMBROILING THE ENTIRE WORLD, THE WAR WOULD CLAIM
SOMEWHERE BETWEEN 70 AND 80 MILLION LIVES, OF WHICH SOME
60% WERE CIVILANS. GERMANY SURRENDERED ON MAY 7, 1945
AND JAPAN ON AUGUST 15, 1945.

Elaine's diary ends on December 7, 1940, one year before the Japanese
bombed Pearl Harbor. Jim Keenan, now engaged, volunteered, and joined
the RCAF on 1 July, 1942. He was activated for initial training in Canada
on 5 May, 1943 and shipped out to England on 3 August, 1943, and was
ultimately posted to the RAF 106 Squadron, Metheringham, where he was
made a tail gunner and completed his training. He became "operational" on
16 April, 1944. Schweinfurt was his 3rd mission.

In addition to the diary, Elaine effects contained several other notes and
letters that provide some insight into her relationship with Jim. It appears
that Jim's talent extended beyond art to include poetry as well. Unfortunately the poem was undated.

"Return to Sender"

As described in Part I, following the war, Elaine burned all of the letters she received from Jim. She told me that she did it because she needed to restart her life. I can only surmise, however, that there must have been some strong attachment to them because, before burning, she transcribed them all. And thankfully she did, because we have a compelling record of this wonderful man.

As we can tell from his letters to her, Elaine was equally faithful in writing to Jim.

If a letter from home arrived for an airmen already reported missing or dead, it was returned to the sender unopened. One such letter was returned to Elaine and was found among the belongings she left for me.

Following the war regulations of time, Elaine's letters were handwritten on flimsy blue folding paper that did double-duty as the envelope. She crammed as much as possible into the available space. The returned letter is reproduced below, in segments, as the folds required the reader to twist and turn the actual paper.

Note the sticker and stamped indication that Jim was reported missing. If it was returned to her before she was officially notified that he was missing, it must have been a shock. If it arrived after, it must have been another painful reminder of his death. Also note that it was letter #172 (both on the outside corner), indicating the order the letter was written. This was necessary because letters often arrived "out of order" due to the vagaries of the delivery during war conditions. As Jim had been in England less than a year, Elaine must have written nearly every day. Note this letter was written just a few days before Jim died. A typed version of the letter is included as written one is difficult to read. I have added brief explanations where appropriate.

Monday, April 24/44   *#172*
Dear Jim

Guess what I saw today – a Lancaster or three. They were flying over the city about 12:45 in connection with the V. Loan. Did they ever make a racket! Everyone was at the doors watching them & it was a thrill just to see them looming across the sky. How I wish I could fly in one of those. Someone said they would be flown overseas as soon as they were finished here & do you know if someone had offered me the chance I would have dropped everything and come along. I hope they have airplanes for cars in our times as I know I would like to fly one. There was a Mosquito [RCAF fighter] over Saturday but I didn't see it. They sure go fast don't they.

Your mother had a letter this morning telling her you were able to buy a camera in London. Mom had already mailed your parcel [a camera] & we called up Mr. Gill but it had already been taken up to the main Post Office & there was no possible chance of getting it. You will have to decide what you wish to do about it. You might as well keep the one you have right now because you have all the film but I wouldn't want you to sell the one I sent because I like it. You could send it home again & I would pay for it. However try it out & see how it works but please don't sell either of them until I know what you intend doing. Perhaps it would be a good idea to use your 828 films up & then sell the one and keep the other. Let me know what you think about it darling.

Rob [Elaine's brother] is taking Ruth to the Spring Fiesta tonight. Remember when we used to go? And the drawing you used to do for it. I sure hope you can get into that work when you come home.

I wish I could do something; I feel so useless just sitting here day after day. It would be wonderful to have a job [she did eventually as a teller at the Royal Bank of Canada] you liked doing & to enjoy your work. The trouble with me is I am not sure what I would like to do & probably would not be capable. I am a Jack of all trades & master of none. It must be wonderful to be brilliant & be able to use your brains.

If God will just give me the chance I shall do my best to make a successful marriage & for that I shall accomplish something at least. Right now I feel as though my life is a horrible waste & that bothers me. That is all for now sweetheart. Please return soon so I can begin my great career.

XXXXXXXXOOOOOOO

All my love Elaine

Not Returned to Sender

The RCAF most often did not "return to sender" packages that arrived after the airman was reported dead. Instead, they distributed the package contents to other airmen, and wrote to the sender explaining the process. Elaine received five such letters over the course of the next several months. Most were addressed to her, or the Ellis family. Frequently the airman receiving the package would write a thank you. Several such letters were in Elaine's effects.

Quote;13-17 Aux.

ROYAL CANADIAN AIR FORCE
OVERSEAS HEADQUARTERS

20. LINCOLN'S INN FIELDS.
LONDON, W.C.2.

27th June 1944.

Dear Miss M.Ellis,

Re: Tobacco Parcel M4A 79794 addressed to
Sgt.Keenan J.P., R.173638.

The above noted parcel unfortunately arrived in the United Kingdom too late to be delivered to the addressee, and therefore the Canadian Overseas Postal Depot has forwarded it to this Headquarters for disposal.

Gift cigarettes which are sold in Canada less the Customs and Excise taxes, and which are admitted to this country duty free when intended for a member of any of the three Services, cannot be returned to the sender at home when the parcel fails of delivery. In the R.C.A.F. these cigarettes are distributed to hospitalized Canadian airmen and to aircrew returning from operations, and this has been done with the parcel sent by you.

It is disappointing that the parcel could not be delivered as you originally intended but it may be a consolation to you to know that your kindness has brought pleasure to other Canadians of the R.C.A.F. serving overseas. I trust that you will approve of the action taken.

Yours sincerely,

(L. S. Breadner) Air Marshal,
Air Officer Commanding-in-Chief.

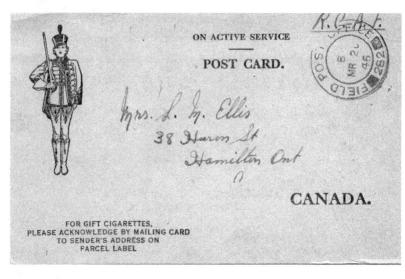

ON ACTIVE SERVICE
POST CARD.

Mrs. L. M. Ellis
38 Huron St
Hamilton Ont

CANADA.

FOR GIFT CIGARETTES,
PLEASE ACKNOWLEDGE BY MAILING CARD
TO SENDER'S ADDRESS ON
PARCEL LABEL

Mar 19/45

Dear Friend
        Recieved carton of cigarettes which are greatly
appriciated and enjoyed so I say thanks a lot keeping fine
hoping this finds everyone there in good health. also hope
business is good that the breaks are with you and not
against you. I am going on seven day leave starting Thurs
Mar 22 nd going to Scotland. They are keeping us quite busy
but will be glad to see Canada again the sooner the better
Well thanks so much for the cigs also for thinking of me
                                    Sincerly
                                    Bill Campbell
                                    RCAF Oversea

Elaine's "Remarks"

Among the items I found in the material Elaine left for me was this single sheet of paper noting her "remarks" on hearing of the invasion in Normandy on June 6, 1944. It is reproduced below. Although the invasion took place only a few months after Jim's death, I was struck by the deterioration of Elaine's handwriting. Without being overly dramatic, I couldn't help but think that the artist in Elaine had lost more than her sense of colour.

Elaine's Mementos

Elaine was what we might refer to today as a "pack rat" or even a hoarder. It was evident that Elaine seemed intent on keeping most everything she had room to store. Among her things was large scrap book with some 60 pages of clippings detailing events with invitations, pamphlets and news items about local Hamilton servicemen, including commissions, marriages and of course notifications of missing in action and deaths, including Jim's.

There are far too many items to reproduce here, but a few were notable and are included below.

Jim's High School Pin

It was common during the war for servicemen to buy pin's or other jewelry for loved ones. These is one of the pins and the bracelet Jim gave Elaine for Christmas, 1942.

BELIEVED KILLED—Mr. and Mrs. J. C. Porter, 63 Fairholt road south, were notified officially to-day that their son, Pilot Officer C. James Porter, R.C.A.F., previously reported missing, must now be believed to have been killed last May 9. Two brothers are serving in the air force.

PRESUMED DEAD — Pilot Officer (navigator) C. J. Porter, son of Mr. and Mrs. C. J. Porter, 63 Fairholt road south, and who was reported missing in May, this year, is now presumed to have lost his life on a bombing foray May 9. He was 22 years old, a graduate of Central collegiate and had been on operations overseas for many months. Intensive raids in which Pilot Officer Porter took part heralded the coming of terrific assaults upon Cologne, Essen and other important targets in industrial Germany during June of this year. Two brothers are serving in the R.C.A.F.

C. James Porter was among Elaine's friends and was often mentioned in Elaine's diary from before the war.

SECOND OF SIX BROTHERS LOST FIGHTING ENEMY

Sgt. Arthur Warnick Is Killed One Year After Death of Flight-Sgt. Eugene

Four Other Sons Are Members of R. C. A. F. and Keep Family Record High

A little over a year ago, six sons of Mr. and Mrs. W. J. Warnick, 133 Stinson street, served with the air force in every quarter of the globe. There were four pilots, a flying instructor and a flight engineer.

Last July, Flight-Sgt. Eugene Warnick, pilot of an R.A.F. bomber, was lost on a raid over Germany. To-day, the youngest of the brothers, Sgt. (flight engineer) Arthur Warnick, is reported to have been killed in a raid on the Continent early in July. He was reported missing July 6, but his death is confirmed in a message just received through the International Red Cross Society.

The splendid record of family service—once unsurpassed in the R.C.A.F.—shines even more bril-liantly to-day. Four brothers, three of them pilots and one a flying instructor, carry on the struggle in which two younger brothers have given their lives.

Twenty Years Old

Sgt. (flight engineer) Arthur Warnick was 20 years of age. He attended St. Patrick's school and Westdale Collegiate and was a life-long member of St. Patrick's Church.

In January, 1941, he left school to enlist in the R.C.A.F., and was in the second class of engine mechanics at the Galt Aircraft School. After advanced training at Camp Borden he went overseas in October, 1941. In the fall of 1942 he remustered to aircrew and after special training was awarded his wing as a flight engineer, in March, this year.

Writing to his parents a few weeks ago, he described a meeting overseas with his brother, Sgt.-Pilot James Warnick, recently arrived in Britain, and four other Hamilton boys whom he had known at school: They were William Hickey, George Christopher, Stanley Morris and David Munroe. The boys were photographed together and had prints sent home to their parents.

Sgt. (Flight Engineer) Warnick leaves, besides his parents, two sisters, Mrs. Leo Moore, of New York, and Miss Lillian Warnick, at home; and five brothers, Flying Officer Paul Warnick, No. 6 I.T.S., Toronto; W. Maurice Warnick, of Hamilton; Sgt.-Pilot James Warnick, overseas; L.A.C. Joseph Warnick, now taking his pilot's course at Centralia, and Warrant Officer Ambrose Warnick, a fighter pilot stationed in India.

Among Elaine's friends, this family lost more than most.

Sgt. James P. Keenan Killed in Action

Sgt. (wireless air-gunner) James P. Keenan, son of Mr. and Mrs. J. G. Keenan, 657½ Barton street east, and who previously was reported missing, is now reported to have been killed in action on a bombing raid. His remains were interred at Chaurfort, France, according to a wire to his parents from the director of records, Ottawa.

Sgt. Keenan

Sgt. Keenan attended St. Bridget's School and Cathedral High School and took a commercial course at Hamilton Technical Institute. At the time of his enlistment he was employed by the National Steel Car Corporation. He was a member of St. Ann's Church and the C.Y.O. there.

Surviving, besides her parents, are two brothers. Sgt. (wireless air-gunner) John J. Keenan and George, at home, and one sister, Miss Bernice Keenan.

SEPT. 23/44

HAMILTON AIRMAN REPORTED KILLED, SECOND IS MISSING

Nov. 22/43

Flt. - Sgt. Mayo Gives Life — Sgt. Crawford Fails to Return From Operations

Flt.-Sgt. Mayo   Sgt. Crawford

One local airman is reported killed and another missing in messages received by next-of-kin over the week-end. Flight-Sgt. William James Mayo, 136 Bay street south, is reported killed on active service in England. Sgt. (air gunner) John J. Crawford, 754 King street west, is reported missing on air operations.

Flight-Sgt. Mayo was the only son of Mr. and Mrs. William Mayo, this city. His wife resides in Toronto. He attended Central Collegiate and Pickering College, Newmarket, and at the time of his enlistment was employed by Cosmos Imperial Mills, Ltd.

He enlisted in January, 1942, and graduated as an air bomber at St. Johns, Que., in December, 1942. Some weeks ago, while returning from a raid on the Continent, his aircraft was forced down into the (Continued on page 11, column 5)

(Continued from page 7) North Sea, but he was rescued by Royal Navy units.

The casualties officer advised that burial was in Regional Cemetery, Cambridgeshire. Besides his wife and parents he leaves three sisters, Mrs. J. A. Cates, Cooksville; Mrs. H. V. Carter, Burlington, and Mrs. F. R. MacDonald, this city.

Sgt. Crawford is the son of Stanley Crawford and the late Mrs. Crawford. His wife is the former Yvonne Downie, of York. He attended Westdale Technical School and was employed at the west end Westinghouse and at the Pratt and Whitney plant, Dundas, before enlistment. He had been overseas since July.

PRISONER—Flying Officer Sydney Alfred Sinclair, son of Mr. and Mrs. John Sinclair, 196 Cannon street east, and who was reported missing on air operations overseas, is reported now to be a prisoner of war in Germany.

Elaine's scrapbook contained more than 60 pages with clippings about friends commissioned, missing, captured or killed.

Escape: Warrant Officer George Collins, Navigator R160042

While this book is about the letters Jim Keenan wrote to Elaine Ellis, it is also very much the story of the shooting down of Lancaster 850. As described in Part I, two other young Canadians, Air Bomber Henry Peebles and Mid-Upper Gunner John Moffat were killed and are buried in the Chauffourt cemetery along side Jim. There were four crew members who escaped: Pilot Gordon Fraser, Flight Engineer Dennis Simpson, Wireless Operator Alex Mackenzie, and George Collins, the Navigator. As it turns out, the escapee's story is very compelling as well.

As described earlier, in my quest to learn the story of Jim Keenan and his last raid, I never found either Dennis Simpson or Alex Mackenzie, and while I did locate Gordon Fraser, the Captain, it was just months after his death. Other than George Collins, I have never been able to contact the families of these men.

My wife Susan, through diligent searching, did find George Collins. We travelled to Canada yet again, and met George and his second wife, Ann. While Ann was quite healthy and full of life, George had obviously been in very bad health. He was only able to give us the barest information about the raid on Schweinfurt; he was struggling to remember many of the details. George also seemed to have difficulty standing. Later in his reading his notes, I discovered why. His feet were badly damaged in his jump from the Lancaster. Many of the effects of the war clearly last a lifetime.

Our meeting with George and Ann was brief, but was well worth it. Ann had meet George well after the war, and knew some of the story. More importantly, George had written, but never formally published his war experiences, with particular emphasis on his escape from the Lancaster and meeting with the French Resistance. Ann gave us a copy.

Not many months after our visit, we received a note from Ann informing us of George's passing. Given the typical age of the Bomber Command crews, and the years since the downing of the plane, I expect that George was likely the last of the crew to pass into history.

Fortunately, Ann gave us permission to tell George's story in his own words. His description of the escape from Lancaster 850, and subsequently from France are excerpted below.

It should be noted that despite the harrowing experiences, this was not the end of the war for George. After returning from France, via Switzerland (a trip that was to take many months), he was sent to India where he served for the balance of the war.

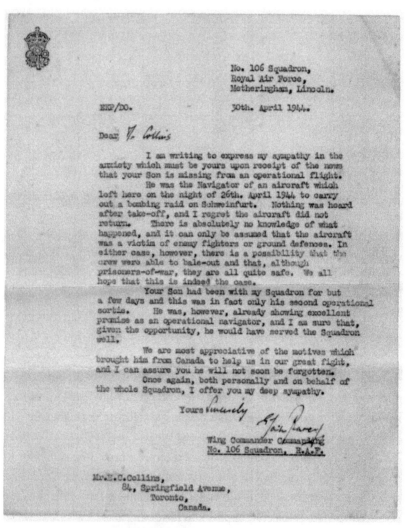

George Collins was originally thought to have been missing.

George A Collins was born in 1932 and raised in Toronto. While in high school he began a life-long interest in technology, excelling in subjects such as math and physics, and as a hobby, built radios, one strong enough to listen to German broadcasts. While attending college, he volunteered in 1942, and spent the next three years with the RCAF/RAF as an operational navigator in Europe and South-East Asia (until October 23, 1945). After the war, he returned to school, completing an undergraduate degree in mining and engineering geology from the University of Toronto in 1946, followed by a Diploma from the Imperial College, London, and a M.Sc. in Geology from the Washington University, St. Louis, Missouri. After a decade of professional experience in Canada, Colombia, and Jamaica, he returned to Washington University and obtained a Ph.D. in Applied Geochemistry in 1960. He later mapped mines in Canada and in several countries around the world, including those in South and Central America and Africa. He also taught economics and mining geology in Canada, Ghana and Thailand. Ultimately, he settled on a small farm in Ontario, coincidentally, not far from Hamilton, the home of Jim Keenan and Elaine Ellis.

On his enlistment, he was given physical and mental tests and assigned for either pilot or navigator training. Ultimately selected as a navigator, he studied "compass, radio, maps, charts, reconnaissance, codes, plotting astro – sextant, stars, loop bearings, astro-compass."

His training took him to various training centers in Canada, the U.S. and Scotland. Perhaps foreshadowing his stealth in avoiding capture, he notes in his remembrances that during sailing to from Canada to England, he was assigned to sleep "in a room with 15 bunks in vertical rows of three. I discovered a steward's cupboard that was unused and locked from the inside. That was where I slept in luxury alone, on a shelf with blankets and pillows."

On completion of his training, he was assigned to Bomber Command, 106 Squadron, in Metheringham, England. After more training, he made his first operation flight to bomb Munich. On the return trip they ran short of fuel and had to land at a RAF base closer to the coast and wait for hours for more fuel to return home to Metheringham.

Clearly, however, the most important event of his war experience was being shot down in the Haute-Marne area of France on 27 April, 1944, on the way to bomb the bearing factories of Schweinfurt, Germany. What follows are excerpts from the written memories of the his first operational flight and, on his second, the escape from the Lancaster, and as he wrote, "the horrors of survival and walking to Switzerland after evasion of capture."

At first he thought he was alone, but noted: *"Pilot and navigator survived the aircraft in flames with fused bomb release cables. Engineer Simpson stole a bicycle and peddled to Switzerland in an RAF uniform."* At one point the French resistance hid three of the airman together. These memoirs by Collins correct some of the incomplete and incorrect information I was given in writing Part I.

Collins notes included three sets of remembrances. Two were shorter, and incomplete, so I have added parts of one memoir to another for continuity. Where possible, I have identified the acronyms, jargon and unfamiliar terms following their first mention. Many of them, however, were not identifiable:

"After the cross-country trips learning to operate new navigation equipment the crew appeared on an "Order of Battle." [to bomb Munich] *It sounds very scary but I can assure you - just another long trip. I couldn't bring my mind to parallel the danger. I didn't get identity tags. We did a Daily Inspection and an N.F.T., a spot of bombing, lunch, then sleep. I scrounged a new oxygen mask from stores. Five o'clock brought tea, then briefing. Cracky,* [British expression meaning something like "Yikes"] *one first trip, ten hours. Straight to work: charts to be drawn up, measurements to be made. An hours work. Then I broke the news to our gunners. Nine hours in a cramped turret, from sunset till dawn, cold with life depending on eyesight.*

Had no chance to see the crew in the Room. The winds [Officers] *came through from Group* [headquarters] *and "Geo"* [George Collins referring to himself] *was busy.*

With the help of the officer in charge of navigation we struggled through the flight plan, Lincoln, Cherbourg, Pons, SW Paris, Lake Annecy, NW Milan, then target.

Airborne – plenty of work to --- to height. Reading up at 15,000 ft. A quick thought of London to the east. With the pack we crossed to France – to starboard of track over Caen. Set course for position near Orleans. Gee [radar] *went near Paris – no Gen.* [information; either good: "pukka gen"; or bad: "duff gen"] *on XF frequency - tried H2S* [early airborne centimetric radar, or "How To See," or "hydrogen sulphide" implying the system "stinks"] *according to the two most popular legends. No dice. Bags of D.R.* [dead reckoning, navigation based on intended track, airspeed and time modified by wind speed and direction] *with B/C winds. Bearings off spot fires. Position definite, a/c for next position. Plenty of comment of the scenery. Mt. Blanc to port, snowcapped. Gunners continually answering questions. OK Jim* [Tail Gunner Jim Keenan]. *OK Don* [Mid-Upper Gunner Donald Moffat]. *Gordon's* [Pilot Gordon Fraser] *trim firm and its all manual from here home.*

A little panic when we couldn't see line of flight markers to position E.T.A. Things started to happen now. Sl's to port – no T.I. Marker [Target Indicator Marker, colored pyrotechnic devices dropped by Pathfinder Forces or lead aircraft to identify targets] *goes down. Run in – fighters SL flack – a deep breath plenty of corkscrews and A/S – loads of comment – I didn't look out!*

Across target at over 200 mph mark. Bombs gone steady for 60 seconds. A minute later I put down timer on target and started A.P.I. Bags of H2S to pass Augsburg. Don reported fighter standing off at spot out of range. Combat maneuvers – shoot it off. Clear of s/l. Dennis [Flight Engineer Dennis Simpson] *is putting more than window down the chute. Homeward bound. DR with A.P.I. and B.C. winds. Easing to Port.*

Did some work with [undecipherable] *turned out duff, passed Paris on wrong side – Gee fix near Dieppe. Crossed coast at 300 mph in shallow dive. In channel – standing by. Gas low. Go for home. Drifting to port, no idea – landed short of satellite of Market Harbour.*

Waited all morning for 100 octane gas. Back at base at 4.30 pm. Sleep, rest, went to dance at Mess. Planned to sleep at night.

Fun at party, a riot with Ma and gang. Dancing, drinking. Up early next morning for DI and N.F.T. of a new kite [airplane] *that we were to use.*

Wrote Jem [or Jimmie, his girlfriend during the war and later his first wife]. *What was to be the last letter for some weeks – what did I say?*

April 26 -27
At 4.30 pm cleared up letters, burned some – put bandage in pocket. Was very careful about things.

Briefing at six o'clock for target. We were to fly "rear Charlie" [last plane in the formation] *low kite black at 15,000 ft. to target. Wind was shifting and increasing on heading.*

Briefings – Schweinfurt
Remember if you navigate.
1. *Use coloured pencils.*
2. *You can use Gee strobes where B for C and C for B.*
3. *Slow down and think*
4. *Remember V.S.C. gives you unaccountable drift if not adjusted correctly.*

5. *Most of your troubles are compass not A/S. check with pilot.*
6. *Don't continue A/P after a turn of over 30 degrees. If you can get a fix.*
7. *Study lakes for H2S, you can use them if you know them.*
    Know Europe, Coasts, Rivers, Cities, Lakes, Defences
8. *Don't use Astic over continent.*
9. *Remember in this order Compass, Airspeed, Windshifts*

At about eight o'clock was working on "flight plan," rest of crew go to kite. I was to follow just before take-off. It was daylight setting course over Lincolnshire without main force. Reading little head of MTA. Dog-leg didn't want to cross coast of France in daylight. Coast of England. English Channel. Coast of France. Slightly port of track. Near Le Havre a/c [or A/C, aircraft] for Cherbourg, enemy territory. Gee fixes to Paris. No H2S fix. Mac working special equipment. Gunners fixed for search. Gee strobe controls go for count. Track lines OK.

Don reports A/C with twin fins and rudders. "not a fighter." Banking search. A/C to maintain track. Langre working on ETA turn. Bash! Boom as if some-one had jumped on floor first with hobnails. Reports of engine failures and fires in bomb bays and main plane. Tried to release bombs near my position. Damn hot! Mac [Wireless Operator Alex Mackenzie] *handed parachute after a/c went west* [presumably this was the Messerschmitt Bf 110 flown by Luft-waffe Grouppenkommander Martin Drewes].

Abandon aircraft.

Moved to front of kite after fixing emergency escape kit in sweater. Attached chute. Bombardier's chute opens in kite. Engineer had left. Hatch jammed at opening. Wriggled through. Chest packs caught finally though minus socks and shoes that went with the slip-stream [the rush of air outside the aircraft].

12:45 midnight. Passed through escape hatch in the nose of the Lancaster, feet first and, as my body wedged, the parachute attached to my chest would not allow me to free past exit. My shoes [were] *torn off in the two hundreds mile-an-hour slip-stream and about that time I figured my legs were also going. Probably ten seconds later I was away of the aircraft minus socks and shoes. Automati-cally I pulled the ripcord in what was now a morgue silence. What a horrible sensation, devilish silence while a huge ball of flame smashed like a meteor on the ground a dozen miles away.*

27.4.1944. 01.00. left aircraft.

Stillness, screaming would have been a relief. My feet were freezing. My chute was ill adjusted and causing a lot of discomfort. I was looking into the black for a spot to land. I couldn't imagine a comfortable landing on the top of a pole or church steeple. A long time passed. I must have opened at about 10,000 ft. - bumps. Hell there it was, terra firma, wet cold earth, a ploughed field. The books say that is the best place to land, but falling on one's back has no future for the spine. The chute was released and pulled into a heap.

Langre – France – south west of a fair-sized town in valley with road fifty feet away. Back twisted in hatch – bad shape. Ate energy pills to get strength to bury chute. Had chocolate. Rested. 0200. Moved up slope to a wooded hill.

Pain grew, my back was worse. I crawled about ten yards to a hedge and went to work on my escape aids with my teeth, my hands were frozen. There was a need for stimulant capsules or I was going to have to pack it in for the duration.

Noise became frequent. Dogs howling and church bells clashing out the quarter hours. Swallowed the capsules, ate a bar of chocolate and started chewing a wad of gum. I watched the searchlights of what I figured was bong – somebody *must be struggling over there.*

Inflated my mae west [or mae, an inflatable life vest worn over flying suit so named because when inflated it made one look like the "pigeon breasted" movie star] *and funny hat. I pulled the silk of the parachute around my feet and legs, they were frozen, and tried to sleep.*

0200 – 0500. Slept in Mae West, cold, damp. Had to sleep. Sunrise, walked 0530 – 0540. Spotted lonely, vacant farm house. Slept in barn 0700. Went out into fields to sleep with the sun on my back.

Hadn't the slightest idea if I slept but some time later I got the urge to scout for a better spot before sunrise. I took a double dose of dope. After burying my chute, set off across the field for a hill one hundred yards south.

My feet were bare, the earth was damp, then some twigs and thistles. Caught on to a trail and carried through the woods, past a fork – carried on straight. Went into the bush off the trail a way. Sat down. Inflated old mae again and after I got over the idea of fatigue and cold - ate a couple of melted milk tablets. I snatched 40 winks.

Woke to the grey before the dawn and carried on through the woods on the old heading south. As the light appeared I hit a second trail, placed mae in a hedge and carried on into open country; a farm with a chapel. Sized the place up. No main road, woods. No jerries [British term for Germans].

My back was dictating policy. When I walked up to the rear door (of the farm house), no answer. "NO! NO!" I reckoned, "cannot break in," so went to the hayrack where I waited until the sun got warmer. Then I went back to the trail, seized mae, made slipper out of same and went up on the mound. Sunned my back to get rid of the rheumatic [sic] *that were setting in from the damp and cold.*

Sat in the sun on a woodpile, admiring a couple poly photos of Jimmie and wondering about what, how and when she would get the grim news. Ate Horlicks tablets [a malted milk candy provided to WW II servicemen as part of survival kit]. *Got thoroughly cheesed.*

A little breakfast of tablets when my curiosity was aroused by a noise. A wood chopper? a little thinking, a collaborator wouldn't be hacking wood. I need-

ed help, food, so started off down field towards the noise. I couldn't see the wood-man even though the noise was close so for some crazy reason started whistling the Marseillaise [French National Anthem], as much for my own morale as for a signal.

Whistling the Marseillaise, walked toward the noise. Talked to old man who was panicking. Had a promise of aid and then he walked away.

Kept on the heading for the woodman and finally saw our man, blue shirt, beret and a flock of white hair protruding. My contact. Those last fifty yards, I walked very slowly - I hadn't the slightest idea who was the most nervous. It was freedom or prison for me, and I suppose a grey – blue sweater, blond hair, blue eyes and a limp could mean Jerry! to my friend.

"Je suis RAF" were my first words as I stared into his eyes. "RAF Bomber tombe."

"Ah, oui," said the frightened man. The old joker was 55 and sure had no way of hiding his fright. He walked away after warning me that the aircraft was a mile west and guarded by Jerry. He also promised me help and food and indicated that I was to sit tight.

I propped myself up on the old man's wood pile and tried to sleep in the sun. The snap [photo] of my fiancé took an hour off my endless time; I knew I was safe and all in one piece. Tomorrow Jimmie would get no letter and think that I was busy at the base. The next day still no letter, she would reckon in time or the following day. What a hell that first week must have been, my mind was whirling. It was practically noon and no wood chopper. I walked along the trail as far as into the field but with increasing difficulty. No woodman! One thing kept me on the spot. If he was helping me he was risking his neck. I had nothing to lose.

I spent the afternoon with no water, no food, and waiting for my wood chop-per. I must make a contact before sunset. Wandering out of the woods I began to realize my back was seizing up and I was forced to use a couple of crutches. Things were gradually shaping up to a map. I had landed on a wooded plateau and the side I was approaching had allotments. In a valley I could make out a village enveloped in a heat haze.

Two Frenchmen were spreading fertilizer. They were young. Whistling. I ap-proached them.

"Je suis RAF" I said to the chap dressed in black.

They were frightened and could not or would not answer but only shrugged their shoulders. These two had no future – no capacity to make a decision. I asked where the kite was. No answer.

Walked out to fields, had a chat with young workers. No help. Walked cautiously toward a village at base of hill.

I dammed those chaps. As I wandered away towards the village they stood and watched me struggling. I sat down at the top of the cliff and eyes stared to hunt for German uniforms in the village. Thirsty, hungry, dirty, chilled, I sat watching two young girls water a flock of sheep. I was next at the well. Before I was able to carry out the decision, a cart passed me and I stopped it. In my best French I asked for help.

This was my break! The chap had been a prisoner of war in Germany 1940 – 1943, he knew, he aided. The next five minutes he had me eating and drinking and asking the name of the village. I remember smiling, France had come to my rescue. They asked me my age. The three Frenchmen who had gathered around me were 18, 20, & 22. France of tomorrow, the heart and the way, they helped me back to the shelter of the woods promising to bring aid at sunset. They left me full of confidence. A handshake. Camarade. Resistance to tyranny!

The old morale soared when a squadron of Fortresses crossed overhead. I checked and wondered. Some of them would be in Blighty [England] in three hours.

Suspicious by nature you should have seen me then. The sun was setting. I kept following the rays as they crept out from my spot, I needed that sunshine. I ended up in a small thicket about one hundred feet from the spot where I had been left. This was a precaution in case I been seen. If the "aid" was trailed to the spot, I would have a chance.

My nerves were going. A dog had run out of the woods straight past me, but my heart dropped back on its natural spot when in the next five minutes no Jerries followed.

Twilight brought me my aid. Whisky for my shattered nerves, food for my crumbling body, and clothes to warm my morale. It was cold!

1900-2000. A man, his brother and his 14-year old son came with clothes, food, liquor and gum boots. I was warm for the first time in 18 hours. I was taken to a vacant house next to a German garage. Food was brought – steak, pie, wine and pudding.

Tremendous spiritual aid was the result of my new comrades; the father was a man of 57 who had tested the full of prison camps. His son, sixteen was mature and had an urge to fly with the French Spitfire squadrons in England. This chap's brother in his late twenties was the very heart of France.

I dressed in civvies was led down the hill in the darkness that had fallen. We worked our way through the gardens around huts to a house. We entered through the barn, up into the kitchen to a backroom. I was left alone, they departed promising more food.

The village was very noisy and my ears couldn't get accustomed to solitude. Hammers clanging along steel, motors lorries and cars revving up. God almighty!! Next door a German maintenance garage. The old nerves unraveled into shreds. My mind flashed back, this chap had said he was a driver, a chauffeur for the Germans, a collaborator! I was in a cold sweat. I couldn't rest. I stood back to the wall and beside the door. Women's voices I could hear. A rap at the door. Three women. Another rap. I opened the door.

"Come in." I didn't wait around outside the door. I sweated blood when they turned and ran away. What a thing to happen! They ran across the road and into a house, outside stood a low-built powerful auto! I literally shook as I cursed under the bed. I came out after the reaction. I prepared the window for a quick exit into the barnyard. The house was surrounded by now. Then the door opened. It was useless to leave. I waited for seconds. Then a party entered the room. Four people, my friends, -- "a coward dies a thousand deaths…..!"

Those women were friends, curious friends of mine -- my comrades', wives and sisters. It was a marvelous sensation, easing to talk to friends. I said I wanted papers for Spain. They talked me out of that. The organization had it all planned. Phase one – they had me leaving for the hills just before the sunrise, after promising me a quiet night.

I couldn't sleep! My nerves were keyed to pitch, so drank myself to sleep on red wine. What a night, cold and miserable. I didn't sleep. I rested for many long dreary hours.

In grey – black mist before dawn, my friend came, with food and liquor. He led me up into the rocky hillside into an open cave. He promised me food after sunrise, and then left.

At nine o'clock a chap came, a farm worker. We were to hunt for my para-

chute after breakfast – eggs, bread, jam, and wine, camp style.

My French was drifting back.

All my sense of direction went for a Burton? [air crew expression for getting killed] *I got back to the chapel and then couldn't figure out, or couldn't find the trail I had used. We kept exploring hunches. Couldn't find the chute. I had the awkward sensation of suspecting myself of being unable to convince these people of my nationality. They were happy, so I talked myself into settling down to eat a heavy lunch. A move was to be made at two o'clock.*

My comrades came and I followed them along the top of the plateau for a mile to clear the district. Then we cut towards the road and made contact with a couple of youths on bicycles. I was given a bicycle, said adieu to my friends and we carried on.

My escort started the conversation in very broken English, enquiring about my crew. He had the "gen." Three had been killed in the crash, and the rest were pinpointed and ...was pulling us together. His description of those that cleared the "chopper" was vague. I couldn't get a clear picture of those that had got away with it. The conversation swung to the "invasion." When? I was supposed to know! Assuring them that the war would be over before the summer had turned into snow. A warning was given to me that if the escort up ahead was stopped, I was to take off in the opposite direction ... It was life and death for my friends. Later I found out that this chap, with khaki shirt and Heidelberg haircut and a Parisian education was a "German collaborator." The poor Gestapo efficient was thick.

We stopped, my comrade and I. A whistle. A reply, and then we quickly placed our bicycles in the long grass and doubled back across a cornfield. There sat a youth of France, the future, small in inches but huge in capacity and radiating confidence. There two Frenchmen spoke of my crew. I could make out three were alive and the others had been buried in a small village close by. The organization was weaving a plan for our safety in the midst of Hitler's fortress.

The "petit comarade" [literally, little friend] took me across a field, down a densely wooded valley, suddenly out of the hazel bushes stood a hut, a barrack made of logs, mud and straw. Where and how, many places was this repeated. Did every village a place to hide the "hunted?" One doesn't ask questions, one waits.

One of the buildings near the crash site where the Maquis, the French Underground, hid the escapees

... the evening sleep came easy as a common reaction to a need. Dawn brought food, eggs, bread, and cheese. The farm worker who brought the basket had a cheerful word Heureuse! [Happy] *Then a smile.*

The solitude of the afternoon sun pouring through was broken by two curious little girls at my door. They ran. Blue uniforms and blonde hair meant only trouble. The incident I told to the "Petit Comarade." I would have to move.

0200-1400 comrades came. Gendarme took me on a bicycle to spot outside [village], *stayed in wood. Overnight.*

The next evening I moved to a house in town that was vacant because of being spotted by a couple of young girls. Slept on straw in kitchen of the old house. All the people brought food.

Spent my time wandering from room to room following the sun as it crept around.

Next stop, the house of the cure [priest], *vacant so the RAF needed a spot. Two staff met me, Gord & Mack. I slept on straw, ate like a king, amused myself following the sun as it moved around the house from window to window.*

Each evening I went down with Petit Camarade for supper. He had things taped and was leading the Resistance in those sections. One evening they brought

Gordon and Mac up to stay with me. We spent our day's playing cards and doing a lot of talking about a lot of things. Home. Life. Death. Flying and after the war. Plenty of food. Gordon was a good cook. We kept shaved and clean. I received a suit and some clothes for a trip.

Evening came to mean the arrival of the "Petit Comrade" and I followed him through the closely packed churchyard across the road and into the Local Committee. Brothers, cousins, fathers, the mayor, farmers and the schoolmaster. I was their contact with England. I was supposed to know the date of the invasion, the spot of the attack before summer. Their forgery committee was hot. Passports and work papers. We were to leave tomorrow, by train.

Photo of Gordon taken in garden, we had group taken, should get a copy apres la guerre est finis [after the war is over].

Rode a bicycle ten kilometer to Chalandray and waited in a darkened station office. A window opened on to the platform. Plenty of Wehrmacht [Nazi Germany's military] *around. Was sitting twelve inches from a muzzle of rifle, too close, took a little more time. My heart missed a beat. I had never seen a German soldier in my life. At that moment my eyes were four feet away from the muzzle of a rifle clutched in the hands of an enemy. He had no reason to be suspicious. I drank a glass full of "eau de vivre"* [literally "water of life," but likely a euphemism for wine], *then I had no reason, none to sustain my knees vibrating.*

A bicycle patrol swept past us. Walked up road to a small suburb. Contact in village was broken, walked back to Vesoul. Sun rise on road, past a road to Luftwaffe depot. Those big tall Aryans who haven't a clue. Our escort was going to buy us train tickets for Belfort. We sat on a stone ledge just outside a church. Had a queer idea that every time a shutter opened, we had been spotted. One man came back from the station and we walked up the hill the fields east of town. Had some food. Walked back to town through a park, spotted lots of Germans.

Oh, they look so serious. Had a look at the Blitzmadchen [German women used for used to support Luftwaffe activities]. *Average girls for basic qualities.*

On Sunday afternoon there was a fair in town. As we walked by I was quite shocked. Plenty of metal. Aluminum saucepans as prizes in games.

We were under convoy of a young Frenchman. A train pulled in for our stop. Ran as train was signaling to go. We followed the leader across the tracks, around the engine and hopped on to the train as it started to roll. open doors, there stood

FRITZ. [A German] *No time to waste. Got on. Stood in vestibule with an "un-teroffizier," a lieutenant, a navy type, going on leave or to Russia. We were just low French types. Yes, me with my blonde hair? Our escort was a good type, cool, student, lawyer*

We had hopped into the arms of a German sergeant major. Not altogether a fatherly type, slightly annoyed at "Frenchmen" being allowed on the same train as the "Herrenvolk." [German expression thought to be referring to the "Master Race"] *Those were my impressions. He was most likely tired, going home on furlough, happy and wanting to get home.*

Is this "eine Wehrmacht Zug [German train]*?" some animal breathed at my neck. Did he really suspect an answer from me. Not little me as I slouched into a corner between two walls. Another shot of Burgundy would have made a favourable impression on my nerves but already I was tipsy. How do you think it feels to stand staring at a blank wall and at a blacked-out light for an hour and a half watching out of the corner of one eye a revolver strapped across the chest of a German officer. The urge was to push him out of the door but valour is never associated with escape. There was also a factor – he had more bullets than we had brains, masses to blow out.*

Trains always get were they are going, so we arrived at the Vesoul, off train, got pass to be on street. It was dark, curfew had to be beaten. The escort got an authorization so we all trooped up and went through the motions and to our surprise without a word got papers also. That is France! Strolling up the cobble streets in our Indian fashion, the three of us had feet trouble, a week and no exercise. We stepped across off a curb into the mist of a cycle patrol with no lights, the Wehrmacht missed. I suppose they figured out we were too close to the station. Two miles on foot in front of the last and dawn broke over two big elms and an old chateau. "Captain B."

The answer came from a window. Captain B doesn't live here anymore. The Gestapo got hot just the day before we did. The chain broke, contact lost. Our escort left us to scout by a broken hedge. What was ... .

We made an accidental contact with a Gunman? German? A French army captain from Paris. Made a contact for a ride from Vesoul to Besancon. When we were walking to the outskirts of the town, we saw the gunman, occupation types, hardly "Herrenvolk." We saw the friends of the European new order. Two

Luftwaffe types, one with automatic rifle and one with rifle and revolver. Pleasant types?

Arrive at Besancon.

7.8.5.1944. Stayed the night in the station hotel. Went to bakery on outskirts next day.

8.5.1944. My birthday. Good food, real hospitality.

11.5.1944. Left for Montbilliard by rail. German police were suspicious but gave no questions, we were soaked in champagne. Had a real confident escort, an electrical engineer. Had dinner in a café on the main street of Montbilliard, went to a vacant house to sleep, Germans had wind up [extremely active] in this spot. Guards were back to back.

12.5.1944. Slept in a house with a complete radio set, we now had the wind up. Plenty of contraband tobacco.

12.5.1944. To a spot 2 km from frontier by way of Audincourt. Pont de Roide, St. Hippolyte. At 400 o'clock in the afternoon our closest spot. Germans were searching the house we were going to enter. Stayed in cow pasture and saw the patrol ride away not a hundred yards from us. The next day at noon we started across the frontier with guide. At 1300 hours we were on Suisse soil. 1400 picked up by patrol of frontier guards.

The French-Swiss frontier, southeast of Lake Geneva was crawling with massive Swiss forts – continuous fields of trip wires made out of steel as strong as piano wire and as thick as 3" in diameter. Two RAF airmen chose to move with me, neither one an officer. By train from Montreux-Aigle (Eagle) on Sunday morning on a local train. S.E. in the Swiss military prohibited zone.

… picked up by the Swiss frontier police. We were imprisoned for 90 days in solitary confinement after crossing the 12km mobility zone from France.

The three young men left the train and began to climb a valley into the mine fields, wire, and crossfire zones of the Swiss forts on the high ground. Taking our bearings on the rising moon, our escape group headed to the ridge of the frontier to occupied France. At sunrise we were in F.F.I. [French Forces of the Interior. The French Resistance after the invasion in Normandy] I had calculated they were clearing the Germans to the west on the south shore of Lake Geneva.

If you have never seen it [French-Swiss border area], *it remains incomprehensible!*

1300. 13.5.1944. Frontier post. Saw Germans at frontier post across the border.

Three nights of celebration: three nights of riots. Where the alcohol came from, one never knows?

[Collins begins to learn war news] *Captured Germans occupying troops were tied to telegraph poles and beaten to a pulp. The most blows were to the head and throat. I could not watch. I knew the reason for the beatings: it was for revenge. The Sunday before our jumping out of Switzerland, the Germans had moved the men, women and the children into a church in Evian, France and burnt the wood and the people in reprisal for F.F.I. raid on the W 100 haus for each soldier. A quick swing around Geneva City and down the route to the south coast of France to meet the Texas #1 Division. Moving at 60mph to cut the Germans from the Italians. A target in the German SW zone.*

1700. Ride to Porrentriay. Slept in old castle on straw pile. Ate Suisse army rations, not bad, not good. The "red cross" changed our money and got us necessities. The soldiers are real friends, not very neutral types.

17.5.1944. Olten central depot and clearing for escapees. Trouble! I swung a deal and got a bed in hospital. They wanted to snip our hair. Nichts! [German for No] *Hold out!*

26.5.1944. Got my bath and passed to Basserdorf for rest of quarantine. Missed Dennis [Fight Engineer Dennis Simpson]. *Had fruit, oranges and bananas. Not much of anything. I will be sending loads of letters to my darling. No cash from government yet.*

5.6.1944. Evening. Am moving to Berne tomorrow, had a talk with our French friends who are going with me.

June 6. 0500. Off to Berne, at station we hear news of invasion. Everyone is in a better mood.

1200. Saw Air attache. News all confirmed. Had lunch, got civic [sic] *clothes. St. Gotthard Hotel. Spent evening at Casino. In hotel for police check at 1000 pm.*

9.6.1944. Left Berne with "tex" after sending cable to Jim.

9.6.1944. Gilon Montreax. Bell… Hotel. Met Dennis and got organized on room.

12.6.1944. Swimming in Vevey in Lake Geneva. Waiting for letters.

14.7.1944. Cable to Jimmie. Darling, don't worry. Mail slow. Will cable often. September is near. All my love. Jimmie Harrison. A marvelous relief: had done a little worrying. It has been 76 days.

20.7.1944. Attempt on Hitler's life. Celebrated my Warrant Officer II. Plenty of cash now. Gordon bought a dog.

29.7.1944. Saturday evening. I went to have a walk up the valley towards Les Avant. The moon made the fir trees vivid, black against a silver sky. I had a chance to dream. 1100 DEST. What are you doing Jimmie? Happy life with my Jimmie.

No cable all week. Last Friday I had a quiet rest on a bench then wandered back to the Bellevue Hotel.

George Collins

30.7.1944. Slept late. Wrote up diary.

August, 1944. In the Hotel Caux, Switzerland, in August, in my miniature command post with a huge map of Europe, I sent my final note in pink colour air letter to clear German censor, to London leading my departure, addressed to a very special lady from girls School who was teaching in East London slum schools down buzz bomb alley. [London's East End was very poor and often the target of the German bombers because of its proximity of the docks.]

6.8.1944. Cable from Jimmie for last week. Today news came through of Americans break at Brest. 200 miles in a week. Home for September.

7.8.1944. Two airmail letters from Dad in Canada. Sent May 31 and June 4. A record somewhat. Most of the chaps haven't had any mail.

9.8.1944. Received Jimmie's watch. Very happy. Wrote letter.

10.8.1944. Telegram from Grantham [Jem's home in England] *today. Sent answer. Did a little invest in camera to take home (64 francs). All OK.*

* * * * *

Later in his narrative, Collins describes his return to England, marriage and eventual assignment to the India.

A quick swing around Geneva City and down the route to the south coast of France to meet the Texas #1 division, moving at 60 mph to cut the Germans from the Italians. At target in the SW zone.

Going south with American armies of 5 divisions headed by 6 Texans, with tens of thousands of Free French. [The French military allies that served outside of France during the war]

– on a two lane National French highway in the Rhone Valley.

With quick airlifts from the coast of France at Frejus, the party of three evaders [presumably his crew mates, Fraser and MacKenzie] *were airlifted by South African Air force B25 bombers to Algeria. With no identification, the RAF provost marshal, military police did not buy our story – NAME, RANK AND SERIAL NUMBER.*

The Americans had taken my story as an Eagle, RAF crew from Detroit, Michigan. I switched my story from the truth to fiction to ride to Algeria, Casablanca to Langham, to Wiltshire, RAF on an executive flight from HQ Cairo on

"The bigger the lie, the better!" If the truth does not fit.

Walking around England with a white shirt, a kaki battle blouse and light tropical shorts with French army boots, 5 years old. This is not the best military dress.

I reported to the RAF in some corner of London and was told to get dressed... The RCAF HQ in London yielded information that lead to a branching of my existence. My life was to change.

I married my sweetheart, in the village church in Colsterworth [a village in England] 2 miles from Woolsthorpe, the birthplace of Isaac Newton, near Grantham, Lincolnshire on November 4th, 1944. We honeymooned at the Castle Hotel, Windsor, UK. A very interesting bill for services, £8, 14s, 6d for accommodation which included room service and all meals.

When I reported back to reality, I received a telegram, "P/O [Pilot Officer] G. A. Collins report to operations NE Europe! ...

This was Christmas and New Years 1944-1945. It was cold and bleak on the west coast of England. The sea was in a grey state with wind speed – rolling up the waves...

Interrogation went like this:

"Why do you not want to fly at night?"

"It's dangerous to my health."

I was posted, with 14 days leave (peace) to RAF Crosby-on-Eden transport Command in the coldest corner of NW England. On the 21st January, 1945...

A very old and wise RAF commander assigned me as a Duty officer whose special duty was to bury "smart and young" but inexperienced pilots.

[Ultimately assigned to RAF, India, along with a pilot he flew with in the UK, Collins continues his narrative]

... F/L Foort, [Collins pilot in India] was a dream pilot – this is his third tour of duty, a grey haired survivor. [F/L Foort] occurs on very page of my log book from January 25th to June 1945 in UK, India and Ceylon. Through snow, sand and monsoons and muck, and Collins survived the tropical rains of India and the deserts of the NW [what is now Pakistan]. We wore clean white overalls with full insights and blue hats to match our eyes.

Counting with my fingers, July, August, September – I decide to go to University to study meteorology, the Science of Weather (the soup which I had been *in sand, water and fire!), the logic was I wanted a posting to Toronto, Canada.*

There was no response from the W/C [Wing Commander] but later I found my complexion was yellow with anemia and liver infection. Today they would call it Hepatitis but in India they called it "sandfly fever." W/C had the orderly Sergeant make out an air ticket on a York (Lancaster Transport) to UK. Clutching the ticket, I left the huge doors of the redstone Imp[erial] courtyard only to fall on my face in the dust. Only the good die young. I survived.

I rode out in style in a metal bucket seat from Delhi to United Kingdom in twenty sectors: ... Cairo, Sardinia to the green grass of Blighty – England.

I had a quick fourteen days of matrimonial leave on an ocean voyage to Halifax and a continental trip in a train bunk for Junior Officers to Toronto.

Next demobilization.

Medical Records. My crushed feet were not recorded on my medical files. They hurt so bad, I did not want to take my shoes off because they would just kill me when I had to put my shoes back on.

When one leaves the service, it takes only 20 minutes...

To enter the RAF Service it takes a whole day...

Upon entering the University of Toronto, I took time to sit back and take stock of my life. There was not one person in my family who had been to University let alone completed high school.

I have been hospitalized... I fought with the F.F.I... I fought with crushed feet... was wounded without hospital care... I was dressed in orange strips of rubberized cloth because I had lost my pants in the slip-stream of the blazing Lancaster... I never put my hands above my head to any German superman... I evaded capture... I NEVER SURRENDRED!

* * * * *

The Maquis and the Survivors from Lancaster 850

The Maquis, the rural guerrilla French Resistance, played a key role in winning the war in France. Their story has been told in books and film, but probably not equal to their contribution. Some famous stories exist, but the role of the Resistance in the area where Lancaster 850 was shot down has not been widely told. Fortunately, a book (in French only, and now out of print) covering the story of the Resistance in the Haute-Marne, provides substantial detail on their exploits. The activities of the Resistance leaders near near Chauffourt and Langres, and the support in the escape of the four aviators of Lancaster 850, were briefly documented in the book, and provide enough information for readers to appreciation for the intrigue surrounding the role they played in this drama. I was able to borrow a copy from the library in Montigny-le-Roi, near Chauffourt, in order to learn about the Resistance in the area. What follows are brief excerpts from the book [translated from the French by Fabienne der Hagopian].

La RESISTANCE en Haute-Marne, (The Resistance in Haute-Marne), pgs.114-115, and 210-214, by Domonique Gueniot, imprimeur-éditeur.

[Note: The names in the French text were left as written. I have added brief explanations in brackets where needed]

"A meeting of the areas managers with the colonel (nobody knew his name) was decided for Easter Monday, April 10th, 1944, early afternoon.

It took place at café Jean Vincent, in Pailly, in a secluded back room. In attendance were: Robert Henry for Langres, René Henry for the NE sector, Henri Hutinet for the SE sector and Roger Tavernier for the SW sector.

The division of the Langres arrondissement in four areas was maintained as well as the person in charge of each area. It was even specified that in order to avoid any confusion and incidents, the sector borders had to be respected without any overlap.

The colonel asked that noncommissioned and commissioned officers, and at least one officer per sector with the ranking of captain or commandant, be found in each sector to take charge of the military commandment for the later development of the Maquis (armed combatting resistants living hidden in the wild to avoid all controls from police, hence the name).

The decision was taken to regroup, under the authority of the colonel, all resistance groups of the arrondissement of Langres, whatever organization they belonged to (this unification would soon be called F.F.I.

FFI banner given to George Collins. Savoie refers to the region
of France near the Swiss border.

The main and crucial task of the colonel was to reestablish contact with
the France Combattante (Fighting France) in England: without weapons, it
was pointless to recruit resistants, and the weapons could only come from
the Allies, by connecting with London. The colonel thought he could reig-
nite this connection through the Bourgogne resistance that he would try to
contact through his nephew by marriage,

François de Montaudoin, that he knew to be a member of the Bourgogne resistance, and who was under the command of Colonel Prats, from
Dijon, FFI chief of Region D, which included Haute-Marne.

Lastly, it was decided from this first meeting, that to protect the secre-
cy of the organization, the main managers would take combat names that
would be the only ones used with new recruits, in all written communications, and these written communication would only be sent via bike mes-
sengers, that each area managers needed to recruit.

Robert Henry de Langres took his first name "Robert" as [his] combat
name, Henri Hutinet (who had a fake ID), also took his first name "Henri",
René Henry took the name "Charles", his middle name, Roger Tavernier
already had a combat name, "Raymond" and the colonel, who lived at Saint
Michel, chose the name "Michel". Until the liberation he was only known
as Colonel Michel.

At the end of the meeting, the colonel smiled under his big "poilu 14-

18" moustache (poilu is "old" French for hair and the nickname given to French WWI soldiers who had big moustaches) and took out of his pocket a guide about the Pailly Castle. He had intended to use the alibi that he was giving us a tour of the area if the German police had inquired about our group.

He gave us a lesson of prudence for the clandestine war in which he was investing himself, body and soul. From the beginning, he had our trust as a calm and resolute leader, always keeping the appearance of a quiet, peaceful man.

II. Plane crashed in Chauffour, April 26, 1944, around 10:30pm

Lancaster British aircraft on a mission to bomb Schweinfurt in Germany – hit by a shell from the German FLAK [originally the French assumed that German anti-aircraft artillery downed the plane]. Out of seven members of the crew, three were killed and four were able to jump with parachutes.

a) Georges Collens:

Sergeant Navigator, Canadian from Toronto, speaking a bit of French. Found at dawn on April 27, 1944 by Léon Pelletier, resistant from Chauffourt, who immediately informs René Henry in Orbigny-au-Mont.

In the afternoon of the 27th, Léon Pelletier, preceded by constable Gosselin from Montigny-le-Roi on a bicycle, brings Collens to a small wooden area near Obigny, on a bicycle loaned by Grandvuillemin (cheese maker at Sarrey) who follows at a distance to bring the bike back on his milk truck.

In the morning of April 27, René Henry alerts the city officials of the area to look for the three other survivors. In the evening of the 27, Jules Voillemin sends his daughter Nelly to inform René Henry that two airmen have been found.

b) Gordon Fraser

Lieutenant pilot, English from Liverpool. Taken in by Mme Déchanet in Lannes, then brought to M. Bélime, tax collector in Rolampont, by M. Rom from Rolampont.

c) Alek Mackensie

Sergeant radio operator, English from Glasgow. Found by M. Felix Prautois, road mender at Charmes, in a grove of trees near the place called "

La Goutte". M. Pratois immediately informed the Bresson of his discovery and Alek was brought to their place. His face was bruised since he had fallen in a tree, arms caught in the ropes and at each sway, his face was hitting the tree trunk.

In the afternoon of April 29, Jean Brosser brought Fraser and Mackensie at Auguste Simon, at the first bridge of the Charmes reservoir, in a truck from his tiles factory.

During the night of April 29, René Royer and René Henry took them to Orbigny-au-Mont where they were hidden in the inhabited presbytery where their mate Collens already was. René Royer, Georges Poisot, Louis Messager and Charles Forgeot brought them food and supplies until Mai 6.

After taking their picture, René Henry had fake IDs made by André Dimay from Chaumont who had a seal from the prefecture.

In the mean time, Roger Page, from Hortes, had alerted the Haute-Saône resistance and was preparing their escape to Switzerland.

They departed during the night of May 6: on foot from Orbigny to Chalindrey where they waited for the train in the office of the train station deputy, an Alsacian who had left Alsace when it was annexed to Germany. It happened that this train that should bring them to Vesoul, was packed with German soldiers. With very English phlegm [note how differently George Collins described the train ride], they settled with Roger Page in nearby cars, among Wehrmacht soldiers, and arrived to Vesoul without trouble. From there, another resistance branch took them to Switzerland where they stayed until the East of France was freed.

d) Alcide Simson

Sergeant Airgunner, British. In the morning of April 28, René Henry is informed that André Roy and his brother Raymond, from Montigny-le-Roi have taken in the fourth survivor: Alcide Simson.

After landing near Poinson-lès-Nogent, he had stolen a bike in the village during the night. He had been found in the morning of the 27, by two masons from Montigny (Mathieu Emile et Galissot), near Bonnecourt, and was hidden that day in the house that they were working on. Brought to Montigny, he was entrusted to the Roy Brothers, iron mongers. In the morning of the 28, Raymond Roy drew him a map to go to a friend of his at Audincourt by bike. This friend would bring him to Switzerland. With civilian clothes on top of his uniform of the RAF, Simpson arrived to destination without trouble and ended up with the same branch of the resistance who helped his friends get to Switzerland.

To appease the owner of the bicycle stolen in Poinson, who was being difficult, and avoid a denunciation, André Roy had to buy him a new bike on the black market (he was later reimbursed by the Colonel Michel on the resistance funds).

The resistance network, ready to react according to needs, had just proven its efficiency."

Gordon Fraser and George Collins returned to Chauffourt many years later to attend a memorial service for their three comrades. Note Collins wearing his FFI banner.

Medals

Military medals (often called decorations in some countries) are awards that symbolize heroism, meritorious or outstanding service or achievement. They have been awarded for centuries in almost all countries. In the event of death, the medals are passed to the family, often the mother. British and Commonwealth medals typically consist of a specific colour ribbon, a metal medallion (typically a star or circle), and occasionally a clasp for special recognition. The medals are to be worn on the left breast in the order (left to right) shown below.

Jim Keenan, Henry Peebles and John Moffat were awarded the identical medals. Their mothers were given a Memorial (or Silver) Cross.

1939 – 1945 STAR

The ribbon is dark blue, red and light blue in three equal vertical stripes. The star bears the initials of George VI on the front side, but without anything on the reverse. This medal is worn first, farthest to the right) and with the dark blue stripe furthest from the left shoulder. The 1939–1945 Star is a military campaign medal awarded to British Commonwealth military personnel who served overseas in WW II (between September 3, 1939 and either May 8, 1945 in Europe or September 2, 1945 in the Far East). RCAF crew qualified after 60 days of service in an operational unit, including at least one operational sortie. A Bomber Command clasp was awarded in 2013 to crews who flew in at least one raid.

AIR CREW EUROPE STAR

The ribbon is light blue with black edges and in addition a narrow yellow stripe on either side. The medal has the initials of George IV on the front with no engraving on the reverse. Worn second, the medal was awarded to British Commonwealth aircrews in WW II who flew at least two months in operations over Europe from bases in the United Kingdom, from the outbreak of the war until D-Day (Normandy invasion, June 6, 1944).

DEFENCE MEDAL

The ribbon has a red stripe with green edges, each with a narrow black stripe. The medal has George VI initials on one side and the Royal Arms of England (three lions and crest) on the reverse. Awarded to British Commonwealth subjects for serving at least six months in the U.K.

CANADIAN VOLUNTEER SERVICE MEDAL

The ribbon is green, scarlet, royal blue, scarlet green; each green and scarlet stripe three-sixteenths of an inch wide. The medal is worn with marching figures on the front. The reverse side has the Royal Arms of England. Granted for those who volunteered for active duty in the Canadian Forces from September 1, 1939 to March 1, 1945. A silver bar with Maple Leaf at its centre was awarded for service outside Canada.

WAR MEDAL 1939-45

The ribbon has a narrow central red stripe with a narrow white stripe at either side, with a broad red stripe at either edge, and two intervening blue stripes. The medal has the image of George VI on the front, and on the reverse, a "British" lion walking on dragon. The Bronze Oak Leaf clasp signifies the medal recipient was mentioned in a dispatch or noted for bravery.

MEMORIAL CROSS

The ribbon is purple, the cross has the initials of George VI on the front and the name, rank and service number of the deceased engraved on the back. A crown is at the top of the cross, with a maple leaf at the foot and the end of either arm. Behind the cross is a wreath. This medal, often referred to as the Mothers Medal, was awarded to next of kin, almost always to mothers and widows on the loss of a son or husband in the war. Although it is illegal for anyone to wear a medal other than the service member to whom it was awarded, wives and mothers were allowed to wear the medal any time.

INSIGNIA

Airmen wore various insignia on their uniforms. Jim Keenan wore three Sergeant strips on his arms with a "Canada" bar (or flash) on the shoulder. On the opposite shoulder he wore an air gunner crest. His officer hat badge featured a crown (gold and coloured accents), a gold metal eagle with spread wings, and gold sheaves.

Memorials

The people of Chauffourt have honored and diligently cared for the three Canadian airmen since the Lancaster went down on April 27, 1944 and buried several days later. The care with which they have honoured them gives real meaning to the expression "we will never forget." It began when they defied the Germans and held a formal funeral. Later, at their own initiative and expense, they erected a stone monument at the crash site.

In addition, the people of Chauffourt have staged periodic memorial services. George Collins and Gordon Fraser were able to attend one of periodic ceremonies. As the years have passed, neither them, nor their families were unable to attend. I had the honour (along with my daughter Carrie) to attend the latest event on April 26, 2014 and assumed the role of "unofficial" representative of the airmen and their families. The ceremony had two official parts, a service at the crash site and their gravesite. Representatives of various military units were present, and four national anthems (Canadian, British, U.S. and French) were played along with remarks from various dignitaries. Monsieur Albert Petit, led the formal events. He has been the inspirational and tireless leader of the memorial efforts.

Members of various military units join the Rick Oliver, daughter Carrie Oliver and M. Albert Petit (center)during the 2014 70th Anniversary Ceremony

The formal events were followed by a reception in the town center under a tent. Most of the people of Chauffourt and nearby villages attended. It included some brief toasts and offered an opportunity to meet and talk with a number of local villagers. I had taken several copies of the first edition of the book which I signed for attendees. Some of the older people we had met on our first visit to Chauffourt were unable to attend but I was able to meet with Jean-Luc Legros whose father had hosted us and related much of the story around the downing of the plane on our first visit. The reception was followed by a luncheon in the town hall, where again, several toasts and remarks were offered to mark the occasion. I was honoured to be asked to speak and did so in French. I also presented to M. Petit a framed tribute to Jim Keenan.

Rick Oliver with M. Albert Petit, the leader of the Memorial activities in Chauffourt.

The most endearing part of the entire event was the unveiling of a new plaque on the monument to the war dead located in the town centre. On our first visit the plague listed the names of the French soldiers from the village and environs who were killed in WW I. The villagers surprised us by unveiling a new plaque that listed the names of Canadians airmen as well. It was the penultimate tribute to the three men buried there.

A Mauling

In addition to the British Bomber Command raids on Schweinfurt and Regensburg (about 110 miles away), the U.S. 8th and 15th Army Air Corps (now the U.S. Air Force) undertook a number of daytime raids on the ball-bearing facilities there. All told, they unleashed some 12,000 tons of bombs on German factories at Schweinfurt, Regensburg and other locations in 40 raids on ball-bearing production facilities. Some two-thirds were dropped on Schweinfurt. The bombing intensity underlines the importance of the city and ball-bearings. The ball-bearing manufacturing facilities Schweinfurt accounted for almost 42 percent of the German production. German engineer had designed significantly more ball-bearings into both civilian and military equipment than equipment designers in other countries. It made the ball-bearing factories of critical importance to the German war effort, and thus a key target for the Allied bomber campaigns.

One particular U.S. raid, Mission 115, was on Schweinfurt/Regensburg on October 14, 1944. Author Martin Caidin, in his book *Black Thursday*, says the raid ranks in importance with the Battle of Gettysburg, Midway and the Battle of the Bulge, among other epic battles, in this case because of the disastrous losses by the U.S. The raid involved 291 heavy bombers, 103 P-47 Thunderbolt support fighters and over 3,000 airmen, who dropped some 724 tons of bombs. The bombers left from a number of different British bases, and typically took about 12 hours from their airbases until their return. They would have encountered fighters such as the Messerschmitt 109/110s, Focke-Wulf FWs and Junkers Ju-88s, as well as ground flak at various points along the route. The raiders' encounter with German fighters over Schweinfurt lasted only 16 minutes, but some 60 B-17 Flying Fortresses (almost 20%) and 600 men were lost. It was the most disastrous battle in the history of the U. S. Air Force. It was in short, a "mauling."

According to Caidin, the "Germans struck at the bombers with savage persistence and incredible courage ... Black Thursday saw the most violent, savagely fought, and bloodiest of all battles in the titanic aerial conflict waged in the high arena over Germany." Several reports from bomber crews, detailed in the book, provide some chilling insights into what it must have been like for the thousands of U.S., and British Commonwealth aircrews in an air attack.

According to Caidin:

"Lieutenant Miles McFann was a navigator aboard the B-17 named the *Paper Doll* on Mission 115; it was is seventh -- and most memorable -- attack of the war. Before training as a navigator he had [piloted] ... little light planes. But he came back from Mission 115 as a pilot simply because there wasn't much choice. The pilot was dead, the copilot badly wounded and bleeding profusely, and the *Paper Doll* had 132 big holes in her. McFann brought the battered Fort down on a strange field ..."

The fighting over Schweinfurt was intense, but the trip home could be hair-raising. One B-17, nicknamed *The Circus* was badly damaged in the raid, and started limping at roof top levels toward home on two engines. As one of the crew reported,

"They were firing everything they had at us. We were so close to them that the noise was terrific. They were firing machine guns and everything else. Troops lined up on the rooftops and in the streets and fields, blazing away with rifles. Their officers were outside, firing pistols. If they'd had more time, they would probably have thrown rocks at us."

Caidin describes the damage and the danger:

"The *Circus* took a terrific beating ... If she was cut up before, she began to fall apart. Pieces of metal curled up on the wings, gaping holes appeared magically in the wings and fuselage, and bullets twanged through the ship like a swarm of bees. ... a waterfall of tracers soared up from the ground and smashed into one of the two remaining engines. The *Circus* faltered visibly ... then struggled on -- carried by only one engine."

The *Circus* crashed into the English Channel just five miles from England, but the crew were quickly rescued by the British. They were, however, among the very lucky ones to go to Schweinfurt and return home.

After the war, it was determined that the raids on Schweinfurt were not particularly effective in halting the German war machine. While very good at destroying buildings (that could be easily repaired) the raids did little to damage production machinery, and when it did, the Germans were very adept at getting them back into production.

According to Max Hastings' compelling account in *Bomber Command*, some 56,000 British and Commonwealth Air Forces' aircrew were killed. By the end of the war, the RCAF was the fourth largest air force in the world.

While 70 years later debate still rages about the efficacy, and even legitimacy, of the bombing campaign against Germany, it was for much of the war, the only means of engaging the enemy. Given the massive changes since WW II in both the kind of wars and the tools of warfighting, we will never see the likes of Bomber Command again.

Rest In Peace

It was nearly 20 years go that I first learned of this story. It has filled me with sadness and regret. Sadness for what might have been; regret that I didn't have the time and resources for a more complete and compelling telling of events. But there is also a positive side. My most cherished memories in learning this history and telling it here, are of the people I met who had lived this story: Jim's family; George and Ann Collins; meeting with Martin Drewes by phone; and most particularly, the people of Chauffourt who held a funeral for the airman in deviance of the Germans, built a memorial, tend the graves, hold remembrance ceremonies, and told me the presence of the graves so prominently in the middle of their small village remind them daily of the sacrifices of three young Canadians.

I think often of Jim and Elaine and wonder what their lives would have been like had he survived the war. Through his letters I came to know and greatly admire him. As for Elaine, I now have an explanation for the sense of "darkness" I had often felt emanating from her for the nearly 50 years I knew her. I know her life was punctuated with periods of happiness, but the arc of her life was one of sadness. I know now that she had compartmentalized and "filed away" many of the memories (even knowing where Jim was buried) and physical items of that period of her life. She was, I'm sure, blanking out the pain. And, although she told me she never saw colour again, I know that she did occasionally express herself in her art. But it was infrequent and never again displayed the vibrancy of her pre-war work.

The principal characters of this story are all gone now: Jim and Elaine; Henry Peebles, John Moffat; George Collins and Gordon Fraser, the members of the Maquis, and, I assume, the rest of the crew of Lancaster 850; and, of course, the German Ace, Martin Drewes.

May they all rest in peace. I know I will when the time comes because my life has been greatly enriched from knowing these people and telling their story.

Many of the items I received from Elaine that she had received from Jim, such as the ring described in Part I, have been returned to Jim Keenan's family. The other items I received from Elaine that are of historic interest, along with the net proceeds from this book, were given to the Canadian Warplane Heritage Museum, near Hamilton, Ontario. Interestingly, the museum features one of only two functioning Lancasters remaining today. The other is at the RAF museum in the U.K.

Rick Oliver
Nashville, Tennessee
2017

For more information or to order additional copies, please visit www.Lancaster850.com

CPSIA information can be obtained
at www.ICGtesting.com
Printed in the USA
LVHW092111190321
681967LV00001B/11